Night-time and Sleep in Asia and the West

The phenomena of sleep and night are experiences that most people take for granted as a natural part of their daily lives. However, both ideas and practices concerning sleeping and night-time are constantly changing and widely differ between cultures and societies. *Night-time and Sleep in Asia and the West* traces the many different associations attached to the night as well as highlighting the diverse sleep patterns and attitudes towards sleep between cultures.

Drawing on case studies from China, Japan, India, Europe and the USA, the contributors address:

- notions of sleep and sleeping time in pre-Buddhist Chinese texts
- the concept of the 'mid-day nap'
- historical developments of sleep patterns determined by socio-economic changes
- the role of sleep in the life of the homeless and the military
- the relationship between fear and sleep
- night-time behaviour of the young in the nineteenth and twentieth centuries

This book suggests that far from being natural phenomena, sleep and night-time are sites of political struggle between groups as distinct as religious leaders, school boards and political parties. The essays here provide an important resource for students of Asian and cultural studies and will also appeal to the general reader interested in such a rarely studied everyday event.

Brigitte Steger is Assistant Professor in Japanese Studies at the University of Vienna. **Lodewijk Brunt** is Professor of Urban Studies at the University of Amsterdam.

Anthropology of Asia series
Grant Evans
University of Hong Kong

Asia today is one of the most dynamic regions of the world. The previously predominant image of 'timeless peasants' has given way to the image of fast-paced business people, mass consumerism and high-rise urban conglomerations. Yet much discourse remains entrenched in the polarities of 'East vs. West', 'Tradition vs. Change'. This series hopes to provide a forum for anthropological studies which break with such polarities. It will publish titles dealing with cosmopolitanism, cultural identity, representations, arts and performance. The complexities of urban Asia, its elites, its political rituals and its families will also be explored.

Dangerous Blood, Refined Souls
Death rituals among the Chinese in Singapore
Tong Chee Kiong

Hong Kong
The anthropology of a Chinese metropolis
Edited by Grant Evans and Maria Tam

Anthropology and Colonialism in Asia and Oceania
Jan van Bremen and Akitoshi Shimizu

Japanese Bosses, Chinese Workers
Power and control in a Hong Kong megastore
Wong Heung Wah

The Legend of the Golden Boat
Regulation, trade and traders in the borderlands of Laos, Thailand, China and Burma
Andrew Walker

Cultural Crisis and Social Memory
Modernity and identity in Thailand and Laos
Edited by Shigeharu Tanabe and Charles F. Keyes

The Globalization of Chinese Food
Edited by David Y. H. Wu and Sidney C. H. Cheung

Culture, Ritual and Revolution in Vietnam
Shaun Kingsley Malarney

The Ethnography of Vietnam's Central Highlanders
A historical contextualization, 1850–1990
Oscar Salemink

Night-time and Sleep in Asia and the West
Exploring the dark side of life
Edited by Brigitte Steger and Lodewijk Brunt

Night-time and Sleep in Asia and the West

Exploring the dark side of life

**Edited by Brigitte Steger
and Lodewijk Brunt**

RoutledgeCurzon
Taylor & Francis Group
LONDON AND NEW YORK

First published 2003
by RoutledgeCurzon

This edition published 2013
by Routledge

2 Park Square, Milton Park, Abingdon, Oxon OX14 4RN

Simultaneously published in the USA and Canada
by Routledge
711 Third Avenue, New York, NY 10017

RoutledgeCurzon is an imprint of the Taylor & Francis Group

First issued in paperback 2013

Typeset in Baskerville by Taylor & Francis Ltd

British Library Cataloguing in Publication Data
A catalogue record for this book is available from the British Library

Library of Congress Cataloging-in-Publication Data
Night-time and sleep in Asia and the West: exploring the dark side of life /
edited by Brigitte Steger and Lodewijk Brunt.
(Anthropology of Asia series)
Includes bibliographical references and index.
1. Sleeping customs–Asia. 2. Sleep–Social aspects–Asia. 3. Night–Social
aspects–Asia. 4. Time–Social aspects–Asia. 5. Asia–Social life and
customs. I. Steger, Brigitte, 1965– II. Brunt, Lodewijk, 1942– III. Series.
GT3000.4.A75 N54 2003
304.2'3'095–dc21 2002156177

ISBN13: 978-0-415-31850-5 (hbk)
ISBN13: 978-0-415-86004-8 (pbk)

Contents

Contributors

Ayukawa Jun is Professor of Sociology at the Kinjo Gakuin University in Nagoya, Japan. His research focuses on the sociology of youth culture, social problems and criminology.

Eyal Ben-Ari is Professor at the Department of Sociology and Anthropology at the Hebrew University of Jerusalem. His most recent research is about the contemporary Japanese military, the Israeli Army and the armed forces of the industrial democracies.

Lodewijk Brunt is Professor of Urban Studies at the University of Amsterdam and in this capacity has been doing fieldwork in India in recent years. In 1999 he produced a TV documentary on the plague epidemic in the city of Surat. His book *Een maniakale stad. Het leven van Bombay* (A maniacal city. Life in Bombay) was published in 2002 by Boom Publishers, Amsterdam.

Li Yi is Professor of East Asian History at Tacoma Community College, Washington, DC. He received his PhD from the University of Washington in the United States. His research interests include social and intellectual studies of modern China. His new book, *Chinese Bureaucratic Culture and its Influence on the 19th-century Steamship Operation*, was published in early 2002 by Edwin Mellen Press.

Irene Maver lectures in Scottish History at Glasgow University. Her book, *Glasgow*, was published by Edinburgh University Press in 2000. She is currently working on a history of Edinburgh. She has also co-edited with Michèle Dagenais and Pierre-Yves Saunier a volume on comparative urban history, *Municipal Services and Employees in the Modern City*, published by Ashgate in 2002.

Chris Nottingham is Director of the Centre for Contemporary History and Reader in Contemporary History at Glasgow Caledonian University. His recent publications include *The Pursuit of Serenity. Havelock Ellis and the New Politics*, published by Amsterdam University Press in 1999, and an edited volume, *The National Health Service in Scotland*, published by Ashgate in 2000.

Peter Rensen is a sociologist. He is now doing PhD research at the University of Amsterdam. His dissertation focuses on the social relationships among the rough-sleeping homeless in Amsterdam. He is also involved in counts of the rough-sleeping homeless in Amsterdam.

Antje Richter is Assistant Professor in the Department of Chinese Studies at Kiel University. She received her PhD in sinology from the University of Munich in 1998. She has recently completed the book *Das Bild des Schlafes in der altchinesischen Literatur* (The notion of sleep in early Chinese Literature), published by Hamburger Sinologische Gesellschaft in 2001, and is currently conducting research on the topic of letter writing in early medieval China.

Brigitte Steger is Assistant Professor at the Department of East Asian Studies at the University of Vienna. She has been awarded the 'Bank Austria prize for the promotion of innovative research at the University of Vienna 2002' for her doctoral thesis on the cultural and social aspects of sleep in Japan. She is currently researching the history of the hour in Japan.

Foreword

Sleep and night-time have attracted very little attention if any until now in traditional ethnographic field studies and monographs and in the studies of social and cultural anthropology.

This is quite astonishing when compared, for instance, with the great interest such studies have displayed in other basic aspects of human life, e.g. eating and drinking. If one takes the questionnaires of the *Atlas der deutschen Volkskunde* (Atlas of German folklore) beginning in 1929 as an example, of the 200 items in this questionnaire about one-tenth are concerned with what we today call ethnological food research. Questions 85 to 87 enquire about the hours that meals are eaten on workdays and on Sundays, the names for these meals, what they are made up of in winter and in summer, and what drinks are consumed with them. Many other questions follow, but not one concerns, for instance, the time one goes to sleep, where one sleeps or where the bed (rooms) is (are) located within the house.

Even with the vast material brought together by this study, the First International Symposium for Ethnological Food Research at Lund in 1970 condemned the lack of methodological studies and welcomed the proposal of the organisational committee of the 1970 European Folklore Atlas in Helsinki to include twenty-four questions on food culture and nutrition in its programme. This project was not realised for several reasons, but food research has in subsequent decades produced a great number of top rank studies from different points of view in Europe and also East Asia, especially Japan.

The contrary holds true for studies on sleep and activities of the night. Most ethnographic monographs ignore this time of day (night). This might be because European scholars tend to ascribe their own European experience (and education) that assigns sleep to the night, to the cultures studied, or maybe they are too exhausted by their daytime research activities to stay awake during the night or too shy to ask the necessary questions. Only very few exceptions come to mind, and without exception they concern descriptions of sexual life, such as the monograph on the Tobriand by Bronislaw Malinowski or that on Japan by Friedrich S. Krauss.

Japan seems to me – and perhaps I am biased here because of my many years of concentration on Japan – to have a culture where research in the fields of sociology, rural sociology, and family structures and kinship had comparatively early – already in the 1950s – noticed, for instance, where within the house and with whom people are sleeping. I am certain that Ruth Benedict's analyses in her carefully considered *magnum opus*, *The Chrysanthemum and the Sword*, have considerably inspired this attention. But this is only a small part of the entire issue and despite the inclusion of such questions in field studies, the information gathered has not been utilised to give us an insight into the social sleeping habits in Japanese rural society, let alone lead to a thorough study of the roles that sleep and night-time play in Japanese culture and society.

If speaking of sleep, insomnia and sleeplessness must also be considered. This is a vital point in studies of Japanese religion. Engelbert Kaempfer reported the story of the Japanese Emperor or Dairi, as Kaempfer called him, locked up in one room of his palace, not sleeping but staying awake day and night to protect the country. In Buddhism it is the Zen tradition that puts great weight on staying awake to meditate, introducing tea as stimulation and thereby contributing one core element to Japanese culture as it is conceived today. Tea, the tea ceremony and Zen meditation are elements of Japanese culture highly esteemed in Europe and the West at the present time. The same holds true also for an element of Japanese material culture connected with sleep: *tatami* (rice-straw mats) and *futon* (mattresses and quilts), the latter to a certain extent replacing the traditional bed in some segments of contemporary European society.

Studies of sleep and the night-time are not entirely non-existent, but reveal only a very limited and incoherent picture. This is the case in traditional and modern Europe, Japan and East Asia, and holds true also for studies in non-industrialised cultures and societies.

The symposium in Vienna organised by Brigitte Steger, Lodewijk Brunt and Ayukawa Jun was an urgently needed and – in light of the studies and workshops in this area which have taken place since 2001 – perfectly timed impetus. It would be a great step to begin correcting this theoretical deficit, and the present volume will certainly set off a new wave of interest and studies in this field, whose importance grows each day and each night in the wake of expanding globalisation and intensified interaction between cultures.

Josef Kreiner

Preface and acknowledgements

In many cultures, sleeping is more or less associated exclusively with the night. The dominant significance of night-time and darkness is thus: to close one's eyes and sleep. As is so often the case, social reality is more complex. This was one of the most obvious, but also most important, realisations of the workshop 'The "Dark Side" of Life in Asia and the West – Night-Time and the Time to Sleep', which was held in Vienna during the initial days of 2001.

To organise an international workshop on topics that are not part of academic traditions is a risky affair. Many questions arose, such as: Will it be possible to recruit sufficient numbers of colleagues to speak from corresponding perspectives? Will it be possible to encourage meaningful discussion and interesting findings?

We express our gratitude towards the persons and institutions that were willing to risk their money, time and energy in such an uncertain enterprise. The Japan Foundation and the European Science Foundation, Asia Committee, provided generous financial support that gave us great encouragement. The University of Vienna, represented by Franz Römer, Dean of the Faculty of Humanities and Cultural Studies, and Erich Pilz, Chairman of the Department of East Asian Studies, offered equally generous hospitality. The workshop took place on the premises of the Department of East Asian Studies and was warmly supported and realised with the help of several students and members of staff. We must also thank our dear and esteemed colleague Ayukawa Jun for his efforts in co-organising the workshop. Our esteemed colleague Josef Kreiner, former Chairman of the Institute of Japanese Studies (predecessor to the Department of East Asian Studies), also joined the workshop and gladly agreed to write the Foreword to this volume.

On the occasion of the workshop we were able to organise an exhibition of beautiful Japanese woodblock prints displaying 'Twenty-Nine Views of the Dark Side'. This selection was chosen from the extended collection of Japanese art that is to be found in the MAK – Austrian Museum of Applied Arts, Vienna. We are grateful to the curator of the MAK's East Asia collection, Johannes Wieninger, who not only arranged for the MAK's first loan of paintings to the University of Vienna, but also offered ample opportunity for us to select the prints and unwittingly helped us sharpen our thoughts on the topics of the workshop. From the exhibition, we chose the stunning print of a bat to be the natural symbol for the workshop. The bat, which stands for good fortune in East Asia, was designed by Bihô (Yoshikuni) from the Meiji period.

From the outset, we decided to incorporate an element of comparison in our workshop in order to avoid ethnocentrism in our discussions. The phenomena of night and sleep were examined by seventeen scholars from ten different countries and fourteen different universities, working from widely different fields and perspectives, i.e. criminology, urban anthropology, mythology, social anthropology, social and political history, cultural studies, and Chinese and Japanese studies. Although the participants were aware of the fact that night and sleep are relatively unknown topics of investigation in the social and cultural sciences with little or no tradition for developing concepts and theoretical notions, they nonetheless presented informative ethnographic material, and, working together, were able to draw interesting theoretical conclusions. They also uncovered a rich area for potential future research. It is easy to recognise the importance of knowing more about phenomena that are central to every person's life, not just for the many practical reasons but also in terms of theory development. How can we make generalisations about human behaviour when we ignore sleep, which makes up roughly one-third of human existence, and when we lack elementary insight into what happens at night in human communities?

We have selected the nine chapters in this volume from the contributions to the workshop. The case studies draw from a great variety of sources, from participant observation and interviews to popular books and media, and from pictures, fiction and non-fiction literature to statistics. They date from 2,500-year-old manuscripts to the latest news on the Internet. Topics range from youth in Japan and mid-day naps in China to nightlife in Bombay and Glasgow and the homeless in the Netherlands, to the way American soldiers are trained to deal with night combat – a chapter that has certainly become more acutely relevant of late. The variety of perspectives and empirical data presented is impressive. Many fresh insights and theoretical notions about these topics were raised, as this volume amply illustrates. We sincerely hope that it will encourage further thinking and research on this wide and dark field.

Finally, we owe a great deal of gratitude to Lisa Rosenblatt and Charlotte Eckler for their painstaking manuscript editing of the chapters, many of which were originally written in English by authors for whom English is not their first language. In cases where Chinese and Japanese transcriptions were used, the Chinese is p'in-yin, the Japanese is modified Hepburn. Names appear in natural order; that is to say, Chinese and Japanese surnames are followed by given names.

Brigitte Steger
Lodewijk Brunt

1   Introduction

Into the night and the world of sleep

Brigitte Steger and Lodewijk Brunt

> Have you ... ever thought of the peculiar polarity of times and times; and
> of sleep? ... Have you thought of the night, now, in other times, in foreign count-
> ries ...? You should, for the night has been going on for a long time.
>
> Dr Matthew-Mighty-grain-of-salt-Dante-O'Connor; in Djuna Barnes
> (1961 [1937]: 80–82)

In recent years, representatives of the social and cultural sciences have increasingly
acknowledged the relevance of the issue of time and time schedules. Most of the
research, however, deals with daytime and waking activities. Especially in the light
of globalisation, and the emergence of the so-called twenty-four-hour economies,
we need to know much more about what is going on outside the '7 to 11' rhythm
that is often considered the framework for our lives. Is this 'outside' time a reverse
time, the meaning of which is completely determined by daytime activities; or, on
the contrary, has the time we can spend on ourselves – our private, personal time –
developed into the only truly meaningful segment of our lives?

Based on the realisation that an exclusive association between sleep,
bedrooms and night-time is a highly ethnocentric notion, in the early days of the
new millennium we invited a small number of researchers to a workshop in
Vienna. The purpose of the workshop was to explore differences and similarities
between cultures and historical periods, including those with strict attitudes
towards the regulation of night-time and sleep and those that reveal a higher
degree of tolerance. Central to our discussion on the 'dark side of life' were
questions of the social, cultural and historical conditions that influence the time
regime of everyday activities in general, and the perceptions of sleep and night
in particular. One of the aims was to explore a new field of study using a variety
of approaches and to counterbalance the diecentric (see below) nature that characterises research in the social and cultural sciences.

For this volume we have selected nine case studies to show what is happening
in daily, or rather nightly, life in different countries, situations and contexts. The
studies concern Asia, Europe and America; not in order to juxtapose an assumed
holocultural Asia with a likewise West, or 'to support some universal theory or
meta-narrative', as Andre Gingrich and Richard Fox put it (Gingrich and Fox
2002: 1), but to enable a comparison of the meaning given to night and sleep

and their interrelationship in different societies and social groups. Throughout the workshop we became aware of the fact that in many respects, differences between European countries can be greater, for example, than between Japan and a specific European country. Moreover, it is not possible to point out precisely what comprises Asian cultures and European cultures, because they have mutually influenced each other throughout the course of history. Chinese culture has had a tremendous influence on the Japanese since the sixth century and Japan is now extending its influence in the reverse direction. So-called 'Western culture', especially the nineteenth century's newly industrialising regions of which Glasgow could be considered a prototype, has influenced Japan and also China during different historical periods. This is true, even if we consider only certain aspects of sleeping habits and notions of the night. Thus, international acculturation processes (i.e. globalisation processes) are not just a phenomenon of our own times.

Naturally, there are limitations to comparison, since the authors all come from very different fields, follow diverse research interests and ask different questions. Most of them originally set out to study something else and have only later realised the significance of the questions of night and sleep to the topic they have been studying. As a whole, the chapters offer a broad range of disciplinary foci. By putting the chapters next to each other, we hope that the differences and similarities in the cultural importance given to night and sleeping behaviour will be visible and theoretical findings will be put into perspective. Nevertheless, all authors develop an argument in their own right. Readers may choose their own order of reading through the book or pick out individual chapters according to their interests.

Despite the close links between the topics, it has become evident that the research practices of people dealing with either sleep or the night are sometimes considerably different. Moreover, as editors, we approach the subject from different particular (sub)disciplines and interests. The night has been a main topic of study for Lodewijk Brunt, an urbanist with a background in anthropology and sociology, whereas Brigitte Steger, a scholar in the field of Japanese studies, has concentrated on the study of sleep. We think it is of heuristic value to handle the two topics separately in our introduction.

Strangers in the urban night

People interested in the 'dark side of life', night-time and the world of sleep would probably be quite disappointed if they were to explore social scientific research traditions hoping to find imaginative ethnographic material, precise social or cultural analyses or inspiring theoretical ideas. Hardly any material exists on these topics. Issues concerning sleep and the night have nearly always been taken for granted and considered natural phenomena as solid and eternal as the weather and the wind. As is the case with many other 'ordinary', everyday topics, the most obvious phenomena escape our attention. The late A. N. J. den Hollander, Professor of Sociology at the University of Amsterdam, quite characteristically said that some scholars seem to know the minutest details about obscure tribes in the Highlands of New Guinea but are completely ignorant as to the everyday life of their housekeeper. Certain subjects simply seem to lack academic 'respectability', and the rewards for interest in them appear few and far between. In the case of night-time and sleep this is quite remarkable since both topics are investigated in other disciplines, i.e. the natural sciences. In addition, the world of art is full of references to the night and sleep, whether in paintings (cf. Haus der Kunst München 1998), musical compositions, dance or other forms. In literature from all over the world, novelists and poets have written about these subjects. William Shakespeare (cf. Noll 1994) is certainly not the only writer whose work nearly overflows with references to the night and its contrasts to the day. And what would children's stories, fairy tales and myths be without the night and its sleeping beauties?

Why is there such a strong case of night blindness in the fields of sociology and anthropology (and likewise in history and the humanities)? Approaching this question by concentrating on the specific field of urban studies may shed light on aspects of the situation in general. Students of urban life have developed numerous concepts and insights into the way people behave in urban public spaces and how they find their way around in a world full of strangers. Human social interactions on streets, in parks and in public facilities, such as waiting rooms, public transportation, theatres and cinemas, have all been theorised. Hardly anyone, however, has thought it worthwhile to consider night-time or the time of darkness as a distinct category. It is of course a difficult matter to define the precise boundary between day and night, but generally speaking it appears as if human behaviour is only of interest when it occurs during the day; or perhaps there is simply no distinction necessary and the existing concepts and theoretical notions are equally applicable to daily and nightly urban social interactions. Yet some central ideas about the ways people relate to each other, for instance Erving Goffman's *civil inattention* (1963) or Stanley Milgram's *psychic overload* (1970), are based on the assumption that people can actually see each other – and their environment – sharply and clearly. Goffman's sociology, for some, is the exemplary study of *face-to-face* interaction. How do these principles of social interaction work if people find themselves in situations where they are not able to see each other so easily, face to face or otherwise?

Spencer Cahill (1994: 9) reviewed a number of influential perspectives on urban public space and made the following observation: 'We all know that an urban park has a public character during the day, but this might only [be] nominally so as soon as darkness sets in.' What are the further theoretical consequences of this insight? Must we ignore the implications and continue to consider the night as just a continuation of the day or does it present a dimension worthy of distinct scholarly attention? It seems rather typical that the author does not say a single word addressing these issues. This lack of thematisation conveys the impression that it simply is not of much interest whether people interact during the day or the night. Could this negligence of the night indeed be ascribed to darkness as a period in which nothing of interest is happening (or at least nothing of interest to practitioners of the social sciences)? Is it a question of short-sightedness on the part of academics?

Insofar as representatives of the social sciences pay any attention to the night at all, it takes place quite casually, as if in passing. As stated earlier, nightlife is not considered an interesting field of study in its own right.[1] However, in our collective consciousness the night has numerous particular associations that penetrate deeply into our common existence. Ordinary dictionaries offer many examples, ranging from fear and hideousness to secret powers and sexual excitement. It is striking that urban dwellers, who are opposed to intrusions of the peace during the night, are apt to ascribe the intruders with characteristics such as 'uncivilised' and 'beastly'. Are 'sleep-breakers' non-human? Matthea Mevissen (1989) cites some typical examples in her study of the environmental effects of night facilities in the centre of Amsterdam. Residents of the city centre, who consider the night a period in which people should sleep instead of roam the streets, complain of being confronted by 'primitive … noises'. They seem to suppose that people who disturb the night are fundamentally lacking in discipline. They point out the frequent occurrence of vandalism, drunkenness, open displays of a wide range of intimate bodily functions and the physical and psychological intimidation of 'decent' passers-by. Each and every one of these associations has a long history in the context of thought about the night.

As is pointed out by Stuart Blumin (1990) in his introduction to the reprinting of George Foster's mid-nineteenth-century reports on the night in New York City, perhaps we should make sharp distinctions between the city and the country when dealing with the urban night. The city never sleeps completely. What this means is put forward by Kevin Coyne (1992: xvi) who compares the urban night with a sleeping human body. The production of necessary goods goes on, in bakeries as well as in steel factories. All kinds of services have to be continued through the night as well: the police are on the alert and in hospitals doctors and nurses are on their night shifts. Innumerable messages are being sent and received, either by telephone, digitally, or through the radio or TV. Transportation of goods goes on or, rather, gets started. 'In the still of the night', says Coyne (1993: xvi), 'we get to know about the basic mechanisms needed to keep human societies running.' In the night, human societies not only function in a concentrated way, but also people are inclined to pursue special activities. Or, as the British author A. Alvarez noticed during his nightly tours with different American police patrols, ordinary tasks take place in a slightly different manner. Police officers take more notice of small details. They assume that most people who are up and about in the night must have a very special reason to do so and this reason is usually highly suspicious (Alvarez 1995: xiv). In Alvarez's terms, the urban night should be considered *free time*. In the evening and night, time is spent on intimate things, being with friends and family, listening to music or reading. But night-time is also meant for excitement and entertainment and for many people this is the moment when 'real life' begins (Alvarez 1995: 259).

The differences between day and night lead to ambivalent feelings. Alvarez (1995: xiii) underlines that 'there is still something not quite right – maybe not even quite sane – about a working life led at night', and Murray Melbin (1987) dedicates a whole chapter to the obstacles and resistance which users of the night have to face; they have to deal not only with the daytimers' inclination to look down on people who are active at night, but also with robbers and other criminals. This must have a far-reaching influence on the way people behave at night, especially in cities. Night people, states Melbin (1987: 73), are much more alert in terms of the strangers they encounter than is customary during the day. They must constantly ask: is the other person dangerous? Goffman's *civil inattention* seems like a risky strategy in these circumstances. It is more likely that fear and distrust lead to avoidance or hostility. In an essay that beautifully articulates the ambivalence of the urban night, Luc Sante (1991: 358) argues that in the dark streets of the city everything that is normally hidden emerges. 'Everybody finds himself in a hazardous situation, everybody is potentially both murderer and victim, everybody is afraid and everybody who is willing is able to frighten others. In the night we are all naked.'

Yet this common realisation of potential dangers seems to have contradictory consequences. When it can be ascertained that the other user of the night is to be trusted, the ensuing feelings of closeness and solidarity are likely to be much stronger than would be the case during the day. 'If not foe, then friend', says Melbin (1987: 73); users of the night are aware of being part of a special situation in which they feel a common identity and a special mutual attraction. On the basis of a number of experiments, Melbin (1987: 80) can tentatively conclude that strangers in the night are easier led to friendship and mutual assistance than daytimers.

It goes without saying that it would be quite difficult – if not impossible – to determine clearly the differences between day and night. We all know that the boundary between the two is quite flexible and depends greatly on the time of year and the culture of the people who make such distinctions. In the Netherlands, for instance, the period in the late afternoon and early evening is called *schemering*. This period of twilight is much longer during the summer than during the winter. It would be a matter of debate whether the *schemering* should be considered as a part of the day or a part of the night. But, in fact, you could say it belongs to neither. Much the same holds for dawn. The association between night and darkness is equally problematic considering the fact that in some parts of the world during some parts of the year there seems to be eternal daylight, and eternal darkness during other parts of the year. Realising the complicated nature of the night (and by implication the day as well), the reading of general (urban) sociological texts becomes rather peculiar, as if the authors were not aware of the existence of the night. This night blindness can be characterised as the diecentrism of the social sciences.

We shall point out how this diecentrism is inherent in some central concepts and notions found in the work of two leading theorists in the field of urban behaviour, Milgram and Goffman (cf. Karp *et al.* 1991; Lofland 1998). Certainly quite similar conclusions can be drawn for the analysis of other theorists in the social sciences.

Diecentrism in urban studies

What is the most pertinent way in which urban dwellers experience urban life? This question is central to a well-known essay by Milgram (1970), in which he applies aspects of systems theory to human beings. According to Milgram, urbanites have to deal with an extraordinary number of impressions coming at them from all sides and at all times. As an illustration he presents us with the following. When people take a ten-minute walk at noon near their urban office, theoretically the chance is for them to encounter roughly 10,000 people. In a big city the number of encounters would be twice as many, whereas in Manhattan this number would even be in excess of 200,000. The possibilities for communication that big cities have to offer extend to near infinite. For the receiver of all these impressions, schematically speaking, this means that impression A can hardly be processed before impressions B, C, D and E announce themselves. According to Milgram, the 'system' continually risks experiencing an overload, or a *tilt*. To avoid this risk, people develop strategies to cope with the pressure, for instance to make choices and put forth priorities. The very core of urban life, Milgram maintains, is constant adaptation to avoid 'psychic overload'. This results in the limited involvement of urban dwellers with other people and a sharp distinction between friends and strangers. In general, people spend little time on impressions and low-priority incidents are neglected altogether. Moreover, urbanites take care to avoid becoming involved in certain types of incidents by developing specialised institutions or by protecting themselves behind impenetrable (symbolic) walls.

This is not the right place to discuss the ramifications of this socio-psychological theory of urban life; we are mainly interested in underlining the fact that Milgram – in stressing the importance of impressions given and received – apparently does not see any reason to wonder whether this 'impression management' might be linked to certain situations or to certain moments of the day or night. Let us assume that it could indeed be possible for people to encounter 10,000 or even 200,000 people during their ten-minute walks through the city centre. Would this not be more realistic if it occurred on a sunny day between 12 noon and 2 p.m. rather than on a rainy night between midnight and 2 a.m. in the outskirts of the city? The very fact that Milgram implicitly assumes that the optimal conditions for so many encounters are always present in cities gives his theory a definitive diecentric character. Daytime is apparently the standard for human existence. What takes place beyond daytime is not mentioned. The notion that cities are sometimes dark, and that this has consequences for the way in which we encounter other people and process our impressions, does not seem to occur, let alone be worthy of theoretical investigation – the (urban) night is not problematised.

Similar objections can be raised to some elements of the theories of Goffman, another outstanding theorist of urban life. A large part of contemporary American 'urban ethnography' – originally developed in the 1970s and extensively published in the journal *Urban Life and Culture* (which first appeared in 1974 and was later renamed *Urban Life*, and still later *Journal of Contemporary*

Ethnography) – reflects Goffman's influence. He is in a league of his own in describing and analysing human interaction in urban situations, based on hundreds of concepts and theoretical notions that he has developed in his influential books and essays. Goffman tries to get to the core of human interactions in metropolitan surroundings by using a 'dramaturgical model'. People's public behaviour is considered a series of 'performances', consisting of more or less subtle forms of impression management. Urban public life is structured and ordered through gestures, eye contact, postures and body movements, although mistakes and misunderstandings take place as a matter of course. Central to Goffman's work is the notion of *civil inattention*, elaborated in *Behavior in Public Places* (Goffman 1963). Civil inattention is a way to show that one is aware of the presence of others in a certain (public) situation, without being particularly interested in what they are doing and conveying the notion that one does not pose a threat to their presence. Public space is by definition generally accessible for everybody; there is no need to ask other people's permission to walk the streets of the city. Pedestrians who encounter each other on the pavement search each other with their eyes when they are at a 'safe' distance, but lower their gaze as they come closer and pass by one another. Civil inattention is a very small, almost invisible, gesture, with important implications. Civil inattention, according to Goffman (1963: 84), 'is probably the most modest of all interpersonal rituals, but yet one which regulates human social intercourse continuously'. It is a delicate form of behaviour which people sometimes try to avoid, for instance by wearing sunglasses, or by glancing sideways at others, out of the corners of their eyes.

Goffman's sociology of public behaviour turns around the activities of watching others and being watched and the observation of subtle gestures and signs. Nonetheless, like Milgram, Goffman seems unaware of the fact that seeing others and being seen by others must be physically possible. In other words, the 'view' must not be obscured by the night. Goffman's sociology and that of his many followers in urban research thus also displays a firm diecentric character.

Studying the night

However shallow the evidence may be in the existing literature, there appears to be firm enough ground for studying the urban night and for the realisation that in many respects social life at night has a fundamentally different character than social life during the day. Many of the themes that seem to be of special interest for studying the night are, in effect, to be found in the contributions dealing with the night in this volume.

As stated before, in the social sciences we lack adequate notions, concepts or theoretical insights for making sense of the night in general, and the urban night in particular. As such this is a specific case of a more general problem, brought to light by the British writer Jonathan Raban (1974). After reviewing the academic literature on the city, he concluded that he could not recognise himself in the kind of world that is projected by planners, architects and urban sociologists: they suppose the city to be completely rational in form and structure whereas in fact we experience everyday urban life in an entirely different way. Much of what goes on in the city escapes us completely and it is almost outrageous to suppose that we would immediately understand the purpose and meaning of a certain building, traffic circle or monument – even if centuries old – by just looking at it. In fact, much of the city, in Raban's words, is 'soft' and instead of seeing the city as some architects or designers would want us to, we project our own images, emotions and desires on the urban environment. For this dimension of the city – its soft side – we lack adequate terms, concepts and theoretical notions.

Although this volume is not conceived primarily as a theoretical treatise in which to develop new concepts and theories, the contributions offer promising ideas that can eventually be used in diverse contexts. Chris Nottingham's policing of the night is a case in point, as it offers interesting consequences for Melbin's central concept of the 'colonisation' of the night (Melbin 1987), meaning the gaining of (productive) time through the extension of daytime activities into the night. Nottingham shows that the colonisation of the night is not just the result of gaining 'productive' time; it is also the result of the extension of expressive and symbolic time. Night is no longer reserved for sleep alone. Like Irene Maver, Ayukawa Jun and Steger, Nottingham has a keen eye for the fact that the groups that colonise the urban night differ from period to period. Whatever groups we have in mind, in the background the political authorities have to make up their minds on how to go about controlling these groups. In Ayukawa's contribution, much weight is given to the new technological devices that help in colonising the night, making it especially difficult to maintain control. Japanese youngsters today are choosing mobile nightspots to spend their time and are otherwise able to escape the control of their parents and the authorities. Their invisibility and autonomy, moreover, are greatly helped by new ideas about human behaviour. Notions such as privacy and individualism offer strong ideological weapons to ward off any kind of unwanted interference by the authorities. In several respects the Japanese youth described by Ayukawa recall one of the fears that Maver raises in her analysis of nineteenth-century nightlife in Edinburgh and Glasgow. The actions of the infamous 'body snatchers' gave rise to associations with the devil and it seems inevitable that for some, the high-speed Japanese youth moving from spot to spot, interconnected by their mobile phones, could also raise similar fears.

Urban nights are not always associated with fear and danger, though. Nottingham shows that one man's fear is another man's fancy. He points to pleasure as the main attraction of city nights and in Brunt's description of Bombay nights he draws attention to the festive atmosphere surrounding the arrival of nightly trains at the stations in the city. Whereas fear is most likely connected to the absence of enough people to turn to in times of danger, in Bombay one is always surrounded by crowds of people, day and night. Brunt also highlights the feeling of solidarity that develops at night when people become co-victims of accidents or power failures. Supported by Melbin's remarks, the idea is raised that night-time solidarity has a special nature. Notions such as the colonisation of the night seem to imply a kind of linear evolutionary course of history. Once parts of the night are colonised it seems to be a matter of time before this process takes over the entire night – a process substantially advanced by globalisation in recent years. Maver offers useful cautionary remarks on this topic. She believes that Melbin is not specific enough with reference to the kinds of people and their value systems in his assessment that lighting has the effect of making the days longer. She writes: 'Whatever the outspoken free-trade beliefs of Glasgow's ruling elite, a libertarian approach to the night was not part of their mind-set.' In much the same vein, Brunt points out that the concept of colonisation does not take into account the state of a city's technological base. Nottingham, however, is very explicit in the presentation of factual developments that can be considered as proof of a reverse trend. 'But there are many services that have gone in the other direction', Nottingham says,

> In Britain the running of the railways on commercial principles has led to the elimination of almost all night trains. … Doctors no longer make night calls except in the most exceptional of all circumstances. The wholesale markets … have now moved to peripheral industrial estates and are entirely self contained.

Referring to the city of Glasgow, where many cinemas, pubs and restaurants have disappeared, home entertainment has been one of the main factors leading to this decline. Nottingham concludes that much of the city centre is relatively empty from about 7 p.m. onwards – time to go to sleep?

Studying sleep

Almost every day we talk about sleep, telling our families how we have slept, or wishing them a good night's sleep. Every child knows what he or she is supposed to do when sent off to bed. Moreover, according to the various time-use surveys conducted worldwide, sleep occupies by far the largest segment of everyday life. Thus it is certainly not irrelevant for us to study how people organise sleep: when, for how long, where and how people are involved in sleep as well as what values and meanings they attribute to it. As long as we are not insomniac or parasomniac (having disturbances during sleep, e.g. sleep walking), sleep is, however, hardly a matter for further consideration. With the exception of related topics such as dreams or the sleeping room and bedding, in social and cultural studies, 'sleep' has been almost completely neglected. The only 'Research Institute on Sleep and Society' of which we are aware is the RISS in Tokyo, a non-academic institute with a three-person regular staff, founded in 1999 by a private company for bedding (cf. Yoshida 2001). Steve Kroll-Smith (2000; 2003) at the University of North Carolina at Greensboro is concerned with 'the social production of the "drowsy person"', whereas Simon Williams (2002) of the University of Warwick is interested in sleep and health throughout the course of a life with particular reference to the boundaries between 'normal' and 'problematic' sleep. Despite its central importance for everyday life, as a research topic sleep – and by implication the person who studies sleep – are hardly taken seriously. Simply mentioning that one studies sleep provokes laughter, amazement and the suspicion that the researcher only wants to justify his or her favourite pastime. In this respect, students of sleep find themselves in the same situation as students of the night. The researcher is associated with various connotations of sleep, such as laziness, self-indulgence and sex.

These ideas attached to sleep are some of the most intriguing aspects of the topic, as the contributions in this volume show. Sleep – as is likewise the case with the night – can be loaded with a variety of meanings. Analysing the sleeping arrangements, night-time activities and the discourse on sleep and the night – as well as the reactions to people who research these topics – reveals attitudes and values embedded in the contexts in which sleep is organised and discussed. Ancient political writings already reveal such attitudes. Antje Richter, in her contribution to this volume, points out that in early (i.e. pre-Buddhist) Chinese literature the 'criticism of daytime sleeping is utilised for rhetorical ends that have nothing to do with sleep' and in certain texts a reference to ' "early to rise and late to bed" suffices to indicate the whole Confucian concept of conduct'. A similar usage of references towards sleep can be observed in present-day China. Li Yi regards the discourse of the mid-day nap as a 'windsock', making visible the changing Chinese attitudes towards communism, traditions, modernisation, work ethics, the West and, more generally, life-styles and values. He shows that when Chinese people argue in favour of or against the habit of mid-day napping, they do so in order to put forward their ideas about working and resting, or their admiration or distaste for the United States. Somewhat less explicit, but easy to depict, are the ideological notions in how-to books on short sleep in contemporary Japan, which Steger presents. Similar to Li's conclusions, she sees the desire to put forward ideologies on work ethics and time use as the primary intention for writing these books, even in those cases where the arguments seem based on 'objective' chrono-biological and medical research.

The recently developed, highly sophisticated sleep logistics of the US military, described by Eyal Ben-Ari, at first glance seem to be dictated by the necessities of the soldiers' bodies and night combat. It is indeed fascinating (and frightening) when he explains that the US Army is now making use of individual monitors, strapped around soldiers' arms like wrist-watches, to make sure they get enough sleep and are prepared for combat, whenever necessary. Yet the determinedness to get a proper recuperating (pill-regulated) sleep as preparation for good performance – something non-existent in East Asian pre-modern history – is striking, as is the lack of consideration of napping. Remarkably, this advanced sleep logistics integrates individual needs with the time structure of the tensest institutions (although they do not measure subjective sleepiness, but rather the amount of sleep a soldier takes). By contrast, the house rules of Amsterdam night-shelters force the homeless to adjust to a rather inflexible schedule and stay in bed the whole night, as Peter Rensen explains. During the day, homeless who make use of the facilities have to refrain from sleeping outright, even when they have nothing else to do. For their integration into society, welfare institutions obviously consider it of great importance that they adjust themselves to a schedule thought proper by the majority of society, according to which the night is meant for sleep and the day for active wakefulness.

The strictness of these regulations would probably be quite strange for a Chinese, Indian or Japanese, who is accustomed to societies that have a much greater degree of tolerance towards daytime sleepers, including those who do so in public. As both Ben-Ari and Rensen emphasise, to understand the sleeping behaviour of a certain individual or group, it is necessary to consider the 'overall logic' of the concerned people, how they handle their lives and what kinds of necessities they have to deal with. To turn the argument around, understanding sleeping behaviour helps us understand some of the central social and cultural notions of a certain individual or group. Since people generally rarely reflect on their sleeping behaviour, this is even more so the case.

Into the world of sleep

When we dig deeper into the topics, however, we face considerable methodological problems. By asking the simple questions 'What is sleep?' and, by implication, 'What are we studying?', we arrive at a dilemma. During sleep, we are generally not aware of the fact that we are sleeping. The waking consciousness is cut off. We might remember dreams and realise that we must have been sleeping deeply and this is precisely because we have no memory of the past few hours or minutes. How, then, is it possible for social and cultural scientists to research sleep? First of all, researchers need to gain awareness of the nature of their subject. Is sleep an activity, as time-use surveys, for instance, imply? Are we not rather passive during sleep? Is sleep a physiological need, or a drive or desire? Or is sleep a behaviour or a state of being? Is it a place we can escape to or is it something that we have to fight against? As will become evident throughout this volume, sleep is not either the one *or* the other. Sleep constitutes itself in the various contexts, as a desire, behaviour, a state of being or an activity. Sleep can be the one *and* the other. This is why we need to investigate sleep within various contexts and from different angles and with a wide range of methods. The authors of the five chapters on sleep collected in this book come from five different disciplines and five different countries. Their research interests are as diverse as one could imagine. Nevertheless, as we will elaborate below, each of their studies is not only enlightening on its own, but as a whole they contribute to a theoretical understanding of the social and cultural phenomenon of sleep and several issues continue to arise in almost every chapter.

One of the obvious contexts of sleep is closely linked to the absence of a waking consciousness; sleepers cannot control the environment, and thus have to find means of protecting themselves. This is even more acute when night-time fears add to the insecurity. Throughout the world, people have built accommodation and fences to keep out animal and human enemies and also the cold or heat, the rain and snow. In addition, humans ensure emotional security for a restful slumber by the presence of those they trust, or by praying and other bedtime rituals. Exactly how emotional security is established differs in the various societies and social groups. Looking at this more closely uncovers the kinds of fears and worries people harbour. It also reveals a great deal about social relations.

In most European countries and North America, sleep is associated not only with the night, but also with privacy. The night is the time for people to go home from their daily jobs and close their bedroom doors. The walls demarcating the house and the separate rooms play the most important role in protecting them. Urban homeless in general, and outside sleepers in particular, are the ones who thus experience this lack of protection most severely. This is crucial in understanding why most of them are chronically sleep deprived, as Rensen makes clear. People hardly find it comfortable to sleep in a public space, either night or day. This is due not only to potential danger, but also to a social environment that has little tolerance for public sleeping. This has not always been the case. Prior to the nineteenth century, co-sleeping in families and even among strangers was common; as was individual daytime sleep, inside and outside the house. Since then, however, most people in Western societies have been trained to sleep alone from early childhood onwards, an exercise that is often accompanied by tears. A teddy bear or other comfort, as well as a goodnight ritual, provide the emotional security that everything will be all right and one is not left alone. In most Asian cultures, private sleeping rooms are the exception rather than the rule. Communal sleeping is quite normal in India, especially in the countryside, but even in big cities like Bombay some people would think it appropriate to invite guests to join them in the afternoon nap. In Indonesia and China the situation is similar. These arrangements are common within the family, and – after a certain age – among those of the same sex, and obviously there is no connotation of immorality. In Japan, too, co-sleeping with family members until a relatively late age has always been very common, regardless of the number of rooms available in the house, as Steger shows in her chapter (cf. also Caudill and Plath 1974; Ben-Ari 1997). Only recently has there been a trend towards providing a private room for children as soon as they enter primary school, and many parents have become extremely insecure about their rights to enter children's bedrooms, even during the day, an issue which points to much more comprehensive social changes, which Ayukawa elaborates. Sleeping in the same space with other people not only provides protection, it also gives a sense of belonging. As American psychologist John Selby points out, 'one of the findings in insomnia research in the last couple of decades has been that insomnia almost always is associated with a disruption of one's sense of communal security and belonging' (Selby 1999: 7).

This comforting social environment, however, can turn into a threat and friends become foes. Thus the Chinese Marquis Zhao, in Richter's example, distrustful of his sleep-talking, always slept alone. Today, outside sleepers in Amsterdam are endangered by the random violence of strangers who – most likely under the influence of drugs or alcohol – find it amusing to urinate on them or let out other forms of aggression on the defenceless persons. They must also fear potential aggression from their fellow homeless, who, on the contrary, at other times provide a protective social environment that allows them to relax and sleep.

Heads of social groups or countries, especially in monocratic societies, have a special, very contradictory role in terms of sleep. On the one hand, they are the ones who have the right to regulate time and in many cultures it would be unthinkable to wake them up before 'the sleep had come to its natural end', as Brian Taylor (1993: 467) puts it. He recalls an incident that took place in the 1980s in Morocco. When Queen Elizabeth II was on a state visit and invited King Hassan to a state banquet, she had to wait several hours for her guest of honour, because nobody dared wake him. Similarly, Chairman Mao suffered from a twenty-eight-hour circadian rhythm and other sleep problems, and forced the people in his surroundings to adjust to him accordingly.

On the other hand, the sleep of the head of a social group might bring this group into a marginal situation. Referring to the statement by Georg Simmel, 'the consciousness of constituting with … others a unity is actually all there is to this unity', American sociologist Barry Schwartz concludes: 'in this particular sense … a society whose entire membership is asleep is, at that moment, no society at all' (Schwartz 1973: 29). Therefore, an exemplary Chinese emperor was to 'forget about sleep' completely, spending 'his nights pondering the welfare of his people and scrutinizing his own rule' as Richter points out. The Japanese emperor was allowed to sleep, yet institutionalised watches represented his rule. 'For some must watch while some must sleep', says Shakespeare's Hamlet (Act III, Scene II). Not only were night watches on duty at the ancient Japanese court in Heian (today Kyoto): a number of ladies in waiting donned in their formal outfits were sitting outside the emperor's bed chamber every night, representing the consciousness of the state (cf. Steger 1998: 21).

Regardless of these differences in the social arrangements of sleep, there is always something private about the matter. Sleep appears to be the most radical disconnection from the social world, which is obvious in the phrase 'one is dead to the world'. Sleep also has an anarchistic potential of self-indulgence that may lead to neglect of social obligations and restraint, especially in connection with sex, alcohol or drugs. Thus in any society, the authorities try to extend their regulations and control of it. At the same time, however, coexistence would cease to be gratifying, or even bearable, if humans were to have no means of regularly isolating or disconnecting themselves from it. This is why '[e]very social organi-sation exhibits structural features which both guarantee the regular performance of duties and insure release from such performances', as Schwartz (1973: 18) points out. Biology itself does not dictate exactly how much sleep is necessary or desirable or when it is scheduled. Instead, this is regulated by negotiation and debate between various groups in a given society. To a great extent these things develop as habits whose original conditions remain unclear and unquestioned.

The regulation of sleeping time rarely goes as far as in China, where 'a right to rest' for the working population was written into the 1950 constitution under Chairman Mao. Li shows that this commonly translated into a three-hour mid-day rest for a meal and nap. Usually, state authorities only indirectly deal with sleeping time by regulating working hours and closing times or by setting a curfew for certain social groups such as in the Hamilton case described by Nottingham. In other cases they make recommendations for a proper sleeping time or for sleeping arrangements. Sleeping time is dealt with at the level of institutions such as hospitals, dormitories, barracks and shelters, or within social groups such as families or households. Steger finds a great number of pre-modern house codes specifying the time to get up and go to sleep. People might find ways of circumventing these regulations such as pretending to be awake by not showing obvious signs of sleep, i.e. snoring or the loss of control over body posture, or through what Rensen calls 'half-sleep' or something similar known in Japan as *inemuri*.

In many societies, we can find a connection between the discussion of time management (or more generally of time use) and sleep. Although the notion that sleep is a waste of time exists in all of the cultures dealt with in this volume, East Asia and 'the West' appear to diverge on the question of why we sleep, and how it should be organised. In her classic monograph *The Chrysanthemum and the Sword*, first published in 1946, Ruth Benedict juxtaposes American and Japanese attitudes towards sleep:

> Americans are used to rating sleeping as something one does to keep up one's strength and the first thought of most of us when we wake up in the morning is to calculate how many hours we slept that night. The length of our slumbers tells us how much energy and efficiency we will have that day. The Japanese sleep for other reasons. They like sleeping and when the coast is clear they gladly go to sleep.
>
> (Benedict 1989 [1946]: 181)

In this statement lies one of the crucial points that become clear when we look at the different case studies in this book. The Americans still appear to be unbeaten in their attempts to make use of chrono-biological knowledge in order to sleep efficiently and to adjust the body to a set of needs. The vanguard of this development is the military. In fact, as sleep researcher Takada Akikazu points out, the questions of how to make night work in general and night combat in particular more efficient have been the prime motors for sleep research, especially in the West (Takada 1993: 66). Ben-Ari, elaborating in this volume on the implication of night combat, explains how the US Army has recently developed a sleep logistics that integrates soldiers' bodies into the institution like 'cyborgs', those 'hybrid machines and organisms that fuse the organic and the technical'. With the help of personal monitors, software and pills, soldiers are put to sleep and kept awake depending on their own sleep history and the needs of the battle. The aim is, as Ben-Ari concludes, to create the 'optimal soldier' through enhancing his or her given physiological and cognitive aptitudes. Not only does the US military work as a model for most military organisations, but, in addition, many high-ranking soldiers from Asia and elsewhere have actually trained in American units. Like the soldiers, ordinary working men and women are eager to function efficiently and effectively while feeling healthy at the same time. They take pills and undertake other measures to overcome jet lag, daytime drowsiness and sleepless nights. Overcoming sleep deficits is also the aim of international chrono-biological and sleep research. Leon Kreitzman, in *The 24 Hour Society*, speculates: 'it is probable that thirty years from now we will have the capacity to design our own cycles for a given set of needs' (Kreitzman 1999: 104). Whether this is promising or frightening is left to the reader to decide.

Today Japanese 'company soldiers', as they have often been called, also try to be efficient in their sleeping habits, although, as Ayukawa shows, many young people radically refuse to share the values of their parents. Western medical and industrial learning, including notions of how to organise sleep, first entered Japan in the second half of the nineteenth century, and again after the Second World War. Eager to catch up with the progress they felt was obvious in European countries and North America, the Japanese also tried to learn from their way of living. They took over the notion of the eight-hour monophasic sleep ideal, but at the same time started to disagree on the optimum length of sleep, a topic which is central to Steger's contribution. In China, there was already a discussion of Western ideas, including those on sleep organisation, in the nineteenth century, but this can be observed more explicitly and radically after Mao's death. Li elaborates on this clash through the example of mid-day naps, which were at the centre of that discussion. Even prior to these East–West contacts, notions on sleep have been contradictory and diverse. Richter explores different ideological traditions in ancient China, but does not find any notion that even resembles the view, often taken for granted, that we sleep in order to improve waking performance. Sleep is either the supplementary counterpart of waking existence, the yin to the yang, the night to the day, or, in the Confucian and Mohist traditions, sleep is seen as a form of indulgence, like sex or drinking, that has to be controlled by the individual. This reasoning is later taken up by Buddhist thinking as well and has found its way into Japan along with other ideological and religious traditions of China.

As we have pointed out before, although some aspects of sleep in Europe and North America can be seen as different from those of Asian countries, no distinctive lines between 'Asian' and 'Western' sleep cultures can be said to exist. Japanese, Koreans or Indians pick up relevant American or European research results as quickly as they are taken up in their own home country. The reverse is also true. Today, melatonin and other sleep-regulating pills and energy drinks are readily available and consumed around the globe to keep up with the demands of busy schedules.

We suggest approaching international, intercultural and historical comparisons of sleep patterns with the help of the typology of sleep cultures that Steger has developed in her doctoral thesis (Steger 2001: 120–130, 241–251), as outlined below.

Sleeping cultures

There are three different ways in which societies organise sleep, categorised in the following typology. The first type is a monophasic sleep culture. Sleep is concentrated in one period with a widespread ideal of an eight-hour nocturnal sleep phase. Healthy adults are not supposed to sleep during the day. In the second type, biphasic sleep determines siesta cultures. This type reveals two set sleeping times, a longer one during the night, and a shorter one usually early in the afternoon. During both periods, the sleep role is protected from social demands to a certain extent. In the third type, a polyphasic sleep pattern characterises napping cultures. People in napping cultures usually have what is called in medical terms their 'anchor' sleep at night, and take individual daytime naps when the situation allows. A high level of tolerance rather than a set time protects their daytime sleep. Generally speaking, the more explicit the demand to be alert at any hour of the day, the more protected must be the sleep role during the night. Although naps help to get over sleepiness caused by sleep deprivation (cf. Inoue 1996: 85), daytime sleep of the biphasic and polyphasic types is not just a compensation for insufficient nocturnal sleep, as implicitly or explicitly underlying most studies on napping. All of these three patterns of distributing sleep throughout twenty-four hours have developed in and of their own right.

In the United States and Northern Europe, monophasic nocturnal sleep is widely taken for granted, and even considered a physiological norm. Swiss sleep researcher Alexander Borbély (1986: 31–33) explains that the human sleep cycle gradually changes from the polyphasic sleep pattern of newborns to the afternoon nap habit of most pre-schoolers and finally to the monophasic sleep of adults. Elderly people again tend to take a nap during the day. Referring to the siesta in the Mediterranean area, South American countries and China, he qualifies this pattern as a cultural tradition and says that 'climatic conditions can … cause adults to maintain the bi-phasic (two-phase) sleep characteristic of preschool children' (Borbély 1986: 35). Thus, he argues that, first, there is a linear development from polyphasic to biphasic to monophasic sleep patterns and that, second, certain circumstances can lead to a deviation from the *normal* monophasic sleep pattern for adults. Internationally, however, monophasic sleep seems to be more of the exception than the rule (cf. Webb and Dinges 1989). Even in Europe, monophasic sleep is a rather recent phenomenon. This becomes evident in paintings such as those of Pieter Breughel the Elder (1525/30–1569) and many written sources (cf. Gleichmann 1980; Sivry and Meyer 1997; Wittmer-Butsch 1990). Not only resting at home, but also public napping were common in pre-modern times. Moreover, despite the ideal, many contemporary Westerners take regular naps. Two developments that had a prominent influence on the formation of a monophasic sleep ideal can be named as: first, industrialisation and the accompanying restructuring of working habits and time discipline (cf., for example, Thompson 1967; Glennie and Thrift 1996); and second, the changes in attitude towards bodily practices in bourgeois cultures, including making sleep more intimate and private (cf., for example, Elias 1997; Sennett 1992 [1974]).

In societies with a monophasic sleep ideal, daytime sleep is generally discouraged and avoided. Sick people, the elderly, children and people performing night-work may violate this rule. On the other hand, the need to protect nighttime sleep is quite strong. Transition periods from the sleeping role to the waking role are comparably long and elaborate. Ideally, the bedroom has the solemn purpose of providing quiet and intimacy for sleep and possibly sex. During the day it is generally not used. Social rules dictate not disturbing sleeping hours, e.g. not phoning early in the morning or late at night.

Siesta cultures – as can easily be seen by the name – are characteristic of Spain and societies with Spanish cultural influences. Seen from the perspective of Middle Europe, climatic influences seem the most obvious motivating factor for this sleep pattern, and indeed sleep often functions as a means of enduring the heat. However, the siesta is neither restricted to countries near the equator, as the example of China shows, nor is it a habit found everywhere in southern regions. Neighbouring Portugal does hardly adhere to a socially set time for afternoon napping, whereas Greece does.

A siesta pattern has many advantages, even for people with a tight schedule. It allows a decrease in night-time sleep (Stampi 1992; Garhammer 1999: 379–381), makes two days out of one (cf. Uejima 1995), reduces accidents caused by drowsiness in the early afternoon and improves productivity (cf. Hecht 1993; Inoue 1996). In siesta cultures there is more tolerance towards late-night activities, since the siesta is an important buffer zone. Moreover, a regular afternoon nap has been shown to decrease the danger of coronary heart disease regardless of the length of sleep (cf. Dinges and Broughton 1989: 306). Nevertheless, in times of globalisation, the siesta is at risk. In a survey conducted in 1996, only 18 per cent of the working population in Spain claimed to have held a siesta the previous working day (quoted in Garhammer 1999: 381). Just like in eagerly modernising China, as elaborated by Li, in Spain the siesta has been given the popular image of leisurely backwardness, which does not fit the image of an advanced member-state of the European Union. A letter to the editors of *Newsweek* protesting about a special report on 'New Faces of Spain' is a prime example of this attitude:

> Your imagery of Spain's old symbols – bullfights, flamenco – don't help your message of a new Spain. Your references to siestas and long lunches are nothing but worn clichés. Spain's 'dark past'? All countries have dark pasts. That is now long behind us. Talk about our economic reality, our social reality.
>
> (A. L. Cangas in *Newsweek* 5 June 2000: 5)

Cangas expresses a common attitude towards the mid-day nap as a kind of relict of a pre-industrial laziness: sleeping during bright daylight is clearly evidence of backwardness, as only diligent, industrious workers are bound to be successful.

Apart from this kind of ideological reasoning, there are also more profane reasons for the decline of the siesta culture. Economic and social reality dictates that global networking and enterprises make it necessary to adjust business hours to an international clock. Shift work – in which the Spanish car industry has a leading role – demands alternating working hours around the clock. 'In an acculturation process, timetables of most working people have been adjusted to the

[Northern] European pattern: This is a general characteristic of the Spanish path to modernity since joining the EU in 1986.' People who work in small-scale service industries and agriculture are still more likely to remain with the siesta pattern (Garhammer 1999: 382). Furthermore, distances from home to the workplace are increasing. Commuting twice a day is increasingly becoming a burden. Therefore, many people avoid doing so. With a growing number of women in the workforce, lunch is no longer prepared for (male) employees when they return home at noon (*International Herald Tribune* 27 December 1999). Thus, they take a quick lunch in a nearby restaurant instead and drink a strong coffee to overcome the 'after-lunch dip'.

Siesta cultures, so it seems, have already had their glory days. Socio-economic developments at the turn of the third millennium, globalisation, international business co-operation, information technology and twenty-four-hour economies threaten many cultures' centuries-old habit of a socially established afternoon resting time. In their paper, Steve Kroll-Smith and Vern Baxter (2003) recognise a decline of the siesta in the southern hemisphere and an emergence of the workplace nap in the northern. They argue that as cognitive labour increasingly defines work in the North, physical, Fordist-type labour is defining it in the South. The 'snooze you lose' motif of the production line is fast eclipsing the value placed on mid-day breaks in Italy, Mexico, Spain and Portugal (Kroll-Smith and Baxter 2003).

Societies with polyphasic sleeping cultures can be found in every continent and under different climatic and socio-economic conditions. Most of the advantages described for the siesta are true for individual napping as well. The main purpose of naps is to help get over the after-lunch energy dip and improve performance. However, the whole of society does not turn in for a lengthy time each day; people do so individually, so they are more flexible in response to irregular needs forced upon them by global networking. There is an additional bonus: people who are trained to use the time available for sleep, whenever it comes, have little or no difficulty falling asleep at any idle moment. Thus, time lags have fewer negative influences on the sleeping quality and jet lag can be minimised.

With regard to napping cultures, at least two kinds of individual daytime sleep can be distinguished. First there is the daytime sleep that is a separation from waking activities, if one finds a quiet place, usually a sofa or a bench, for a nap; and second, there is a socially distinct form of napping, which in Japanese is aptly called *inemuri*. *Inemuri* is composed of the Chinese characters for *i(ru)*, to be present, and *nemuri*, sleep (in the physiological sense). That is to say, *inemuri* does not imply a certain body posture, duration or EEG pattern (particular amplitude of the brainwaves); rather, its main characteristic is that the sleeper is present in a situation that is meant for something other than sleep. Today this expression is typically used for sleep during lectures or meetings, at a party or in a discotheque, when riding in a train as well as when driving (which is a main cause of accidents). Socially, *inemuri* is not necessarily regarded as sleep in the sense that the sleeper is not completely 'dead to the world'. In order theoretically to understand *inemuri*, we find it helpful to refer to Erving Goffman's concept of 'involvement within the situation' (Goffman 1963: 36–38), although he is not necessarily writing about sleep: 'Involvement refers to the capacity of an individual to give, or withhold from giving, his concerted attention to some activity at hand' (43). Goffman differentiates between *main* and *side*, and between *dominant* and *subordinate*, involvements. A side involvement is an activity that can be carried out in a fashion 'without threatening or confusing simultaneous maintenance of a main involvement', such as humming while working (Goffman 1963: 43). Thus, when one retires to bed or to the sofa for a nap, sleep is the main involvement. Yet it is possible to regard sleep while riding a train as a side involvement. Sleep does not harm the main purpose of the trip, i.e. moving from point A to B (although a problem might arise if the slumber is so deep that one misses the station to get off). In comparison:

> A dominating involvement is one whose claims upon an individual the social occasion obliges him to be ready to recognize; a subordinate involvement is one he is allowed to sustain only to the degree, and during the time, that his attention is patently not required by the involvement that dominates him.
>
> (Goffman 1963: 44)

In the case of *inemuri* at a lecture, a meeting or a party, sleep can be seen as a *subordinate* involvement. The *dominant* involvement is that of the situation one is in, such as the social gathering. The main characteristics of such a subordinate involvement are that the body idioms remain the ones appropriate to the situation at hand and the activity (in our case the sleeping) has to be stopped as soon as the dominant involvement demands active contribution (cf. Goffman 1963: 43–79).

Whether this form of napping is accepted or not and how it is evaluated is highly ambivalent. Rules regarding daytime sleep are hardly explicit, and even for those raised within a certain culture they are sometimes difficult to obey. Rensen shows this ambivalence when he writes about half-sleep. Even in societies that exhibit tolerance towards daytime as well as public sleep, like in China, Japan or India, there are many occasions when obvious sleep during social activities is not allowed. And there are intercultural differences as well.

> Since the involvement idiom of a group appears to be a learned conventional thing, we must anticipate one real difficulty in cross-cultural or even cross-subcultural studies. The same general type of gathering in different cultures may be organized on the basis of different involvement obligations.
>
> (Goffman 1963: 37)

Indian author Khushwant Singh, who in his autobiography seems to be satisfied characterising the Indian Rajya Sabha (the equivalent of the English House of Lords) as a place to fart and sleep (Singh 2002: 334), was not at all satisfied with the behaviour of some of the students he taught during his professorship at the University of Hawaii. His memories of the period are quite ambivalent, to say the least. None of the students knew anything about India. He writes:

> I had to make my lectures very elementary and fill them in with as many anecdotes as I could unearth. Particularly upsetting were two Nisei Japanese girls who would start nodding with sleep as soon as I started speaking. It became a challenge keeping them awake. I failed in this task.

What is permitted in the highest of India's political institutions is obviously not allowed in Singh's classroom, for he concludes: 'I wreaked vengeance on the girls by failing both of them on the mid-term papers.' When they came to his office complaining about this he taught them a lesson: 'How would you feel if, while you are talking to a person, he or she fell asleep? It is most off-putting' (Singh 2002: 225). Later the girls dropped out of the course altogether. This example would indicate that Indians regard a classroom as a situation where sleep as a subordinate involvement cannot be tolerated, even though public sleep (as a main and as a side involvement) can be readily observed. In Japan, although we find the attitude that *inemuri* is in fact regarded as non-commitment to work, the general attitude is that as long as active participation in the situation is unnecessary, why shouldn't one take a nap? Formally, one has to fulfil the duties of attending the session or lecture, but informally there are a number of ways to cope. As one informant explains, 'We Japanese have the Olympic spirit. Taking part is what counts' (Matsubara Akira, personal communication).

In light of the twenty-four-hour society and globalisation, as Steger shows, ever more authors in Japan regard polyphasic sleep models including *inemuri* as the most adequate way to organise sleep in contemporary societies. They advise active use of day and night, to succumb to sleep any time the body demands and circumstances allow. We must conclude from the book at hand, however, that although napping is becoming popular in other countries as well, the idea of *inemuri* has not yet become global. The following scene, observed by a woman chairing an international meeting in Rome on 27 November 2000, illustrates this point: 'I had a meeting in a hall with two Japanese, and they were dosing off regularly. Reaction by the French: they probably have digestive problems. The Americans: No, jet lag!' (L. F., personal communication).

Note

1   However, there are signs of a process of rethinking. From 15 to 18 March 2001, a few months after the 'Dark Side' workshop, the conference 'Night and the City' took place at McGill University, Montreal. From 14 to 17 August 2002, the 7th Biennial Conference of the European Association of Social Anthropologists in Copenhagen also included a half-day workshop 'When Darkness Comes: … Towards an Anthropology of the Night', organized by Burkhard Schnepel (to be published as a special issue of *Ethnos*).

Bibliography

Alvarez, A. (1995) *Night. Night Life, Night Language, Sleep, and Dreams*. New York and London: W. W. Norton.

Barnes, Djuna (1961 [1937]) *Nightwood*, with an Introduction by T. S. Eliot. New York: New Directions.

Ben-Ari, Eyal (1997) *Body Projects in Japanese Childcare. Culture, Organization and Emotions in a Preschool*. Richmond, Surrey: Curzon Press.

Benedict, Ruth (1989 [1946]) *The Chrysanthemum and the Sword. Patterns of Japanese Culture*. Boston: Houghton Mifflin.

Blumin, Stuart M. (1990) 'George G. Foster and the Emerging Metropolis', in George G. Foster (ed.) *New York by Gas-Light and Other Urban Sketches*. Berkeley, CA, and Oxford: University of California Press, 1–63.

Borbély, Alexander (1986) *Secrets of Sleep*. New York: Basic Books.

Cahill, Spencer E. (1994) 'Following Goffman, Following Durkheim into the Public Realm', in Spencer E. Cahill and Lyn H. Lofland (eds) *The Community of the Street*. Greenwich, CT, and London: JAI Press, 3–19.

Caudill, William and David W. Plath (1974) 'Who Sleeps by Whom? Parent-Child Involvement in Urban Japanese Families', in Takie Sugiyama Lebra and William P. Lebra (eds) *Japanese Culture and Behavior. Selected Readings*. Honolulu: University of Hawaii Press, 277–312.

Chiba Yoshihiko (1996) *Karada no naka no yoru to hiru. Jikanseibutsugaku ni yoru atarashii chūyakan* (Day and night in the body. New views on day and night through chrono-biology). Tōkyō: Chūō Kōronsha (*Chūkō shinsho 1315*).

Coyne, Kevin (1992) *A Day in the Night of America*. New York: Henry Holt.

Dinges, David F. and Roger J. Broughton (1989) 'The Significance of Napping. A Synthesis', in David F. Dinges and Roger J. Broughton (eds) *Sleep and Alertness. Chronobiological, Behavioural and Medical Aspects of Napping*. New York: Raven Press, 299–308.

Elias, Norbert (1997) *Über den Prozeß der Zivilisation. Soziogenetische und psychogenetische Untersuchungen. Erster Band: Wandlungen des Verhaltens in den weltlichen Oberschichten des Abendlandes* (On the process of civilization. Sociogenetic and psychogenetic investigations. Vol. 1: Transformations in behaviour in the worldly upper-classes of the West). Frankfurt am Main: Suhrkamp.

Garhammer, Manfred (1999) *Wie Europäer die Zeit nutzen. Zeitstrukturen und Zeitkulturen im Zeichen der Globalisierung* (How Europeans use their time. Time-structures and time-cultures under globalisation). Berlin: Edition Sigma.

Gingrich, André and Richard Fox (eds) (2002) *Anthropology, by Comparison*. New York and London: Routledge.

Gleichmann, Peter R. (1980) 'Einige soziale Wandlungen des Schlafens' (A few social transformations of sleep), *Zeitschrift für Soziologie* 9(3): 236–250.

Glennie, Paul and Nigel Thrift (1996) 'Reworking E. P. Thompson's "Time, Work-discipline and Industrial Capitalism"', *Time & Society* 5(3): 275–299.

Goffman, Erving (1963) *Behavior in Public Places. Notes on the Social Organization of Gatherings*. New York and London: The Free Press/Macmillan.

Haus der Kunst München (1998) *Die Nacht* (The night). Wabern-Bern: Benteli.

Hecht, Karl (1993) *Besser schlafen - schöner träumen* (Sleep better, dream sweeter). Düsseldorf and Vienna: ECON Taschenbuch.

Inoue Shōichi (1996) *Hirune no susume. Tanjikan suimin no fushigi* (Recommendation to take a mid-day nap. The mystery of short-time sleep). Tōkyō: Ie no Kōkyōkai.

Karp, David A., Gregory P. Stone and William C. Yoels (1991) *Being Urban. A Sociology of City Life*. New York and London: Praeger.

Kreitzmann, Leon (1999) *The 24 Hour Society*. London: Profile Books.

Kroll-Smith, Steve (2000) 'The Social Production of the "Drowsy Person"', *Perspectives on Social Problems* 12: 89–109.

Kroll-Smith, Steve (2003) 'Popular Media and Excessive Daytime Sleepiness. A Study of Rhetorical Authority in Medical Sociology', *Sociology of Health and Illness* 6(25).

Kroll-Smith, Steve and Vern Baxter (2003) 'Napping on the Job. A Sociology of Employees, Time and Dormancy', Paper presented at the Southern Sociological Society Annual Meeting, New Orleans, April.

Lofland, Lyn H. (1998) *The Public Realm. Exploring the City's Quintessential Social Territory.* New York: Aldine de Gruyter.

Melbin, Murray (1987) *Night as Frontier.* New York: The Free Press.

Mevissen, Matthea (1989) *De Amsterdamse horeca tussen beleving en beleid* (The Amsterdam amusement sector – between experience and policy). Amsterdam: University of Amsterdam, Centre of Environmental Law.

Milgram, Stanley (1970) 'The Experience of Living in Cities: A Psychological Analysis', *Science* 167(13): 1461–1468.

Noll, Marcus (1994) *An Anatomy of Sleep. Die Schlafbildlichkeit in den Dramen William Shakespeares* (An Anatomy of Sleep. Sleep imagery in the dramas of William Shakespeare). Würzburg: Königshausen & Neumann.

Raban, Jonathan (1974) *Soft City.* London: Hamish Hamilton.

Sante, Luc (1991) *Low Life: Lures and Snares of Old New York.* New York: Farrar, Straus, Giroux.

Schwartz, Barry (1973) 'Notes on the Sociology of Sleep', in Arnold Birenbaum and Edward Sangrin (eds) *People in Places. The Sociology of the Familiar.* London: Nelson, 18–34.

Selby, John (1999) *Secrets of Sleep. Natural, Pleasurable Techniques Designed to Help Cure Insomnia.* New York: Excel.

Sennett, Richard (1992 [1974]) *The Fall of Public Man.* New York and London: W. W. Norton.

Singh, Khushwant (2002) *Truth, Love and a Little Malice: An Autobiography.* New Delhi: Ravi Dayal Publisher and Penguin Books India.

Sivry, Sophie de and Philippe Meyer (1997) *Die Kunst des Schlafs. Eine kleine soziale, symbolische, medizinische, poetische und liebevolle Geschichte des Schlafs* (The art of sleep. A little social, symbolic, medical, poetic and caring history of sleep). Vienna: Brandstätter.

Stampi, Claudio (ed.) (1992) *Why We Nap. Evolution, Chronobiology, and Functions of Polyphasic and Ultrashort Sleep.* Boston: Birkhäuser, 184–196.

Steger, Brigitte (1998) 'Kodai Nihonjin wa itsu neteita ka' (When did ancient Japanese sleep?), in Sepp Linhart and Inoue Shōichi (eds) *Nihonjin no rōdō to asobi. Rekishi to genjō* (Work and leisure of the Japanese. Past and present). Kyōto: Kokusai Nihon Bunka Sentā (Nichibunken sōsho 16), 13–33.

Steger, Brigitte (2001) '(Keine) Zeit zum Schlafen? Eine soziologisch-anthropologische Studie' ((No) time to sleep? A study on sleep in Japan from the perspective of social and cultural sciences), Doctoral thesis, University of Vienna.

Takada Akikazu (1993) *Nemuri wa hyakuyaku no chō* (Sleep is a universal remedy). Tōkyō: Kōdansha.

Taylor, Brian (1993) 'Unconsciousness and Society. The Sociology of Sleep', *International Journal of Politics, Culture and Society* 6(3) (Spring): 463–471.

Thompson, E. P. (1967) 'Time, Work-discipline and Industrial Capitalism', *Past and Present* 38: 56–97.

Uejima Keiji (1995) 'Kairaku wa aku ka? Shiesuta. "Ichinichi ga nido aru" seikatsu mankitsu' (Is relaxation bad? Siesta. The satisfying life that 'makes two days out of one'), *Asahi Shinbun* 20 November (evening edition).

Webb, Wilse B. and David F. Dinges (1989) 'Cultural Perspectives on Napping and the Siesta', in David F. Dinges and Roger J. Broughton (eds) *Sleep and Alertness: Chronobiological, Behavioral and Medical Aspects of Napping.* New York: Raven Press, 247–265.

Williams, Simon J. (2002) 'Sleep and Health. Sociological Reflections on the Dormant Society', *Health. An Interdisciplinary Journal for the Social Study of Health, Illness and Medicine* 6(2): 173–200.

Wittmer-Butsch, Elisabeth Maria (1990) *Zur Bedeutung von Schlaf und Traum im Mittelalter* (On the meaning of sleep and dream in the Middle Ages). Krems: Medium Aevum Quotidianum.

Yoshida Shūji (ed.) (2001) *Suimin bunka-ron* (Treatise on sleeping culture). Tōkyō: Heibonsha.

2 Sleeping time in early Chinese literature

Antje Richter

Chinese people do, of course, sleep – like all human beings, or rather like all warm-blooded creatures. In China, however, this fact becomes evident to a visitor more quickly than it does in Western countries. Especially in the early afternoon it is easy to observe people sleeping in public, sometimes in the most surprising postures and locations, and not only in a context of poverty or rough living, but obviously as a habit common among quite respectable people. This peculiarity has long caught the attention of Western visitors to the country. In the chapter 'The Absence of Nerves' from his nineteenth-century book, *Chinese Characteristics*, Arthur Smith observes:

> It would be easy to raise in China an army of a million men – nay, of ten millions – tested by competitive examination as to their capacity to go to sleep across three wheelbarrows, with head downwards, like a spider, their mouths wide open and a fly inside!
>
> (Smith 1894: 94; cf. Liu 1995: 51–76)

Over the course of the twentieth century the situation has hardly changed, as Li Yi points out in his chapter appearing in this volume. The habit of mid-day napping has never really suffered a setback despite the ups and downs in its ideological evaluation. Western visitors are still puzzled by the sight of sleeping Chinese and there is hardly a book of prints on China that is without a photograph of one or more picturesque sleepers.

Turning to early Chinese literature for an explanation of this distinctive sleeping behaviour – as I did when my fascination with sleeping Chinese became rather persistent – I discovered that sleep plays a marginal role in early Chinese texts. There is no god of sleep like Hypnos in ancient Greece, no comprehensive investigation like Aristotle's *On Sleep and Wakefulness* (*De somno et vigilia*), no god like Vishnu, sleeping before the dawn of creation in the Hindu context, no motif of a 'Sleeping Beauty' as is common in the West from early Greek poetry to German fairy tales. Indeed, there are many early Chinese texts that go without even mentioning sleep or sleep-related subjects. The topic thus shares the fate of other private matters in early Chinese literature whose scarcity or absence is a well-known and often lamented fact. Thus, it is not surprising that, for the most part, the topic of sleep has remained unexplored in sinology, with the exception of its most impressive aspect, dreaming (cf. Brown 1987; Eggert 1993; Liu Wenying 1993).

Despite the apparent scarcity of sleep as a topic in early Chinese literature (in texts that were written before the third century AD) there is a wide range of more or less prominent notions about sleep and sleeplessness: first and foremost, the topic of the appropriate sleeping time, i.e. the question of when to sleep and for how long.[1] Except in medical or lexical texts, sleep as such, however, is hardly ever treated as a topic that is explicitly reflected upon. If it is referred to at all, it is usually just mentioned in passing without the intention of giving information about the subject. A closer look at these secondary or implicit references to sleep reveals that they are mostly to be understood as rhetorical devices conveying different ideas in texts of different persuasions. The following investigation will thus introduce and analyse the main notions of sleeping time in early Chinese literature, and enquire into their rhetorical functions, emphasizing intertextual relations.

I would like to begin with a few remarks on the lexical ambiguity of some designations of 'sleep' in early Chinese literature. There are only two words in classical Chinese that primarily denote 'sleep'. Of the two, the general one is *mei*. The other, *shui*, means specifically 'to fall asleep or take a nap while sitting'. While both *mei* and *shui* are rare in classical Chinese, the designations *qin*, *wo* and *ming*, probably secondary, are quite common. Their capacity to denote 'sleep' is derived from prominent characteristics of that state – either from lying down (*qin*, *wo*) or from closing one's eyes (*ming*). In the case of *qin*, for instance, it is very often unclear whether it means 'to sleep' or 'to go to bed' or just 'to retire to (or stay in) one's private chambers'. Another lexical feature that adds to the semantic problems that may arise from these ambiguities is the use of euphemisms, motivated by the desire to veil the state or the sphere of sleep. Not only might *qin*, *wo* and *ming* have originally been euphemisms, but there is also the widespread use of figurative phrases such as 'to approach the cushion' (*jiu zhen*), 'to join the eyelashes' (*jiao jie*) or simply 'to rest' (*an*, *xi*, *xiu*) or 'to dream' (*meng*). On the other hand, not only were euphemisms used to avoid an explicit expression for 'sleep', but 'sleep' itself was also used as a euphemism. Compared to sex and death, it was obviously regarded as the 'lesser evil'. Since they share some characteristics or connotations, sleep was employed to veil the spheres of sex and death. Both aspects are common in European languages as well.

Medical writing: sleep as a natural phenomenon

A most remarkable discrepancy in early Chinese literature surfaces between texts that regard sleep as a natural phenomenon and texts that focus on the social implications of sleep. Concerning the evaluation of sleep, the medical texts in *The Yellow Emperor's Inner Canon* (*Huangdi Neijing*, *c.* first century BC) seem to be fairly impartial: sleeping and waking are regarded as equally valued counterparts. This balance results from correlating sleeping and waking with macrocosmic phenomena such as night and day, winter and summer and, finally, *yin* and *yang*,[2] which are, in principle, on an equal footing with respect to each other.

In the medical texts of *The Inner Canon*, sleep is explained, like any other bodily function, by the condition of the physiological *qi* – 'energies that make the vital functions possible' and 'follow regular cycles of activity' (Sivin 1987: 46–53). While the vital energies may basically be characterized by the complementary aspects *yin* and *yang*, *yin-qi* and *yang-qi* are not regarded as fixed opposites but also as temporal phases of a cyclical process.

As there is no systematic discussion of the nature of sleep and wakefulness in *The Inner Canon*, the basic understanding of these phenomena in this compilation must be extracted from scattered references in the elaborations on different kinds of illnesses. The following remarks are taken from a passage that explains excessive yawning:

> *Yin* rules the night, at night we sleep [*wo*]. … If *yang-qi* is exhausted [*jin*] and *yin-qi* is flourishing [*sheng*] we will fall asleep [*mu ming*], if *yin-qi* is exhausted and *yang-qi* is flourishing we will wake up [*wu*].
>
> (*Huangdi Neijing* 1986: *Lingshu* 28.2/349)

First, the relation of *yin-qi* and *yang-qi* is described as determining sleep and wakefulness. Sleep, as well as the night, is correlated with *yin*, the dark, soft, turbid, moist, female, passive, latent, etc. In the same way, waking must be correlated with *yang*, bright, hard, clear, dry, male, active, overt, etc.[3] In traditional Chinese medicine, thinking in terms of *yin* and *yang* renders irrelevant the question felt to be most pressing in modern Western medicine, 'Why do we sleep?', a question that was also posed by Aristotle (384/3–322/1 BC) in his *De somno et vigilia* (454b). There simply had to be a counterpart to waking and to *yang* – where there is *yang*, there must also be *yin*. Within this concept, the discussion of a possible regenerative function of sleep is quite irrelevant, as are suggestions for ascetic behaviour, such as sleep reduction.

Second, the night is regarded as the appropriate time for sleep. Sleeping and waking are regarded as healthy when they are 'intact' in the literal sense of the word; when the macrocosmic rhythm of night and day corresponds with the individual microcosmic rhythm of sleeping and waking. The human rhythm of sleeping and waking is thus described as a reflex of the governing cosmic rhythm of night and day. This correlation is also mentioned in the famous and at times elaborate descriptions of the body as a microcosm, found in early Chinese literature (cf. *Chunqiu fanlu* 1994: 13.2/58; *Huainanzi* 1992: 7/55). In *The Inner Canon*, the relevant statement reads:

> Heaven has day and night [*zhou ye*], man has sleeping and getting up [*wo qi*].
>
> (*Huangdi Neijing* 1986: *Lingshu* 71.2/446)

As already suggested, sleep is embedded in the annual cycle of *yin* and *yang*. A chapter of *The Inner Canon* that concerns appropriate personal behaviour during the four seasons gives the following, among other more general, instructions for sleep:

> During the three months of spring ... go to sleep late and rise early [*ye wo zao qi*]. During the three months of summer ... go to sleep late and rise early [*ye wo zao qi*], do not be weary of the sun. ... During the three months of autumn ... sleep early and rise early, be up with the cock [*zao wo zao qi, yu ji ju xing*]. ... During the three months of winter ... sleep early and rise late, be sure to await the sunlight [*zao wo wan qi, bi dai ri guang*].
>
> (*Huangdi Neijing* 1986: *Suwen* 2.1/10)[4]

According to this macrocosmic setting of sleep, in times of rising and dominant *yang* it is suitable to sleep little, whereas in times of rising and dominant *yin*, sleep should be extended. The general recommendation goes: sleep at night – be it short or long – and stay awake in the daytime. Observing these recommendations results in significantly varying sleeping times over the course of a year – at least in northern China. The close correlation of sleep and night merges the two aspects of sleeping time – when to sleep and for how long.

It would, however, be misleading to presume a conceptual consensus in the Chinese medical tradition, even on a seemingly simple issue such as sleep. This is neither the case within *The Inner Canon* – which is, after all, a heterogeneous collection of medical texts – nor in the received medical texts from outside this tradition. Occasionally the discovery of tomb texts provides glimpses of the diversity of opinions that must have existed. With regard to sleep, the manuscript *Ten Questions* (*Shiwen*), buried in the second century BC and excavated in 1976 at Mawangdui in southern China, offers a fresh and unique understanding. It displays the teachings of the famous physician Wen Zhi, which do not confine sleep to night-time nor pair it with *yin*, but allocate to it both an explicitly capital role and functions that are clearly associated with *yang*.[5] The physician declares that 'sleep [*wo*] ranks first' in the 300 chapters he has written about the Way (*dao*). When questioned by King Wei of Qi (reigned 356/334–320 BC, cf. *Shiji* 1989: 46/1888–1892) about why he holds sleep in such high esteem, Wen Zhi explains:

> Sleep causes food to be digested and medicine to flow through the body. The relation of sleep to food is like that of fire to metal. That's why a single night without sleep cannot be compensated by a hundred days. ... For this reason, men of the Way will venerate sleep.

The metaphor paraphrasing the impact of sleep on food employs the distinctive *yang*-phase fire: sleep dissolves food just like fire melts metal. Wen Zhi's ascription of physiologically positive effects to sleep may be exceptional in early Chinese medical literature but it is reminiscent of Western interest in the function of sleep. Regarding the adjustment of sleeping time to the rhythm of *yin* and *yang*, Wen Zhi's outlook likewise goes beyond the scope of *The Inner Canon*. Referring to his statement that 'a single night without sleep cannot be compensated by a hundred days', the king, a notorious pleasure-hunter, asked:

> 'I am habitually fond of drinking until late at night, am I then not prone to sickness?' Wen Zhi replied: 'This cannot do any harm. Among the birds and beasts some go to sleep early and rise early [*zao wo zao qi*] and others go to sleep late and rise late [*mo wo mo qi*].'
>
> (*Mawangdui Hanmu boshu* 1985: 150–151)

Wen Zhi seems to dissolve the correlation between sleep and night, which is presumed not only in *The Inner Canon* but also in most of the received non-medical literature. His flexibility concerning sleeping time could be merely a clever move in order to comply with his counterpart's personality or to avoid the king's possibly dangerous annoyance at being contradicted.[6] Leaving aside *The Inner Canon* as a standard of assessment, it seems nevertheless more probable that the understanding of sleep accidentally preserved in this manuscript represents just another facet of what is probably a vast and heterogeneous body of lost medical teachings of early China. While the texts of *The Inner Canon* closely correlate sleep and night, which are equally associated with *yin*, in *Ten Questions* Wen Zhi breaks up this close correlation and attributes a capital role and positive physiological functions to sleep.

Political writing: sleep as a socially relevant phenomenon

A different picture results if the sleeper is not, as in medical literature, viewed primarily as a warm-blooded creature subject to the laws of nature, but, rather, as a social being as occurs in political and ideological writing. Sleep is socially relevant since a sleeping person is temporarily inaccessible to the demands of participation in social life. To ensure a high degree of availability, sleep is subject to diverse restrictions and constraints, which often render inappropriate *The Inner Canon*'s advice to sleep at night. Diverse as these restrictions may be, they are all traceable to temporal interferences. Even uncomfortable sleeping conditions that apparently intend to induce sleep of a poor quality – such as 'sleeping on a bed of straw, the head resting on a lump of earth' (*qin shan zhen kuai, Liji* 1992: 38.1/159), as required by certain mourning rites – in the end actually result in less sleep.

While every adult is expected to curb sleep to a certain degree for the sake of his or her duties (including self-cultivation), this demand is socially differentiated. This negative conception of sleep is common to the majority of early Chinese literature. It links factions of writing that otherwise are not at all concordant, texts later ranked as the Confucian canon, didactic and historical literature, Mohist and, with some modification, also Legalist writings.

The awareness of sleep as social or, more accurately, antisocial behaviour is heightened by the fact that it is very often directly or indirectly associated with different kinds of pleasure. The 'sweetness' (*gan*) of sleep[7] may consist in the rather passive pleasure of waning strain. By falling asleep, one not only withdraws from the outside world and social responsibilities but also from one's own consciousness, an action that now and then may appear perfectly desirable.[8] The only definition of sleep found in early Chinese literature selects 'not knowing' or 'unconsciousness' (*wu zhi*) as the most distinctive feature of sleep:

> Sleep is the intelligence not knowing of anything [*wo zhi er wu zhi ye*].
> (*Mozi* 1988: 40/65, cf. Graham 1978: 280)

In sleep, the intelligence (*zhi*), the faculty of 'knowing' (*zhi*), is not employed: generally one neither perceives nor feels nor thinks. Expositions of the motif of sleep as a refuge, where one no longer 'knows' of the world and one's self, are to be found in the *Book of Songs* (*Shijing*), a collection of songs from the eleventh to sixth century BC. The following song is an impressive example:

> There is a hare who moves slowly, the pheasant fastens in the net.
> In the early part of my life would that I had not acted [*shang wu wei*]!
> In the latter part of my life I have met with a hundred sorrows,
> would that I could sleep and not stir any more [*shang mei wu e*]!
>
> There is a hare who moves slowly, the pheasant fastens in the trap.
> In the early part of my life would that I had not taken action [*shang wu zao*]!
> In the latter part of my life I have met with a hundred grieves,
> would that I could sleep and not wake up any more [*shang mei wu jiao*]!
>
> There is a hare who moves slowly, the pheasant fastens in the snare.
> In the early part of my life would that I had not been busy [*shang wu yong*]!
> In the latter part of my life I have met with a hundred calamities,
> would that I could sleep and not hear any more [*shang mei wu ting*]!
> (*Shijing* 1995: 70, cf. Karlgren 1944: 194)

The situation of the unknown singer must be desperate indeed. He does not couch his desire to escape the hundredfold sorrows of waking life in the wish for a positive change – nor even for comforting dreams, at least – but in the wish for the numbness of sleep. Desolation is expressed most strongly by the wish 'not to wake up any more', which comes close to a wish for death: death as well could provide the desired absence of sorrows.

In addition to the idea of a passive refuge, sleep is associated or mingled with the active pursuit of sensual pleasures. It is therefore frequently set in a context of undue indulgence in eating, drinking, sex and music. In early Chinese literature, these four belong closely to the sphere of sleep since they usually occur in the same places – bedrooms or private chambers – and since they are often pre-sleep or post-sleep activities.

Apart from this local and temporal intermingling of sleep and sensual pleasures – which is already sufficiently suggestive – some texts also establish causative relations. Excessive indulgence in drinking, for example, has to be compensated for by sleeping longer, which may have devastating effects on the performance of

social duties. As in political and ideological writing the person under consideration is generally the ruler of a state, his indulgence evoking the politically
dangerous situation in which the state is virtually without a ruler. The coupling of
sleep (generally accompanied by other sensual pleasures) with the neglect of
duties is a widespread motif in didactic and historical writings, where it serves as a
rhetorical pretext for remonstrations appealing to the ruler's sense of duty. One of
four similar remonstrations of Yan Ying (Yanzi, *c.* 589–500 BC) to Duke Jing of
Qi (reigned 547–490 BC), recorded in *The Springs and Autumns of Master Yan* (*Yanzi
chunqiu, c.* fourth to third century BC), may exemplify this aspect:

> Duke Jing had drunk wine and become intoxicated. When three days later
> he got up again, Yanzi attended the audience and asked: 'Did you suffer
> from a hangover?' When the duke answered in the affirmative, Yanzi said:
> 'In antiquity, when drinking wine, people were content to move their vital
> energies [*qi*] and to meet friends. ... That's why outside there were no
> complaints about the government and inside there was no disorderly
> behaviour. Now you drink so much wine in one day that it takes you three
> days to sleep it off [*qin*]. Outside there are complaints about the government
> of the state and inside your entourage raises disorder. ... I wish you would
> moderate yourself!'
>
> (*Yanzi chunqiu* 1993: 1.3/1–2)

Although the ruler's absence is very aptly represented by his sleep, it is obvious
that sleep itself is not the point. The focus of the argumentation is political; the
reference to sleep merely serves to illustrate a political point, in this case the
proper behaviour of a ruler.[9]

The association of sleep and drunkenness is rather persistent in early Chinese
literature (cf. *Lienüzhuan* 1993: 6.7/55–56; *Hanfeizi* 1982: 7.2/21–35/738,
19.4/4–34/759, 22.15/1–11/771). Sleep and drunkenness seem to intensify
each other, 'drunken sleep' signifying both exceptionally deep sleep and very
heavy drunkenness. The association appears to be based not only on a causative
relation (i.e. drinking promotes sleep) but also on the supposition of an intrinsic
affinity of both states. The affinity probably lies in the desire to be relieved of
consciousness, which can be accomplished by both sleep and drunkenness.
Incidentally, drunken sleep was to become an important topos in Chinese literature, especially in poetry.

Although textual references to sleeping time are complex propositions, they
can be conveniently differentiated according to the two aforementioned questions: when to sleep and for how long? An investigation of the textual evidence
concerning the first question discloses a certain imbalance. While the approval of
sleeping at the right time – during the night – is hardly ever emphasized, the
disapproval of sleeping in the daytime is a much more conspicuous topic.[10]

The Inner Canon's cosmologically based demand to sleep at night is rarely
emphasized in the political literature. Obviously, it is as unnecessary to insist on
an adequate amount of sleep as it is to insist on drinking enough wine. There is

some evidence that sleeping at night was simply presumed, not least for the sake of public security. The *Book of Rites of the Zhou* (*Zhouli*, compiled *c.* third century BC) mentions the position of night watchmen (*si wu shi*, *Zhouli* 1993: 5.34/72), whose duty was to enforce the curfew, though no details are given. Indirect confirmation of the fact that sleep at night was simply taken for granted may be drawn from references to night activities that are expressly characterized as such – often associated with secrecy or even insidiousness (cf. *Zhanguoce* 1992: 73A/30, 324/165, 399/192) – or from the concession of exceptional situations that allow one to depart from the usual night's rest.[11] Another indication of the assumption of night-time sleeping may be found in the *Canon of Mountains and Seas* (*Shanhaijing*). In this book of mythical geography, features like absolute sleeplessness or deviation from the natural rhythm of sleeping and waking are only ascribed to strange and decidedly non-human creatures, which live at the borders of the empire, far away from the centre and the ruling power.[12]

The relative prominence of the disapproval of daytime sleeping might have been triggered by a famous anecdote included in the *Analects* (*Lunyu*, *c.* fifth to third century BC), linked to Confucius and Zai Yu,[13] one of his disciples:

> Zai Yu had a lie-down in the daytime [*zhou qin*]. Confucius said: 'Rotten wood cannot be carved, nor can walls of dirty earth be whitewashed. What can be expected from Yu?' Confucius said: 'Formerly, when I listened to other people's words I trusted in their behaviour. When I listen to other people's words now, I watch their behaviour. I changed [my attitude] because of Yu.'
>
> (*Lunyu* 1995: 5.10/10)

As taking a nap in the daytime is, of course, not a sufficient reason to condemn a person so severely, commentators have speculated on the exact nature of Zai Yu's stay in his private chambers. However, regarded in the light of his availability to the demands of society, it does not matter whether Zai Yu was actually taking a nap or having sex or just being idle (cf. Steger's contribution in this volume). It is the unjustified withdrawal from public life at a public time that counts. The only justifications for being in bed in the daytime are given in the following passage from the *Book of Rites* (*Liji*, compiled *c.* first century BC):

> If somebody stays in his inner [chamber] in the daytime [*zhou ju yu nei*] it is legitimate to inquire after his health. If somebody stays outside at night [*ye ju yu wai*] it is legitimate to condole with him.[14] That's why the gentleman will not spend the night outside without sufficient reason. Unless he is fasting or sick, he will not stay in his inner [chamber] day and night [*bu zhou ye ju yu nei*].
>
> (*Liji* 1992: 3.37/14)

This passage maintains that by merely considering somebody's whereabouts at certain hours, it is possible to decide whether somebody is ill or in mourning. Considering how little we really know of early Chinese life, it is impossible to know whether ritual regulations like these reflect actual habits or whether they are ideologically motivated attempts to establish such conventions.

A closer look at other references to Zai Yu in the *Analects* reveals that he 'enjoys the dubious distinction of having been criticized by Confucius on more occasions than any other disciple', as Lau (1992: 248) puts it. He is even denied humanity (*ren*), the central Confucian virtue, on account of his 'unfilial' criticism of the strict mourning rites proposed by Confucius (*Lunyu* 1995: 17.21/50). Zai Yu thus appears to serve as a negative model.

Confucius's abhorrence of daytime sleeping invited not only doubt and straightforward protest – like that of Wang Chong (27–*c*. 100) in his voluminous treatise *Weighing of Discourses*[15] – but also more subtle forms of contradiction. In a superbly ironic anecdote, which has come down to us in the compilation *The Springs and Autumns of Lü Buwei*,[16] Confucius himself is depicted as 'having a lie-down in the daytime' (*zhou qin*). Moreover, in order to probe the decency of his favourite disciple, Confucius feigns sleep and then even a dream, thus resorting to a considerably indecent trick himself. This anecdote might be exposing Confucius's harsh disapproval of daytime sleeping to ridicule, but all the same, it argues in line with the impropriety of this practice.[17]

Thus in both the *Analects* and *The Springs and Autumns of Lü Buwei*, criticism of daytime sleeping is utilized for rhetorical ends that have nothing to do with sleep. Talking about sleep serves as a pretext to convey distinctive ideological opinions that go beyond the private sphere of sleep: in the case of the *Analects* as regards the evaluation of central virtues like filial piety or humanity, in the case of *The Springs and Autumns of Lü Buwei* as regards the evaluation of Confucius. Since the widespread disapproval of daytime sleeping encountered in early Chinese texts is set in a context of ideological argumentation, it may not be interpreted as bearing testimony to an equally widespread custom of daytime sleeping. In the absence of relevant reliable data, any hypothesis on the existence of a napping or siesta culture in early China can only be speculative.

A similar pattern can be observed in an episode reported by Ban Gu (32–92) in the *Book of the Han Dynasty* (*Han shu, c.* 100). This official history discloses an imperial nap, that of Liu Xin, Emperor Ai of the Han (25–1 BC, reigned 7–1 BC) with his favourite, Dong Xian (23–1 BC):

> Dong Xian usually went to sleep and got up together with the emperor [*chang yu shang wo qi*]. Once they had a lie-down in the daytime [*zhou qin*] and Dong Xian lay just on the emperor's sleeve. Dong Xian was still asleep when the emperor wanted to get up. As he did not want to disturb Dong Xian, the emperor cut off his sleeve and got up. So far reached his grace and love.
>
> (*Han shu* 1990: 93/3733–3734)

The story became rather famous and the 'cut sleeve' turned into a common metaphor for male homoerotic relationships (cf. Vitiello 1992). The historian, however, certainly does not hand down this episode to inform his posterity of the 'grace and love' of Emperor Ai or to promote the idea that a lover's sleep should be protected from disturbances. It is not even daytime sleeping or the existence of a favourite as such that is disapproved of, but the submissive character of the emperor's relationship towards Dong Xian, as it is unworthy of an emperor. In another episode, Ban Gu tells of Liu Xin's irresponsible handling of the mandate of heaven in a more direct way: he reports that the emperor offered to abdicate the throne in favour of Dong Xian, who in the course of his liaison with the emperor had acquired immense political powers (*Han shu* 1990: 93/3738). In light of the impending fall of the Han dynasty at the hands of Wang Mang, whose Xin dynasty was to last from 9 BC to AD 23, the emperor's negligence appears abominable.

As regards the second question concerning sleeping time – how long one should sleep – textual evidence indicates a certain social differentiation. Generally speaking, severity in terms of sleep duration increases with the social rank of a person, the top of the hierarchy ideally being sleepless. Whenever sleep is mentioned in connection with the exemplary ruler, it is in the negative; in other words, he is depicted as being awake at night as he is expected to spend his nights pondering the welfare of his people and scrutinizing his own rulership – an idea that might confuse Western readers who are used to associating sleep with a clear conscience, at least in the sphere of politics.[18]

A passage in the *Records of the Historian*[19] shows sleepless King Wu (reigned 1049/45–1043 BC), founder of the Zhou dynasty, being visited by his younger brother, the Duke of Zhou (*fl.* 1042–1036 BC), who is obviously just as sleepless. They subsequently converse on the problem of how to secure heaven's support for the rising power of the Zhou in a historically vital situation:

> When King Wu had arrived in Zhou he could not sleep [*bu mei*] at night. Dan, Duke of Zhou, went to the king's place and said: 'Why is it that you cannot sleep?' The king replied: 'I tell you: … As until now I have not secured heaven's support how could I have time to sleep [*xia mei*]?'
> (*Shiji* 1989: 4/128–129; cf. *Yi Zhoushu* 1992: 44/20–21)

An important quality of this specific kind of insomnia is its effortlessness. For a gentleman it is not difficult at all to stay awake as the power of his virtue makes him 'forget to sleep at night' (*ye ze wang mei*),[20] like other physical needs that disturb ordinary people:

> The gentleman's longing for humanity and righteousness is such that by day he forgets to eat and by night he forgets to sleep [*junzi si ren yi zhou ze wang shi, ye ze wang mei*]. At sunrise he gets down to work, in the evening he scrutinizes himself [*ri dan jiu ye, xi er zi xing*], thus cultivating his personality.
> (*Da Dai Liji* 1992: 5.2/33)

There is a great distance between *The Yellow Emperor's Inner Canon*'s modest advice to sleep at night and the exalted image of the sleepless gentleman presented in texts of Confucian provenance, as in the *Book of Rites of the Elder Dai* quoted

This discrepancy is brought about by different perspectives. Political
not concerned with the well-being of individuals but with their
socialization. Thus, they favour the submission of one's personal needs
to the needs of others. The effortless renunciation of sleep attributed to the ruler
also appears to be motivated by a politically relevant intention. The sleeplessness
of the ruler or gentleman proves and heightens his aloofness: while all men are
equal before sleep, he is not.

The comparatively mild reduction in sleeping time, exemplified by the phrase
'early to rise and late to bed' (*su xing ye mei*), does not adhere to *The Inner Canon*'s
'neutral' evaluation of sleep either. 'Early' generally refers to the concrete time of
the 'cock's crow' (*ji ming*), i.e. well before sunrise, whereas 'late' less specifically
means 'late at night'.[22] Nevertheless, in terms of sleep, 'early to rise and late to
bed' is the most frequently encountered instruction in texts of Confucian persuasion, from the *Book of Songs* through to the official histories (cf. Steger concerning
Japan). It appears to be the minimal demand for all sorts of people; in other
words, the first step on the way to socialization. This minimum concession is
required from everybody except small children,[23] apparently as a prerequisite for
proper conduct of proficient rulers, of men that are regarded as filial sons and of
devoted wives alike. However, to label someone as one who is 'early to rise and
late to bed' is not primarily intended to give information on his or her sleeping
habits but to characterize the degree of commitment to his or her respective
business. Again, sleep itself is not the point.

In pre-imperial times this pattern of characterization also appears in Mohist
writings with an openly anti-Confucian tendency. These texts even modify the
formula 'early to rise and late to bed' according to various factions of society (cf.
Mozi 1988: 9/9, 25/37, 32/55–56, 37/61). By Han times, though, when the
Mohist school had vanished, 'early to rise and late to bed' had become something of an exclusively Confucian label and was adopted with growing
frequency. This does not mean that only Confucians used it. The formula occurs,
for instance, in the Daoist compilation *Master of Huainan*,[24] where it is put to
exemplary use. The infamous villain Zhou, last king of the Shang dynasty,[25] is
reported to have been annoyed and disturbed by the success of his rival, King
Wen of Zhou, who threatened to win over the people of the Shang empire.[26]
The king of the Shang is notorious for 'banquets of the prolonged night' that are
said to have turned 120 days into a single night (*Lunheng* 1996: 25/107).
Imminent danger moves him to consider embracing a different way of life as a
remedy for the impending ruin of the state:

> If I rise early in the morning and retire late at night [*su xing ye mei*] I will be a
> match for [King Wen] as regards conduct. But [if I do so] my heart will be
> embittered and my body will be weary.
>
> (*Huainanzi* 1992: 12/114)

This unpleasant prospect alone drives Zhou to dismiss the idea. Remarkably,
'early to rise and late to bed' suffices to indicate the whole Confucian concept of

conduct. As with the other occurrences of the formula in the *Huainanzi*, 'early to rise and late to bed' serves to enhance or mark a typically Confucian context – in other words, it is something like a theme song, which is then nonetheless utilized in serving the respective rhetorical ends of the Daoist compilation.

Unlike the minimal demand 'early to rise and late to bed', the earlier mentioned quality of being spontaneously able to 'forget sleep' is ascribed exclusively to the perfect ruler or gentleman. I encountered just one passage in which this phrase was applied to the common people. Notably, this application was accompanied by a complete shift of meaning. The sleeplessness that had otherwise been the adornment of the perfect ruler was now inappropriate and thus condemned. When the common people 'forgot sleep', this was deemed a manifestation of their suffering: in other words, a symptom of an inadequate ruling authority (cf. *Zuozhuan* 1995: Zhao 19/371).

High-born but less virtuous men may try to keep awake at night as well, but since they act on pure volition and lack the necessary inherent quality to 'forget sleep', they must either do violence to themselves or fail. The eminent Warring States politician Su Qin (d. *c.* 320 BC) is described as having pierced his legs with an awl till the blood ran off at his heel just to keep himself from falling asleep while at study.[27] This act of self-mutilation earned him the honorary name of 'Master who pierced his legs' (*Cigu xiansheng*, cf. *Beitang shuchao* 1962: 97/50) and an immortal place as a model student in numerous Chinese encyclopaedias. He is even granted a line in a text as short as the popular primer *Three Character Classic*[28] – alongside a brother in spirit, by the way, who lived about 700 years later and is famous for having tied his hair to a roof beam in order to feel pain when nodding off (Huang Peirong 1995: 200). The pre-eminence of Su Qin's learning covers up both the selfishness of his motives – he was driven by personal ambition only – and the dubiousness of his measures (cf. Steger on sleep reduction and studying).

Doing violence to oneself is – in a similar way to military bravery – a highly questionable measure in Confucian terms as it contradicts the central virtue of filial piety, which demands keeping one's body intact. While self-mutilation is thus rare in the context of early Chinese texts, it becomes much more common after the advent of Buddhism in China. The most prominent example in our context is the assumed founder of the Zen school in China, the Indian monk Bodhidharma (*fl. c.* AD 520), who, according to an apocryphal account, is said to have so hated the interruption of meditation by sleep that he cut off his eyelids.

In pre-Buddhist Chinese literature there appears to be only one example of an attitude similar to that of Su Qin's: Youzi (*c.* 508–457 BC), a disciple of Confucius, who allegedly scorched his palms to fight off sleep while at study. Commenting on Youzi's approach to self-discipline, the Confucian philosopher Xunzi[29] concludes:

> The perfect man – why should he have to force himself or overcome himself or guard himself?
>
> (*Xunzi* 1996: 21/105)

For Xunzi, Youzi's intention of doing away with sleep is not questioned. Rather, he looks down on those that have to employ such drastic methods in order to achieve their intentions. Once again, sleep itself is not the point. The attitude towards sleep merely serves as a convenient indicator of the extent of a person's self-control and self-discipline.

The application of forcible measures to reduce sleeping time is not a widespread topic in early Chinese literature and appears to occur merely as an extreme. It nevertheless seems to represent a general implicit tendency to devalue sleep as a waste of time. The following anecdote from *The Springs and Autumns of Lü Buwei* may serve to clarify this point:

> Ning Yue was an ordinary man from Zhongmou. When he had become weary of the troubles of ploughing and sowing he asked his friend: 'What can I do to get away from this weariness?' His friend replied: 'There is nothing better than studying. If you study for thirty years, you may succeed.' Ning Yue said: 'I ask for fifteen years. When others rest I will not dare rest and when others sleep I will not dare sleep [*wo*].' In fifteen years he was tutor to Duke Wei of Zhou.
>
> (*Lüshi chunqiu* 1994: 24.5/158)

Ning Yue's story illustrates well the disregard of sleep compared with the manifold opportunities and promises of waking – from this point of view, sleep is only accepted as a necessary evil. This perspective even extends to the views of Yang Zhu (*c.* 395–*c.* 335 BC), who, despite enjoying the label of 'hedonist', also regards sleep as time lost for 'real life':

> Yang Zhu said: 'A hundred years is the maximum of longevity. To live to an age of a hundred years is not even achieved by one man in a thousand. Supposing there was one: in the arms [of his mother] in infancy and in drowsy old age, about half of the time is taken. The nightly suspension by sleep [*ye mian*] and the daily waste of time when awake, again take about half of the time. Pain and illness, grief and weariness, loss and failure, sorrow and fear again take about half of the time.'
>
> (*Liezi* 1996: 7/38)

The long line of miserable equivalents to sleep makes Yang Zhu's point very clear: only life that can be consciously enjoyed is worth living. As he strives for nothing but individual pleasure, Yang Zhu's intentions differ completely from those of his Confucian, Mohist or Legalist adversaries who focus on the well-being of the community. Nevertheless, on the path towards their respective ends they all share a deep concern about 'losing time' and utilizing one's life span as fully as possible.

As regards the perception of sleep in Legalist writings, they share some of the perceptions described above; for instance, they similarly view sleep as a state that should, to a certain extent, be reduced. However, the Legalist approach to sleep differs from that displayed in Confucian or Mohist writing. It is characterized by distinctive features that arise from the Legalist sensibility towards control and execution of power. As falling asleep involves a temporary abandonment of one's faculty of control and self-defence, the sleeper delivers him- or herself not only to sleep but also to the mercy of those around that are awake. This weakness can cause the loss of property or well-being or even life: murder in bed also occurs in early Chinese literature (cf. *Lienüzhuan* 1993: 5.1/41, 5.15/50; *Zuozhuan* 1995: Zhuang 8/44; on fears related to sleeping see also Rensen in this volume).

But this is not the only reason to mistrust sleep. Alongside the latent danger from without, there is also danger from within: during sleep, the self-control of bodily functions is at a very low level. There is neither a guarantee against unpleasant dreams nor a way to influence one's words or deeds. In well-known episodes of *Master Han Fei*,[30] this multiple uncertainty drives Zhao, Marquis of Han,[31] to take unique measures after decisive talks with his political advisers:

> He never refrained from sleeping alone [*du qin*] as he was afraid others could find out about his intentions through the words he might utter in his dreams.
> (*Hanfeizi* 1982: 34.21/816)

One of the core issues of Legalist thinking – taking strong actions against the slightest violation of the law – is illustrated by another instance of Marquis Zhao's totalitarian consequences taken in apparent trifles: his famous punishment of the managers in charge of the Marquis's caps and cloaks who violated their respective areas of responsibility while the Marquis was asleep. The keeper of caps covered the sleeping Marquis with his cloak, while the keeper of cloaks failed to do so. They were both executed (*Hanfeizi* 1982: 7.2/738). Considering the rhetorical function of sleep, it proves here to be a pretext or dramaturgical vehicle for triggering probation, similar to the anecdote of Confucius feigning sleep in *The Springs and Autumns of Lü Buwei*. Under examination is not only the loyalty of the officials but also the success of the ruler. His sleep serves as a criterion for the effective implementation of his laws, which should ideally work like laws of nature, needing neither supervision nor even intervention. When this ideal is reached, it is finally proper to 'sleep on a high pillow' (*gao zhen er wo*). This genuinely Legalist metaphor transcends and relieves the intense mistrust of sleep as a sphere largely beyond human control. 'Sleep on a high pillow' was widely employed as a metaphor for the absence of danger and the redundancy of control or intervention in historical and didactic writing of Han times.[32]

Summing up the attitude towards sleep in texts of Confucian, Mohist and Legalist provenance results in a surprisingly homogeneous picture of the mistrust of sleep. Implicit restrictions concerning sleeping time are manifold: no one should sleep during the day; everyone should go to sleep late and get up early; the gentleman should be able to forget sleep and other physical needs effortlessly. However, as these notions are set in a context of ideological argumentation, they serve primarily rhetorical purposes and do not necessarily tell us anything about actual sleeping behaviour in early China. A similar scepticism should be applied to the various aspects of sleep reduction. The uncertainty regarding the representational faculty of the received literature of early China might perhaps be gradually diminished in future by the vast quantities of manuscripts discovered in the last decades awaiting reading and comprehension.

Daoist writing: sleep as a counter-conception

A completely different approach prevails in the Daoist compilation, *Master Zhuang*,[33] where sleep is characterized as a positive counter-conception in both literal and rhetorical respects – certainly not in the sense of recommending sleep but in the sense of a refutation of society's claim to control and instrumentalize the individual. In radical contrast to the Confucian, Mohist and in part also the Legalist praise of waking, the *Zhuangzi* emphasizes that there is only a relative distinction between the states of waking, dreaming and sleeping.

The famous story of Zhuang Zhou's bewilderment about whether he was dreaming he was a butterfly or whether the butterfly was dreaming it was Zhuang Zhou (*Zhuangzi* 1988: 2/7), is joined by likewise notable anecdotes praising dreamless sleep – the only true absent-mindedness. Dreaming, after all, is still a kind of subjective mental activity that is only relatively distinct from waking and doubtless still bears the marks of civilization and ego alike. In the *Zhuangzi* and other Daoist texts, the attribute of dreamlessness is projected onto the Daoist ideal of True or Perfect Men (*zhen/zhi ren*) who lived before civilization began.

> The True men of antiquity slept without dreams and awoke without sorrows [*qi qin bu meng, qi jiao wu you*]; they did not relish their food and breathed from very deep.
>
> (*Zhuangzi* 1988: 6/15)

In the *Zhuangzi*, the fundamental inconsistency of human consciousness that sleep reveals is not regarded as dangerous (as in the Legalist writings) but as promising because it may provide a temporary liberation from the restrictions of waking perception and consciousness and thus from the limitations of subjectivity. For this reason, sleep could serve as a metaphor for meditation, like in the story of Master Beiyi who was overjoyed and started singing when he discovered that his disciple Nieque had fallen asleep – not only during the daytime, but in the middle of a lesson on the Way (*dao*).[34] The story of Beiyi's delight at his disciple's sleep may well allude to Confucius's disapproval of his disciple Zai Yu when he found him sleeping during the day, subtly offering an alternative to Confucius's obsession with utility.

The suitability of 'sleep' as a metaphor for meditation lies in the intellectual emptiness of sleep, especially of dreamless sleep. The following words, put into the mouth of the legendary Yellow Emperor, address this idea concisely:

> Not to think, not to ponder, therein lie the beginnings of knowing the Way.
>
> (*Zhuangzi* 1988: 22/57)

The *Zhuangzi*'s attitude towards life and death displays a similar impartiality as that towards waking and sleeping, an impartiality that is moreover characterized by a complete absence of anxiety. Whereas the close association of sleep with death usually causes a mistrust of sleep – which may even be expressed as a warning to sleep on one's back, like a corpse (cf. *Lunyu* 1995: 10.24/25; *Lunheng* 1996: 68/302) – in the *Zhuangzi*, the same close association serves as an expression of a markedly different attitude to life. The *Zhuangzi* values a deep trust in life in its wholeness; that is, including both waking and sleeping, being alive as well as being dead – in this respect sharing the 'impartial' cosmological perspective of the medical texts in *The Yellow Emperor's Inner Canon* (cf. *Zhuangzi* 1988: 6/17, 18/46). In a playful discourse with his friend Hui Shi (*c*. fourth century BC), triggered by the topic of a great useless tree, Zhuang Zhou praises uselessness, including sleep, which is very often regarded as a waste of time:

> Now, if you have that great tree and feel sorry that it is so useless, why don't you plant it somewhere where there is nothing or on a wide open field and enjoy yourself in doing-nothing at his side or roam in sleep [*qin wo*] beneath it? It won't die an early death by axe or cleaver; nothing will harm it. If you are of no use at all, why should there be hardship and trouble?
>
> (*Zhuangzi* 1988: 1/3)

Presenting his idea of life, Zhuang Zhou allows a day – spent in doing nothing and roaming – to fade away in sleep, thus granting sleep its place on the level of everyday life as well, not only as a metaphor of meditation.

Summary

Early Chinese texts of different persuasions share the treatment of sleep as a marginal subject. However, if this subject is mentioned, it always enhances the genuine characteristics of and contrasts between the different concepts of life and a person's role in society, which texts ascribed to the different so-called 'schools of thought' maintain. While the naturalist or cosmological perspective taken in medical writing results in an impartial treatment of human sleeping and waking, the political writings of Confucian, Mohist or Legalist provenance are generally partial: they explicitly or implicitly favour waking and disregard or even despise sleep, as they view man in a social rather than cosmological perspective. The *Zhuangzi*'s impartiality towards waking and sleeping appears to counter this widespread and dominant attitude on the philosophical as well as rhetorical level.

As references to sleep thus reveal important aspects of the respective notions of life, it is possible to infer the main rhetorical aims of a text from one of the central anecdotes concerning sleep. Confucius's contempt for Zai Yu's lie-down in the daytime suggests the strict subordination of the individual to social requirements that is so characteristic of Confucianism. The Marquis of Han's concern about the inevitable loss of control in sleep evokes the Legalist obsession with control and the execution of power. Yang Zhu's disregard of sleep as a waste of time reveals the utilitarian traits of his so-called hedonistic attitude towards life. Beiyi's delight when his disciple Nieque suddenly falls asleep proves the *Zhuangzi*'s trust in the wholeness of life, including the inconsistency of human consciousness in sleep.

Notes

1 For a comprehensive analysis of the notion of sleep in early Chinese literature, see Richter (2001).
2 On the concepts of *yin* and *yang*, see Graham (1986).
3 The only explicit correlation of sleep and *yin* in early Chinese literature is expressed in *Qianfulun* (1995: 28/53). Implicit correlations are to be found more often, e.g. in *Chunqiu fanlu* (1994: 13.3/59), *Huainanzi* (1992: 3/19), *Lunheng* (1996: 64/285) or *Taixuanjing* (1995: 2/1, 86/61).
4 Cf. the so-called 'monthly commands' (*yueling*) in *Liji* (1992: 6/38–50), *Lüshi chunqiu* (1994: 1–12/1–62) and *Huainanzi* (1992: 5/39–49).
5 A description of the main features of the manuscript is found in Harper (1998: 28–29). For references to Wen Zhi (*fl. c.* 343–301 BC) in the received literature, see *Lüshi chunqiu* (1994: 11.2/54) and *Lunheng* (1996: 24/98–99).
6 Incidentally, to suppose fear or opportunism on the side of Wen Zhi would be out of tune with the *Lüshi chunqiu*'s (1994: 11.2/54) account of his undaunted death at the hands of King Wei's grandson, King Min of Qi (reigned 300–284 BC).
7 Cf. *Huainanzi* (1992: 6/51, 7/57, 20/215 (*gan wo*)) and *Zhuangzi* (1988: 24/67 (*gan qin*), 32/89 (*gan ming*)).
8 The withdrawal, which is typical of sleep, has been remarked upon by Western thinkers as well. The pre-Socratic philosopher Heraklitos (*c.* 500 BC) declared that in sleep, man is removed from the shared empirical world of the day and immersed into a world of his own (cf. Mansfeld 1986: 1/234). Two millennia later, William Shakespeare (1564–1616) in *A Midsummer Night's Dream* (III/2) wrote of 'sleep, that sometimes shuts up sorrow's eye, / steal me awhile from mine own company'. Sigmund Freud (1856–1939) in his *Introductory Lectures on Psychoanalysis* (1916/1917) coined the term 'narcissism of sleep' and remarked that the psychological nature of sleep consists in an 'interruption of interest in the world'. He adds: 'Our attitude towards the world … appears to have the consequence that we are not able to endure it without interruptions' (cf. Freud 1940–1968: 11/84–85).
9 This connection has been pointed out by Harbsmeier (1995: 355), concerning eroticism in Chinese poetry. Other examples for remonstrations that draw on sleep are to be found in *Zhanguoce* (1992: 307/155–156) and *Lienüzhuan* (1993: 2.1/12).
10 A similar attitude appears to have been common in ancient Greece. Demokritos (460/459–*c.* 400 BC) regarded daytime sleeping as an indicator of bodily disorders, confusion, idleness or a lack of spiritual education (cf. Mansfeld 1986: 2/ 265).
11 Exemptions from night's rest were granted in cases such as travelling to the funeral of one's parents (*Liji* 1992: 35.2/155) or during thunderstorms (*Liji* 1992: 13.5/80).
12 Cf. *Shanhaijing* (1994: 17/74). Parallels may be found in the records of the ancient Greek historiographer Herodotos (*c.* 484–425 BC).
13 Confucius, i.e. Kong Qiu, courtesy name Zhong Ni (551–479 BC); Zai Yu, courtesy name Ziwo, alternative name Zai Wo (*c.* 520–481 BC).
14 The *Book of Rites* and other early Chinese texts of Confucian persuasion maintain that – especially after the death of one's parents – an enormously complex and graduated system of mourning instructions should come into effect and last for up to three years. The essentially ascetic mourning instructions aimed at marking every aspect of life of the person under consideration as mourning. Of course, this also referred to

sleeping behaviour: the mourner should no longer sleep in his private chamber but spend the night outside, alone in a hut near the grave of the deceased, and should go without comfortable pillow or mattress.

15 *Lunheng*, *c.* 100. Regarding Confucius's condemnation of Zai Yu, see *Lunheng* (1996: 28/124–125).

16 *Lüshi chunqiu*, compiled *c.* 240 BC under the auspices of Lü Buwei (290–235 BC), former Chancellor of Qin. On Confucius's 'lie-down in the daytime', see *Lüshi chunqiu* (1994: 17.3/102).

17 In Confucian political writing, apart from the above-mentioned exceptional situations, falling asleep during the day appears to have been considered unsatisfactory in any case, even if no withdrawal into the inner chamber is mentioned. In a passage of the *Book of Rites*, a discussion between the Marquis Wen of Wei (reigned 424–387 BC) and Zixia (i.e. Bu Shang, 507–*c.* 420 BC) is recorded. The marquis asks Zixia the reasons for his failure to listen attentively to the ancient music in a ritual context: 'When in my correct attire I listen to the ancient music, I am only afraid to fall asleep [*wo*]' (*Liji* 1992: 19.24/102). In this case as well, inattention to one's duties is expressed through a reference to sleep.

18 An exemplary case may be the sleeplessness that Shakespeare ascribes to Brutus before the murder of Caesar (*Julius Caesar* II/1).

19 *Shiji* (*c.* 100 BC), completed by Sima Qian (?145–?86 BC).

20 There are a number of variants or synonymous expressions, e.g. 'lie down but cannot sleep' (*qin er bu mei*, *Zuozhuan* 1995: Zhao 12/353), 'do not find rest on pillow and mat' (*bu an zhen xi*, *Lüshi chunqiu* 1994: 9.2/44), etc.

21 *Da Dai Liji*, allegedly compiled *c.* first century BC.

22 Variants of synonymous expressions comprise 'be early for the morning audience and retire late' (*zao chao yan tui*, *Zhanguoce* 1992: 461/226), 'sleep late and rise early' (*ye qin su xing*, *Mozi* 1988: 9/9), 'go out early and come home late' (*zao chu mo ru*, *Mozi* 1988: 9/9), etc.

23 In the *Book of Rites* children are explicitly exempt from the strict adult time regime: 'Children [may] go to bed early and get up late [*zao qin yan qi*], just as they like' (*Liji* 1992: 2.5–6/73).

24 *Huainanzi*, compiled before 139 BC at the court of Liu An (?179–122 BC), King of Huainan.

25 Di Xin (reigned *c.* 1086–1045 BC), last king of the Shang, is commonly referred to by the abusive name Zhou. Cf. *Shiji* (1989: 3/105–110).

26 King Wen of Zhou (reigned *c.* 1099/1056–1050 BC), cf. *Shiji* (1989: 4/116–119).

27 *Du shu yu shui, yin zhui zi ci qi gu*, *Zhanguoce* 1992: 40/13–14). Cf. *Shiji* (1989: 69/2241–2248).

28 The *Sanzijing* (compiled *c.* thirteenth to fourteenth century AD) is made up of 356 lines of three characters each.

29 Xunzi (i.e. Xun Kuang, alternative name Xun Qing, *c.* 340–*c.* 245 BC), author of a text of the same title.

30 *Hanfeizi*, a collection of writings by the Legalist philosopher Han Fei (*c.* 280–*c.* 233 BC).

31 Marquis Zhao of Han (reigned 358–333 BC) is something of a model ruler for Han Fei, as acting on the advice of Shen Buhai (*c.* 400–337 BC), he was the first to employ modern Legalist methods of government in Han Fei's native country.

32 Cf. *Hanfeizi* (1982: 26.1/780 (*gao zhen*)), *Zhanguoce* (1992: 133/65 (*gao zhen er wo*)), *Chunqiu fanlu* (1994: 6.6/26 (*an zhen er wo*)).

33 *Zhuangzi*, a heterogeneous collection of Daoist writings that are partly ascribed to the philosopher Zhuang Zhou (*c.* 365–*c.* 290 BC).

34 Cf. *Zhuangzi* (1988: 22/58). Concerning the legendary figures of Beiyi (alternative name Puyizi) and Nieque (traditionally dated to the middle of the third millennium BC), cf. *Gaoshizhuan* 1: 1a–2a.

Bibliography

Aristoteles (1997) *Kleine naturwissenschaftliche Schriften (Parva naturalia)*, trans. Eugen Dönt. Stuttgart: Reclam.

Beitang shuchao (*c.* 630), comp. Yu Shinan (558–638). Taipei: Wenhai (1962), 2 vols.

Brown, Carolyn T. (ed.) (1987) *Psychosinology: The Universe of Dreams in Chinese Culture*. Washington, DC: Woodrow Wilson International Centre for Scholars.

Chunqiu fanlu (*c.* 100 BC) in D. C. Lau and Chen Fong Ching (eds) (1994) *A Concordance to the Chunqiu fanlu* (The ICS Ancient Text Concordance Series 21). Hong Kong: Commercial Press.

Da Dai Liji (*c.* first century BC) D. C. Lau and Chen Fong Ching (eds) (1992) *A Concordance to the Da Dai Liji* (The ICS Ancient Text Concordance Series 6). Hong Kong: Commercial Press.

Eggert, Marion (1993) *Rede vom Traum: Traumauffassungen der Literatenschicht im späten kaiserlichen China* (Münchener Ostasiatische Studien 64). Stuttgart: Steiner.

Freud, Sigmund (1940–1968) *Gesammelte Werke*, ed. Anna Freud, 18 vols, London and Frankfurt am Main.

Gaoshizhuan, comp. Huangfu Mi (215–282), in *Sibu beiyao*. Shanghai: Zhonghua (1927–1937).

Graham, A. C. (1978) *Later Mohist Logic, Ethics and Science*. Hong Kong: Chinese University Press.

Graham, A. C. (1986) *Yin-Yang and the Nature of Correlative Thinking* (IEAP Occasional Paper and Monograph Series 6). Singapore: Institute of East Asian Philosophies.

Han shu (*c.* 100), comp. Ban Gu (32–92). Beijing: Zhonghua (1990 [1962]), 12 vols.

Hanfeizi (*c.* third century BC), in Zhou Zhongling *et al.* (1982) *Hanfeizi suoyin*. Beijing: Zhonghua.

Harbsmeier, Christoph (1995) 'Eroticism in Early Chinese Poetry: Sundry Comparative Notes', in Helwig Schmidt-Glintzer (ed.) *Das andere China. Festschrift für Wolfgang Bauer zum 65. Geburtstag*. Wiesbaden: Harrassowitz, 323–380.

Harper, Donald (1998) *Early Chinese Medical Literature: The Mawangdui Medical Manuscripts* (Sir Henry Wellcome Asian Series 2). London: Kegan Paul.

Huainanzi (second century BC) in D. C. Lau and Chen Fong Ching (eds) (1992) *A Concordance to the Huainanzi* (The ICS Ancient Text Concordance Series 9). Hong Kong: Commercial Press.

Huang Peirong (1995) *Xinyi Sanzijing*. Taibei: Sanmin.

Huangdi Neijing [Suwen & Lingshu] (*c.* first century BC) in Ren Yingqiu (1986) *Huangdi Neijing zhangju suoyin*. Beijing: Renmin weisheng.

Karlgren, Bernhard (1944) 'The Book of Odes', *Bulletin of the Museum of Far Eastern Antiquities* 16: 171–256.

Lau, D. C. (1992 [1979]) *Confucius: The Analects (Lun yü)*. Hong Kong: Chinese University Press.

Lienüzhuan (*c.* second to first century BC) in D. C. Lau and Chen Fong Ching (eds) (1993) *A Concordance to the Gu Lienüzhuan* (The ICS Ancient Text Concordance Series 14). Hong Kong: Commercial Press.

Liezi (*c.* third to fourth century AD) in D. C. Lau and Chen Fong Ching (eds) (1996) *A Concordance to the Liezi* (The ICS Ancient Text Concordance Series 44). Hong Kong: Commercial Press.

Liji (*c.* second to first century BC) in D. C. Lau and Chen Fong Ching (eds) (1992) *A Concordance to the Liji* (The ICS Ancient Text Concordance Series 2). Hong Kong: Commercial Press.

Liu, Lydia H. (1995) *Translingual Practice: Literature, National Culture, and Translated Modernity – China, 1900–1937*. Stanford, CA: Stanford University Press.

Liu Wenying (1993 [1989]) *Meng de mixin yu meng de tansuo*. Taibei: Xiaoyuan.

Lunheng (*c.* 100) in D. C. Lau and Chen Fong Ching (eds) (1996) *A Concordance to the Lunheng*, 2 vols (The ICS Ancient Text Concordance Series 41). Hong Kong: Commercial Press.

Lunyu (*c.* fifth to third century BC) in D. C. Lau and Chen Fong Ching (eds) (1995) *A Concordance to the Lunyu* (The ICS Ancient Text Concordance Series 33). Hong Kong: Commercial Press.

Lüshi chunqiu (*c.* 240 BC) in D. C. Lau and Chen Fong Ching (eds) (1994) *A Concordance to the Lüshi chunqiu* (The ICS Ancient Text Concordance Series 23). Hong Kong: Commercial Press.

Mansfeld, Jaap (1986) *Die Vorsokratiker*. Stuttgart: Reclam.

Mawangdui Hanmu boshu, vol. IV (1985) Beijing: Wenwu.

Mozi (*c.* fifth to fourth century BC) in William Hung *et al.* (eds) (1948) *Mozi yinde* (Harvard-Yenching Institute Sinological Index Series 21). Beiping: Harvard-Yenching Institute. (Reprinted Shanghai: Guji, 1988.)

Qianfulun (second century AD) in D. C. Lau and Chen Fong Ching (eds) (1995) *A Concordance to the Qianfulun* (The ICS Ancient Text Concordance Series 36). Hong Kong: Commercial Press.

Richter, Antje (2001) *Das Bild des Schlafes in der altchinesischen Literatur* (Hamburger Sinologische Schriften 4). Hamburg: Hamburger Sinologische Gesellschaft.

Shanhaijing (*c.* fifth to third century BC) in D. C. Lau and Chen Fong Ching (eds) (1994) *Concordances to the Shanhaijing, Mutianzizhuan, Yandanzi* (The ICS Ancient Text Concordance Series 22). Hong Kong: Commercial Press.

Shiji (*c.* 100 BC), comp. Sima Qian (?145–?86 BC). Beijing: Zhonghua (1989 [1959]), 10 vols.

Shijing (*c.* eleventh to sixth century BC) in D. C. Lau and Chen Fong Ching (eds) (1995) *A Concordance to the Maoshi* (The ICS Ancient Text Concordance Series 29). Hong Kong: Commercial Press.

Sivin, Nathan (1987) *Traditional Medicine in Contemporary China: A Partial Translation of Revised Outline of Chinese Medicine (1972) with an Introductory Study on Change in Present-day and Early Medicine*. Ann Arbor, MI: Center for Chinese Studies, The University of Michigan.

Smith, Arthur H. (1894) *Chinese Characteristics*. New York: Fleming H. Revell.

Taixuanjing (*c.* first century BC to first century AD) in D. C. Lau and Chen Fong Ching (eds) (1995) *Concordances to the Fayan, Taixuanjing* (The ICS Ancient Text Concordance Series 38). Hong Kong: Commercial Press.

Vitiello, Giovanni (1992) 'The Dragon's Whim: Ming and Qing Homoerotic Tales from *The Cut Sleeve*', *T'oung Pao* 78: 341–372.

Xunzi (*c.* third century BC) in D. C. Lau and Chen Fong Ching (eds) (1996) *A Concordance to the Xunzi* (The ICS Ancient Text Concordance Series 45). Hong Kong: Commercial Press.

Yanzi chunqiu (*c.* fourth to third century BC) in D. C. Lau and Chen Fong Ching (eds) (1993) *A Concordance to the Yanzi chunqiu* (The ICS Ancient Text Concordance Series 15). Hong Kong: Commercial Press.

Yi Zhoushu (*c.* fourth to second century BC) in D. C. Lau and Chen Fong Ching (eds) (1992) *A Concordance to the Yi Zhoushu* (The ICS Ancient Text Concordance Series 12). Hong Kong: Commercial Press.

Zhanguoce (*c.* third century BC) in D. C. Lau and Chen Fong Ching (eds) (1992) *A Concordance to the Zhanguoce* (The ICS Ancient Text Concordance Series 1). Hong Kong: Commercial Press.

Zhouli (*c.* third century BC) in D. C. Lau and Chen Fong Ching (eds) (1993) *A Concordance to the Zhouli* (The ICS Ancient Text Concordance Series 13). Hong Kong: Commercial Press.

Zhuangzi (*c.* fourth to second century BC) in William Hung *et al.* (eds) (1947) *Zhuangzi yinde* (Harvard-Yenching Institute Sinological Index Series 20). Beiping: Harvard-Yenching Institute. (Reprinted Shanghai: Guji, 1988.)

Zuozhuan (*c.* fifth to third century BC) in D. C. Lau and Chen Fong Ching (eds) (1995) *A Concordance to the Chunqiu Zuozhuan*, 2 vols (The ICS Ancient Text Concordance Series 30). Hong Kong: Commercial Press.

3 Discourse of mid-day napping

A political windsock in contemporary China

Li Yi

It is not clear when and how taking a mid-day nap began to develop in human society, but throughout the past millennium it has become deeply ingrained in many cultures, such as the Chinese culture. Not only has the practice of mid-day napping been a matter of life-style, but also the intellectual reflections on it have remained an integral part of the greater realm of political thinking. Particularly seen in light of the motto established by the rapid modernisation of the past two centuries, 'time is money', the practice of sleeping in the middle of a day rather than working inevitably arouses acute questioning. Is it simply a waste of one's golden time, irresponsible to one's self, family and society, or is it a good and necessary way to reach a better life? What standard should we use to assess the validity of arguments made either to maintain or abolish the practice? What social and political conditions have shaped such standards? Different answers to these questions inevitably lead to controversy and intellectual discourse. In my approach to these issues, I will focus on the discourse of mid-day napping in China between 1980 and 2000, and examine the larger political and social significance reflected in the discourse.

The Chinese have radically changed their attitudes towards mid-day napping during the last two decades of the twentieth century. Through much of the 1980s, carried away by a sense of urgency for modernisation, many criticised the practice. The critique peaked in 1984 when the government announced an official change in the work schedule, shortening the lunch break from three hours to one hour. Beginning in the late 1980s, however, with increasing complications in their modernisation programme, the Chinese began to question the merit of this change in their traditional life-style. Towards the mid-1990s, the discourse seems to have taken another turn. As a result of the increasing diversification of society, the once politically loaded discourse was overshadowed by the concern of economic growth, and napping became largely a matter of individual choice. Such swift changes of attitudes towards mid-day napping, I have found, reflect the frustrations experienced in efforts to catch up with the West, and remain consistent with the fluctuations of the larger China–West relations. Furthermore, in arguing for mid-day napping, some critics do not see the practice simply as isolated behaviour but an organic link in the social system as a whole. Thus, they touch upon the notion that sleep is a continuation of daytime activities rather than an interruption. These diverging understandings of mid-day napping reflect two different approaches to the role of sleep in our lives. Should it be marginalised and even sacrificed to achieve more during the day, or should it be a necessary preparation for increasing daytime achievement? The controversy has existed for centuries, but it became significantly sharpened by the rapid social transformation in recent decades. China is certainly by no means the only country that has experienced such discourse. A preliminary comparison of the discourse in China with the discourse in other countries with a siesta tradition, therefore, will shed more light on the issue of modernisation.

Mid-day napping in China and the start of a discourse

On 28 July 1980, an article by Linda Mathews appeared in the *Los Angeles Times*: 'It's the Law: The Nap – China Rests on Tradition'. The article started with a story that an American engineer visited an oil rig in the South China Sea, which was equipped with what at the time was probably state-of-the-art technology. To his surprise, all the Chinese workers turned off the machines at noon and went off for lunch, followed by a nap, or *xiuxi* as they call it. This American engineer commented that this practice was unthinkable in the West, for precious machines like this must run twenty-four hours a day to maximise efficiency and profit. Mathews continued with other similar stories, thoroughly venting the frustration that Westerners must have periodically encountered while doing business in China. 'Resident foreigners who brush up against *xiuxi* daily often come to cringe at the mention of the word, for it has become an all-purpose excuse for bad service and delays', said Mathews (*Los Angeles Times* 28 July 1980).

Mathews was by no means alone in having this reaction to mid-day napping in China; most visitors during the 1970s could not miss noticing the practice. Typically, from Monday to Saturday a bell would ring at 11:30 a.m., signalling the beginning of the lunch break. The street would soon be packed with people on their bicycles rushing home from work. With kids coming home for lunch, parents usually prepared a meal more formal than noodle soup. After the dishes were cleaned around 12:30 p.m. there came a time that characterised what was then an idiosyncratic feature of Chinese society: the time for a mid-day nap. The Chinese took their napping quite seriously. Compared to full-scale sleep at night, napping was shorter and therefore simpler: people would not wear their pyjamas, for example. But they usually took off their jackets and long pants and opened up folded quilts. Children who were not willing to follow the norm would be under some parental pressure. It would be a social blunder to visit someone during the naptime, for you might catch your hosts in their under-clothes. To avoid napping beyond the time to get back to work, people usually set the alarm to go off around 2 p.m. The next half-hour or so would witness a scene common in the morning rush hours: the street was once again packed with people who were on their way back to work.

The Chinese thus lived their lives following a rhythm in which their daily routine was split in two by a three-hour lunch-and-nap break. Almost immediately, all government services and most businesses would cease functioning during those three hours, and even the street under the noon sun became quieter. Although Mathews adopted 'China rests on tradition' as the subtitle to her article, she actually singled out the socialist system as the major source of the practice. She argued that with the 'iron rice bowl' guaranteed by socialism, it was impossible for anyone to get fired. She quoted the leader of a Singapore trade mission, stating 'the Communists have taken a naturally industrious people and made them lazy' (*Los Angeles Times* 28 July 1980). It is apparently a feeling that Mathews herself shared.

Mathews' interpretation was not accidental given the fact that 1980 was a time when the ideological rift of the global Cold War had not yet faded. But she has seen only one side of the coin. The practice of mid-day napping, in fact, resulted from a long cultural tradition over the past few thousand years. Daoists would encourage nap-taking for they believe that humans should restrain from deliberate efforts to change the world and let nature take its course. But in the Confucian tradition napping was condemned, because Confucians maintain that the ideal man should always exert himself to seek the best for his family and society. In her article in this volume, Antje Richter has carefully documented the different stands in ancient Chinese literature towards sleep, and the controversy surrounding napping appears consistent with the development of Chinese political thought. Beginning in the period of the Song (960–1279), Daoism and Confucianism gradually merged into congruence. As part of this greater cultural trend, taking a nap was no longer a reserved privilege for the free-spirited Daoist; instead, it became common for the literati in general. The Chinese scholar Shen Jinhao has suggested that the mid-day nap contained profound aesthetic and cathartic values for the Song literati (Shen 1995: 3). This reconciliation of the two previously opposing views on napping set a pattern that was to affect the orientation of the Chinese literati in the later era: one could be both a tight Confucian official and a loose Daoist philosopher at the same time. The personality of Zhuge Liang, a hero in the late-Ming vernacular novel *The Romance of Three Kingdoms*, illustrates this point particularly well. When times were right, he was a Confucian, making his best effort to manage the state and pacify all under heaven. But when times were adversarial, he would withdraw into his own world, drinking, chanting and enjoying a mid-day nap. No doubt, napping is by no means an invention of the communist leaders who took over China in 1949; it has always been an important part of tradition.

A new edge was added to the controversy surrounding mid-day napping in the early twentieth century when crises, both foreign and domestic, once again put China in a difficult situation. In their long search to escape from the crises, some Chinese began to lose their faith in the traditions that had brewed them. During the 1910s, a small group of students who had returned from studies abroad started a new cultural movement, one in which they blamed China's weakness – as witnessed in repeated military defeats – on traditional culture. In an effort to abandon traditional culture, the practice of mid-day napping, along with foot binding, was condemned as a trademark of Chinese 'backwardness'.

The loudest voice of this wholesale attack on tradition belonged to Hu Shi, who returned to China and served as a professor of philosophy at Beijing University after earning his doctoral degree from Columbia University at the age of 24. Drawing on his rich experiences of living in the United States, Hu singled out Chinese tradition as the factor dragging his country down while other countries were racing towards modernisation (Chow 1981; Schwarcz 1990). Many other people followed the direction that Hu had spearheaded, such as the writer Lu Xun, who is known for his criticism and critique of traditional Chinese culture. This kind of questioning attitude towards tradition remains influential in the Chinese intellectual world, and we can still hear its echo in 1970s Taiwan when Bo Yang wrote and published a book, *The Ugly Chinamen* (Bo 1991).

This round of attacks on tradition took place at a time when the West constituted a source of the crises, and therefore the discourse of mid-day napping was consistently linked with the intellectual current of Westernisation. This current was nonetheless quickly diluted in China and submerged under a stronger current, nationalism. Under the flag of nationalism, a variety of social forces gathered, including a reviving traditionalism and rising communism, and it was the combined effort of these two that finally triumphed. Such nationalist sentiment was so strong that it wiped out most of the initiatives to learn from the West, as epitomised by the 'one-sided' diplomacy of the People's Republic. As far as the practice of mid-day napping is concerned, the communist authority identified itself as a regime of the working class and thus wrote in Article 49 of its 1950 constitution, 'The working people have the right to rest'. The traditional practice of napping, as part of 'rest', was legally protected for the first time under the shadow of communist ideology. After an ugly break-up with the Soviet Union in the late 1950s, Mao Tse-Tung led the country on a radical road of revolutionary isolation, which China followed till Mao's death in 1976. During these two decades when foreign influence of any sort was reduced to a minimum, the earlier attack on the practice of napping, which had never been fully fledged to begin with, also waned.

With little significant challenge, the practice not only remained common but became increasingly obsessive in Chinese society. Most Chinese apparently took this phenomenon for granted, giving little thought to it and rarely talking about it. Mao Tse-Tung himself might not necessarily take naps due to his behavioural abnormality consistent with his rebellious personality. As a close observer revealed, Mao had a different biological clock: while others functioned following the cycle of a twenty-four-hour day, Mao's cycle was a twenty-eight-hour day (Li Zhisui 1996). Most other political leaders, such as Deng Xiaoping, took naps without questioning it any further (Mao 2000: 146). While Mathews blamed the Chinese napping culture on the socialist system, the Chinese leaders saw it as a necessary ingredient of the 'good life' under the socialist system, and thus gave it further justification (*Renmin Ribao* 20 December 1958). More importantly, to have a good life, taking a nap was not an end in itself; it was instead the means by which to achieve the end, i.e. a better functioning society. In the rural areas where napping was also popular, for example, the leaders often placed the practice in a broader socialist scheme. A 'planned rest' was necessary for a 'planned production', according to the rural leaders (*Renmin Ribao* 29 December 1958). For the Chinese, the better rest acquired through mid-day naps was thus for the ultimate purpose of demonstrating the superiority of the socialist system.

If the practice of mid-day napping in China was at all confirmed during the communist rule, it was probably the unique social structure there that made it easier to practise. In most Western countries, commuting between work and home would be an obstacle if one chose to go home to take a nap in the middle of the day, but in China this presented less of a problem. People who study contemporary China are familiar with the term *danwei*, or 'work unit'. It may be a factory, a school, a service or a government agency, usually in an urban area. But what differentiates a Chinese *danwei* from what we commonly know of as a 'business' is that the Chinese *danwei* provides not only jobs for its members, but also most major services such as medical care, nursery facilities and, most importantly, housing. In other words, workers and their families usually live in flats assigned to them by the *danwei*, which usually builds the residence near, or within, its territory. This arrangement makes it possible for the workers to go home quickly at 11:30 a.m., and return to work by 2:30 p.m. after a nap. It must be emphasised that this type of arrangement, which turned out to facilitate the practice of mid-day napping, was not originally intended for that purpose. It was simply part of the great socialist experiment.

Mathews launched her criticism in a unique moment of Chinese history. In the late 1970s, the Chinese bid adieu to their earlier revolutionary isolation after the death of Chairman Mao. The price of the previous experiment was high, for the revolutionary fire burnt out not only material resources but also the enthusiasm of an entire generation. As if awakening from a long mid-day dream, the Chinese suddenly found that, compared with the developed countries, their lives were ones of poverty, no matter how they romanticised them. After the new leadership under Deng Xiaoping nailed down the fulfilment of the so-called 'modernisation in four fields' as its national goal, the country took an abrupt turn. It began to abandon much of its past in which it had once taken pride and to embrace the West, the enemy that it once sought to bury, in the hope of acquiring vitally needed resources for modernisation. Corresponding to this turn, the theory of 'wholesale Westernisation' gained a new momentum, and the feeling that anything Western was surely better than anything Chinese quickly developed and became widespread, particularly among the youth and intellectuals. A popular joke, that the moon in the West is rounder than in China, perfectly exaggerated such feelings. The tendency continued and intensified through the early 1980s. As a result of the open door, discos and democracy found their way into the once tightly closed country, and accompanying them was a call to abolish the traditional practice of mid-day napping, a practice that many Westerners frowned upon.

Prior to Mathews' article, many Chinese had already begun to poke fun at the issue of modernisation in a cultural and political context, particularly those in the academic world. Luo Yuanzheng and Xue Yongying, for example, suggested in the January 1980 issue of the Chinese journal *Economic Management* that loafing on the job had brought the economy to the brink of collapse in previous decades. 'Too many workers are not motivated to work hard and do only the minimum amount of work necessary', they found (Luo and Xue 1980: 1). This voice represented a widespread and still-growing feeling among intellectuals who believed that inertia, which was epitomised by mid-day napping, was what kept them behind the rest of the world. This early Chinese discourse of inertia often bears an influence from politics in the top leadership at that time, for the critics tended to put the blame on the 'Gang of Four', and accused them of nourishing such loafing. But the self-criticism by the Chinese signalled the inception of an ideological shift from the previous revolutionary radicalism to a moderate reformism, the guideline that the Communist Party's Third Plenum in 1978 clearly identified for the nation (Hsu 1985: 800).

It is this unique historical context that has assigned a significant role to Mathews' criticism. She not only addressed a general dissatisfaction with a tradition, but also questioned how soon, if ever, the Chinese would modernise their country. People in other countries with siesta traditions take mid-day naps too, but they tend to work later in the day, while the Chinese usually had a six-hour workday, Mathews pointed out (*Los Angeles Times* 28 July 1980). Although she missed the fact that the Chinese then had a six-day workweek, she made her point clear that the practice was a barrier to efficiency. In this way, she touched upon one of the most sensitive nerves in the Chinese mind: would they ever achieve the national goal of modernisation? More provokingly, Mathews contrasted the ethnic Chinese from Singapore, Hong Kong and Taiwan, who began to enjoy the fruit of economic success, with the Mainland Chinese, where phenomenal poverty was rampant. This contrast only confirmed the sense of the Mainland Chinese that their poverty was not because of their genes; it must be due to some cultural and political reason. And now the question was what should be changed and how to change it.

The great discourse of mid-day napping

Linda Mathews' criticism of the Chinese culture was presumably not the first of its kind. In fact, beginning in the 1950s, China-watchers in the West witnessed constant criticisms of the Chinese tradition and the socialist system that the Chinese practised. Compared with these other criticisms, Mathews' appears to be tackling only a minor aspect of her target. Rarely, however, had a Western work generated a reaction from the Chinese world, as did Mathews' article. Following its publication, the Chinese started a great discourse of mid-day napping, and the discourse revealed their juxtaposition in modernisation and their understanding of the role of napping in the social system.

Mathews undoubtedly brought to the surface China's long-fermented rejection of its immediate past, and focused attention on the practice of mid-day napping. With all of its loaded meanings and sarcasm and published at the moment of a major transition, Mathews' article became a trigger for a more severe battle over the legitimacy of napping. Highly conscious of the fastest way to modernise and attentively watching the gestures of the West, the Chinese would certainly not miss such criticism. On 21 August 1980, the *People's Daily*, the flagship of the Chinese media, translated and reported Mathews' article. By comparing her original article with the Chinese translation, it can be seen that the latter skipped the criticism of socialism but highlighted the frustrations of foreign visitors with the low efficiency in China. Such a selection in translation is natural considering the present state, but even the incomplete translation of a Western China-watcher's work sufficiently alarmed the Chinese. In the months that followed, responses to Mathews' criticism from different quarters of Chinese life developed into a great discourse of the merits of the practice of mid-day napping.

The discourse centred on a rivalry between a pair of sharply opposing opinions. One opinion was against Mathews' criticism. According to this opinion, many aspects of life in China, including residence, diet and work, were too harsh for the Chinese people. For example, physical labour, which remained the main form of labour output among the workforce, consumed so much energy that they had to take a nap to recover from exhaustion. Chinese meals were also much lower in nutritional value than meals in the developed countries. So it was not that they had too much rest; rather, they did not have enough of it. Some people argued against Mathews' criticism from a different perspective. They insisted that as a foreigner, Mathews did not truly understand the Chinese culture. It was true that inefficiency was widespread in China, they maintained, but it was due to some deficiency in the system and poor quality of the leadership because of the 'Gang of Four', and not due so much to the practice of taking a nap. So merely abolishing the practice would not help to improve the situation. For them, it was hard to accept the fact that Mathews, a foreigner, had pointed a finger at a particular aspect of Chinese culture, and they went so far as to blame the *People's Daily* for transmitting this criticism to Chinese readers.

On the other hand, Matthews' criticism did not lack support from Chinese readers. Many of them felt that she was right on target, and agreed that taking a nap was entirely a waste of time. They argued that it was necessary to take some break in the middle of the working day, but it is questionable whether the practice of napping would be as popular and lengthy as it was at the time. A more radical wing of this opinion held that in the era when China was falling far behind the developed countries, it was desperately in need of a forced march to catch up. Furthermore, these critics maintained that napping was not only a waste of resources and capital, but also made it hard for China to match the pace of the developed countries. The critics apparently believed that such a march was vital for modernisation. The editor of the *People's Daily* soon summarised these two sharply diverging reactions to Mathews' criticism, and introduced them to a wider readership (*Renmin Ribao* 18 September 1980).

Contrasting these two different reactions has epitomised two different attitudes towards tradition. The first reaction emphasises that Chinese society has its own idiosyncratic features and should not blindly follow the Western way. Taking into consideration diet and the nature of labour, those who held this opinion clearly did not treat the practice of mid-day napping as simply isolated social behaviour. Instead, they focused on the connection between the rest and one's normal functioning, highlighting the necessity of the former for the latter. In addition, these critics suggested that abolishing the age-old practice of napping would have more of a symbolic than an actual meaning. At the centre of this concern was the view that the practice was a link in the entire system by which Chinese society operated; its abolition would inevitably result in a malfunction in many other social sectors. Lunch service, for example, was singled out as a major problem: if napping was abolished, how would the working people have enough time for lunch as they had to wait in a long line to get to the lunch window? For these critics, abolishing napping was not as simple as replacing a part in a machine; it was a move that would affect the working of the whole system. Clearly, this discourse was in essence a continuation of that of the late nineteenth century, when the Chinese faced the question of how far China should go in adopting Western ways in building a stronger and richer society.

The second reaction, on the other hand, represents a view that in order to modernise the country, China must abandon its tradition and adapt itself to the modernisation paradigm set by the developed countries. This argument was implicitly, if not explicitly, based upon the assumption that the Western path of modernisation was universal, a path that the Chinese must follow. For them, the practice of napping was an element of tradition unfit for the pace of the modern world, and therefore should be abolished. The discourse continued throughout the next few years without clear results. For the Beijing government, whether to abolish napping constituted one of the many dilemmas in its modernisation project; although a very small one compared with others, it was still similar in nature. On the one hand, maintaining consistency by honouring tradition had a twofold meaning: it was not only a question of maintaining the spirit of independence but also vital for social and political stability. On the other hand, as the clock of the century ticked its way towards the end, the anxiety about catching up with the developed countries ruthlessly overwhelmed Chinese leaders. After repeated deliberation, on 26 November 1984, the State Council officially announced that beginning on 1 January 1985, the mid-day break for government workers would be cut from three hours to one hour. The decision clearly stated that this change of the work schedule was to meet the needs of modernisation both at home (*duinei*) and abroad (*duiwai*), and to promote working efficiency (*Renmin Ribao* 26 November 1984).

What explains the side that the government finally picked in the ongoing discourse is, obviously, the timing. The early 1980s were a time when the communists had just escaped from the Cultural Revolution, which had burnt out the faith of many Chinese people, and the new leaders hoped to acquire an additional legitimacy by promising the people a better life in the decades to come. Moreover, it was a time when China had just restored normal relationships with the United States after hostility for almost three decades, and new expectations were on the rise with the cementing of a new relationship. For China, the economic success of the West, particularly the United States, represented its own future, regardless of how it would get there. The anxiety to catch up, accompanied by fresh trust in the West, underlay the decision-making of the leaders in Beijing.

It is also interesting to note that it was the government that took the lead in moulding social practice. On 27 December 1984, an article by Ma Wenfei and Fan Zhengxiang appeared in the 'science mailbox' column of the *People's Daily*, replying to a reader's question on whether less napping time would affect health. In the article, Ma and Fan made three points. First, they argued that taking naps was merely a habit that could be changed. Quoting from some unidentified sources, they stated that in the morning one's analytical capacity was at its peak and the afternoon was good for memory, while night-time was best for sleeping. A fully scheduled day would ensure better sleep at night. Second, they pointed out that not everyone takes naps. The examples given here include those in the service industries, as well as many great people such as Zhou Enlai, Napoleon, Karl Marx and Thomas Edison, who Ma and Fan said never took naps. Again, Ma and Fan did not specify where they got the information, but the point they wanted to make is that staying up all day would not harm one's mental and physical health. Finally, they maintained that while taking a break in the middle of the working day might be necessary, one nonetheless did not have to sleep. They suggested what they called 'active rest', namely taking attention away from routine work by focusing on other things. While writing *Das Kapital*, Karl Marx would turn away to do some mathematical exercises to rest his mind when he became tired, instead of taking a nap, according to Ma and Fan (*Renmin Ribao* 27 December 1984).

It is hard to identify exactly who Ma and Fan are, but the *People's Daily* is a government-controlled newspaper, and the government usually passes its messages to the people through the newspaper. As I have already outlined, however, although the socialist system in China organisationally facilitated the spread of the traditional practice of mid-day napping, the practice was not part of the government's explicit political programme. Despite the government's authoritarian nature, its disciplining power was significantly weakened during the Cultural Revolution, and a major tone in the aftermath was to rebuild its authority (Xin 1996). This new tone was in harmony with the sense of urgency to recapture time wasted by the 'Gang of Four', a repeated voice of the times that reflected the overwhelming anxiety to catch up with the developed countries. The fact that the government attempted to change the course of a social practice using the media under its control was consistent with its more assertive role in the social realm.

The State Council's decision to change the work schedule was followed by cheers from some sectors of society, with the strongest support coming from the intellectuals. Around the mid-1980s, a discourse on the socialist life-style was under way in the academic world. A common theme consistent in this discourse was the comparison of the Chinese and Western life-styles. Emerging in this comparison was a consensus that the Western life-style was one of efficiency, and that with a supposedly more advanced socialist system, China must have better efficiency (Pei 1987: 1; Peng 1986a: 5). Whether or not to abolish mid-day napping thus became closely linked to a higher-level theoretical debate. For some scholars, this comparison has a more profound significance, one in which they see the importance of 'historical, modern and world consciousness'. Peng Ding'an suggests, for example, that the socialist life-style should be the most modern, and represent the future of humankind (Peng 1986a: 1). All these arguments seem to have suggested the necessity to develop a life-style different from the old one. The most explicit support for the official change of the working schedule was an article by Jin Zhe and Chen Shejun, who argued that a modern concept of time was essential for a modern life-style, and that the abolition of napping was a significant move for developing a modern life-style (Jin and Chen 1985: 1). Thus, by the mid-1980s, the call to abolish mid-day napping reached its zenith; it was accepted by many in the society, and was actually put into effect by law with the visible hand of the government.

This does not mean, however, that there was no resistance. Just below the surface of overwhelming support for the change, dissent was gathering. On 18 December 1985, Sheng Hongzu, a social critic who wrote for the 'current events' column in the *People's Daily*, published an article dismissing the practice of mid-day napping. In the article, he sarcastically claimed that he would raise both his hands to support the change of work schedule, but at the same time he sharply picked out a few things with which he would be concerned when the change was implemented. Among these was the problem of lunch service. Most of the *danwei*, or work units, in China had their own lunch services for their members, but these services were usually not very good. A major problem was the long wait before one could get to the window. (I myself remember as a student in Beijing University that to purchase lunch was an experience similar to battle.) Sheng now pointed out that with the abolition of napping the problems of the lunch service would become more acute and must be tackled (*Renmin Ribao* 19 December 1984). In this respect Sheng was not alone. A week later, Li Gengcen, another critic, wrote to the *People's Daily* to address the same problem (*Renmin Ribao* 27 December 1984). These reactions to the change in the work schedule are apparently a continuity of the negative reactions to Mathews' criticism. The State Council was undoubtedly fully aware of the resistance. In order to soothe the feelings of unease that the change might arouse, the State Council particularly emphasised that this change would also leave government workers with more time for study, domestic chores and social life (*Renmin Ribao* 27 November 1984).

The great discourse on the practice of mid-day napping in response to Mathews' criticism clearly reflected the nature of the timing in the early 1980s. The two opinions in the discourse derived from two different interpretations of the role of napping in social life; that is, how necessary it was and to what degree it could be sacrificed. The anxiety to catch up with the developed countries, which prevailed in the discourse, was quite common among countries such as China, which were later to enter modernisation. In addition, the Chinese settled their discourse with an executive order from the State Council, a fashion common in many developing countries when addressing social and economic issues. This settlement was only temporary, however, for resistance was by no means entirely subdued. In fact, the voice of resistance was merely submerged under the much louder cry for modernisation. It was destined to resurface in due course.

New turns in the continuous discourse

The Chinese discourse of mid-day napping continued after the official change of the work schedule in 1985. On the one hand, the change undoubtedly represented the interests of those modernisation-minded people eager to catch up with the West. On the other hand, the majority of the Chinese people who had been accustomed to taking a break for a nap felt that the change interrupted the rhythm of their normal lives. When the job of catching up went smoothly and as long as relations between China and the developed countries that it sought to emulate remained stable, support for the change seems to have held its course. But in the late 1980s, economic reform reached a bottleneck and Chinese–Western relations stumbled through a stormy period. Against this new background, different opinions began to surface and the discourse took a new turn – centred on the merits, and therefore apparent lack, of napping.

Resistance to abolishing mid-day napping continued to brew among the Chinese people. It is interesting that the first one who stood against the government's decision was once again a China-watcher in the West. In the article 'I Don't Detest a Siesta', Braden Phillips expressed his regret that the Chinese had officially abolished mid-day napping, arguing that China, like many other siesta countries, may not be an industrial giant, but siesta is not the cause. He pointed out that all that was necessary was to add the length of the snooze to the end of the working day, and there would be no loss of competitive edge. Inspired by Bertrand Russell's call for a four-hour workday, Phillips urged fitting a half-hour nap into our busy lives (*New York Times* 18 January 1985). Phillips' view on siesta probably represents a feeling towards modernisation in a post-modernisation era, a feeling that many Chinese might not have shared. This time, however, the *People's Daily* did not report on Phillips' article, and it is not clear how the Chinese would have reacted.

Nevertheless, the Chinese did not have difficulties finding their own reasons to defend the practice of napping. Noticeably, their opposition to abolishing the practice by this time took on new perspectives. Instead of narrowly regarding napping as being cultural and habitual, they now argued for it from a biological point of view, and found fuel to support their view in modern science. In 1988, Da Di published a short article in a popular medical magazine, *Scientific Life*, where he quoted what he claimed to be a discovery of German sleep specialists. According to his explanation, the discovery showed that a person could stay awake for only four hours, and that the body demands a rest once the four hours ends (*Kexue Shenghuo* 1988: 8). The defence for mid-day napping grew stronger from the perspective that the practice was a biological need. Tan Jiwen introduced his readers to the research of scientists in Greece and Britain who stated that taking mid-day naps would reduce the risk of heart attack by 30 per cent, and that this was why siesta countries in the Mediterranean region have a lower rate of heart attacks (*Zhongguo Shangye Bao* 1988: 7). Since these writers intended their articles for popular readers, they did not specify the sources of the scientific discoveries. But the fact that they turned to Western science and technology to play a tune disharmonious with the officially sponsored 'catch-up-with-the-West' programme demonstrates an interesting dilemma in China's modernisation.

A second perspective that the pro-napping writers took was to argue for the practice following the line of tradition. The first to speak from this perspective was Shao Weiguo, who in 1987 published an article in a popular medical magazine. In his article, Shao gave the example of Zhao Tingdong, a man from the Qing era (1644–1911) known for his longevity, to show that the best physical nourishment (*yangsheng*) was to follow the natural course and rest in the afternoon. In the end, he stated that napping was vital for one's physical health and spiritual well-being, and argued that it should not be sacrificed for any reason (*Dazong Yixue* 1987: 9). Liu Zhanwen and Zhu Ming wrote that napping was a human practice corresponding to the cyclical motion of nature, and the mid-day nap was based on a profound understanding of the harmony between humankind and nature (*Dazong Jiakang* 1989: 12). It is hard to tell who these writers are, but they certainly share one thing in common. Their message is very clear: the traditional practice of mid-day napping contains reasonable elements, it is not simply a waste of time, and to learn from the West is not to trash the entirety of China's own traditions.

Carried away by this trend, some writers even romanticised the practice of mid-day napping. For them, it was not so important whether or not the practice would hinder the modernisation programme. Rather, the practice remained so highly integrated into Chinese daily life that it became part of the beauty of living. In 1988, Chen Youcai wrote a poem entitled 'mid-day napping':

> The air is exhausted, no longer carrying songs;
> the shade is exhausted, penetrating into the earth under my feet;
> my eyes are exhausted, resting upon the fence of eyelids,
> remaining is only my day dream,
> that follows grape vines up to the blue sky.
> (*Renmin Ribao* 8 December 1988)

Like his predecessors in ancient times, Chen assigned in this poem an artistic value to napping, a mathematically immeasurable value. As a serious campaign contingent with the modernisation effort, the call for abolishing mid-day napping thus ran into strong obstacles.

In the late 1980s and early 1990s, more articles appeared in newspapers and magazines calling for a legitimate status for napping. This reverse from the previous tone of the discourse was not an isolated phenomenon. It was not because the Chinese had better exposure to modern science, or because they had developed some new taste for their own past; instead, the reverse course echoed frustrations that the Chinese encountered in their efforts to modernise. The early 1980s witnessed the burning desire of the Chinese to learn from the West and thus brought them into an unusual closeness, which constituted one important condition for the soaring call for ending mid-day napping. As some Western China scholars indicated, in the 1980s many Chinese intellectuals regarded Westernisation as the only means for China to modernise (Zheng 1999: 76). But it was not easy to develop a truly close relationship with the West, due to the profound differences in many aspects. Pouring into China was not only technology and capital, which the Chinese leaders hoped for, but also discos and democracy, which they did not want. The partnership between China and the West therefore was one filled with uncertainties even at its inception. The movement to cleanse this capitalist spiritual pollution was launched in 1983, followed by many others aimed at ridding the Chinese people of the influence of 'bourgeois liberalism'. The thriving expectations and drive for rapid modernisation were thus replaced by hesitation and reluctance. Meanwhile, the reform to develop a market economy to connect China with the West began to show its limits and side effects. Less government planning and control, for example, resulted in numerous errors and rampant corruption. All these difficulties led people to question whether the Western path was the right one for successful modernisation. As such questioning deepened, it touched upon the bigger question of whether the Western way was the right way for China to follow, or whether the Chinese model was worth holding onto. Battles ensued as the country was deeply divided on these questions, and the massive student demonstration in Tiananmen Square was in fact a result of an accumulation of these battles. In this larger and changing political climate, the discourse of mid-day napping also began to show some corresponding fluctuations. The question of whether the practice should be continued or discontinued thus transcended its original scope.

Indeed, the military crackdown of the student demonstration in 1989 probably marks the lowest point for the movement that steadily pushed support for abolishing the mid-day nap. As relations between China and the West stumbled through a rocky period, many Western-inspired social reform projects, such as the one to end napping, also gradually faded away. The hidden message was very readable: just because the people in the West do not practise mid-day napping, or just because foreign China-watchers were criticising the Chinese for taking naps, it does not at all mean that the Chinese would have to give it up. The fact that it became popular to see values of mid-day napping in the light of tradition clearly demonstrates this mentality, which in turn resulted from the confusion and uncertainty in modernisation.

The early 1990s saw yet another gradual but fundamental change in the political climate in China. After a period of rigid control in the intellectual world that essentially muted politicised discourses like the one on mid-day napping, the wind started to blow the other way in 1992 when Deng Xiaoping began touring the southern provinces. He urged the people to set aside the once-vehement ideological debate and focus on economic growth. 'Economic development is the right cause', he stated, reasserting his well-known 'cat theory' that 'regardless of whether a cat is white or black, so long as he catches mice, it is a good cat'.

Economic growth was once again identified as the top priority in the national agenda, and society was again reactivated. The emphasis on economic growth during the early 1990s, however, was not simply a repetition of that in the 1980s. In the first place, as a result of the military crackdown, most people tended to shun, if not become indifferent to, politics. Many people who were once excited by the sacred fight for democracy now lay down their Molotov cocktails and picked up their briefcases, finding great opportunities for their talents in the business world. In fact, such a depoliticised pursuit of economic gain was exactly what Deng Xiaoping wanted the Chinese people to follow. Second, compared with the 1980s, the rapid growth of the economy in the 1990s saw a much reduced role for state enterprises. It was the private sector, which had grown considerably in the past decade, which was surfing on the tide. By the late 1990s, the private sector in China had achieved stunning growth. It currently employs an increasingly large portion of the labour force, and generates roughly half of the state revenue, compared with the insignificant numbers in the early 1980s (Borthwick 1998: 429). In other words, if in the 1980s it was necessary for the elite to steer or influence the public mind towards efficiency, in the 1990s the public began to sit behind the wheel. Some scholars defined this phenomenon as a retreat from the public into the professions, a post-modernist formula (Xu 1999: 57).

Under these circumstances, the Chinese discourse on napping gradually faded as a hot topic in the media. The overheated economy between 1992 and 1996 provided ample opportunities for people to get rich, which quickly attracted popular attention, and the fast-paced privatisation and favourable policies for the so-called 'socialist market economy' allowed the idea of 'time is money' to become established without much effort. For the people who worked in the growing private sector, what set their timetables was neither the national goal of modernisation, nor some old customs that they observed. Rather, it was the strong drive to make the best of this opportune time. Chen Jiayuan, a Beijing University student who served as my assistant during my research trip in the summer of 2000, mentioned that his parents no longer took mid-day naps. He explained that the reason for this was that they were among the stock market players, a new social configuration emerging since the stock market was reopened in Shanghai. These players would not take a nap as long as the wheel of fortune was spinning. Even the millions who remained in the state enterprises and government offices were carried away to one degree or another by this widespread trend. It has subsequently created a wave known as 'going down to the ocean', meaning laying down their 'iron rice-bowl' guaranteed by the socialist system and participating in the private business world.

The heated discourse on mid-day napping thus took a turn that echoed this changing political climate. Instead of arguing back and forth with messages loaded with political and ethical meanings, critics now tended to address more practical aspects of the issue. In his article 'A New Kind of Mid-day Nap', Zhang Xiaoping maintains that napping was but a habit of individual choice; if you choose to take it you should take it before lunch, which may be more beneficial than after lunch (*Zhongguo Tiyu Bao* 2 September 1992). Yu Bojun wrote to coach his readers on the four best ways to take a nap. First, one should not take naps immediately after lunch, as it would hinder digestion. Second, napping should not last more than one hour. Third, the right position for napping should be to lie down on the right side, which would facilitate breathing. Fourth, older people and those with low blood pressure should not take a nap (*Jinwan Bao* 16 May 1993). Many other people approached the subject in a more scholastic way, like Chen Kunyou, who studied different ways of taking naps, and concluded that the best way to nap is for about ten to twenty minutes after lunch (*Jiankang Bao* 5 July 1994). These writers derived their statements from a wide variety of sources, and the authenticity of their ideas was undoubtedly subject to scrutiny. But the point here is not whether or not they were right in what they argued, but the fact that the central concern of the discourse was no longer the same as in the 1980s. The political content in the discourse was largely unloaded, replaced by the technical aspects of taking a nap. This shift of concern clearly corresponds with the major rhythm of life in China.

Contrary to the 1980s, most of the articles on mid-day napping during the 1990s appeared in small and apolitical newspapers and magazines. The size of their readership is not clear, or how much they influenced readers, but the subject undoubtedly ceased to be a political one. The new central concern in the fading discourse during this time became the quality of life. Cao Zhongqiang, for example, suggested that one would live a better life by taking naps (*Dazong Yixue* 1995: 11). Liu Zhaohua also stressed that a short nap may secure a better mood and higher spirit for the remainder of the day (*Kexue Shenghuo* 1997: 2). Clearly, the practice and the discourse have become increasingly marginalised in the political concerns of the public. After the mid-1990s, however, articles on the subject, although rare, still appeared occasionally in newspapers and magazines. In 1999, for example, Zou Zhiliang introduced readers to new research done by Israeli scientists, which suggests that the mid-day nap may be deadly for the elderly (*Meiri Qiaobao* 2 December 1999). It has generated almost no significant response from its audience. This is not to say that people in China will no longer take mid-day naps; rather, as society has become increasingly diversified, fewer and fewer people continue to think of it as a vital issue related to the future of the nation. Instead, the siesta has become a decision made at the level of the individual, rather than a subject of debate in the public arena.

The Chinese discourse in the light of comparison

China is clearly not the only country in the world where mid-day napping has been practised. In the Spanish-speaking world, the term siesta reveals its high degree of popularity. China is also not the only country that has gone through the process of modernisation. In much of what we call the 'West', namely the developed nations, the same process was completed a century earlier. Looking across the world, an interesting pattern for comparison emerges for the examination of the Chinese discourse on mid-day napping. In the West, during the same period of time, it appears that the issue of whether or not to take naps rarely posed a serious question to the populace. But in the 1990s, people there became more concerned about their well-being than the need for economic success, and their view on the siesta also changed. The curve of the changing attitudes in the West also reflected a different state of the society there, and revealed a gap between the one in China and that in the West.

Generally speaking, until the 1980s there were two different approaches to the siesta culture, one positive and the other negative, similar to those in China. For many, the siesta represents an exotic culture, believed to have developed in association with the local diet. The Dominican Republic is known as 'the nap capital of the Caribbean', for example, where people take their lunch and siesta seriously. 'This sleepy, steamy, three-hour calm between coffee-hopping Dominican mornings and rum-infested Dominican nights is excellent proof of the symbiotic relationship between food and human biological rhythm', as Daisanne McLane suggests. McLane admits that coming directly from Manhattan where the word 'lunch' generally precedes 'meeting' or 'hour', the tropical enlightenment knocked her out like culinary jet lag (*New York Times* 25 August 1991). Others may have a more critical view and often relate the siesta to poor work ethics, laziness and low productivity. But they also point out that other siesta countries differ from China in that the people there tend to work until early evening to make up for the missing hours after taking a long mid-day nap (*New York Times* 18 January 1985). A striking difference between the discourse of the subject in the West and that in China is that in the West it remained mellow, was rarely loaded with political spices, and did not involve the authorities.

Towards the late 1990s, however, the volume of discourse in the West increased as many critiques aimed to promote nap-taking at work. This change was probably largely a result of the accumulation of knowledge regarding the importance of napping for the human body. Most of the research done during the 1980s, as followed keenly by the Chinese, provided a firm justification for the siesta on biological grounds. For example, German specialists discovered that a rhythm in the human body alternates between sleeping and waking in four-hour sequences (*Toronto Star* 6 June 1987). Interestingly, Chinese critics of mid-day napping quoted this report in the magazine *Popular Medical Science* (*Dazong Yixue* 1987: 9). Japanese researchers also found that taking a three-and-a-half-hour nap at work was a novel way to help shift workers deal with the disruption of their sleep cycle (*Toronto Star* 8 January 1988). The underlying message in these reports was that if humans are genetically programmed to take naps, what is stopping them? More significantly, scientists approached the subject not only from a biological point of view, but also from a psychological perspective. The Californian psychologist Ernest Rossi wrote a book, *The 20-Minute Break: Using the New Science of Ultradian Rhythms*, which elaborates on how the afternoon nap could increase creativity and productivity. It is from this perspective that the issue of siesta begins to attract wider attention among the populace in developed countries. For capitalist-minded people, exhaustive means by which to maximise profit seem to be yielding to a more important concern, a sense of well-being. In

1997, for example, 42 IS Consulting, a computer consultancy based in Berkeley, California, viewed a regular siesta as a fundamental part of doing business. 'Not only do we allow it, we encourage it', said P. M. Clary, a spokesperson for the company (*Toronto Star* 13 December 1997).

Meanwhile, similar voices were heard in a wider scope. A number of books have been published, such as Bill Anthony's *The Art of Napping at Work* and *Power of Sleep*, and Dr Lucille Pezek organised the Canadian Centre for Stress and Well Being (*National Post* 27 November 1998). The Spanish, who were once anxious to catch up with their richer neighbours and let their siesta tradition disappear, are now said to be resuming it (*Vancouver Sun* 1 April 2000). Some shrewd business-people there even put the siesta up for sale – by setting up a place for rent on an hourly basis to people who want to take a nap – as some nosy journalists later discovered (*Central European Times* 3 February 1999). Not everyone is carried away by this trend, though. Some German bosses, for example, would frown if their workers were to take a brief snooze at work, according to observers. When asked whether his company offers employees recreation rooms to have a nap, the German chairman of the major US computer company IBM answered, 'We see no need for this' (*Deutsche Presse-Agentur* 10 August 1998). This type of resistance, however, appears very weak in the wake of the overwhelming campaign to give the mid-day nap a legitimate place in daily life. As Sue Bailey properly indicates, 'Sleeping during work hours still carries the stigma of laziness. But more employers are waking up to the idea that naps can increase productivity' (*Toronto Star* 14 May 1999).

The point Bailey makes here is significant. The completion of modernisation in developed nations allowed the people there to divert more of their attention to matters other than economic growth. This diversion in turn reinforced the call to give the siesta a legitimate place, for it arguably nourishes people's physical and spiritual well-being. However, if the argument was only that a siesta was good for the well-being of an individual, there would still be room for the capitalists in a free market economy to say, 'Hey, we did not force you to make the sacrifice!' But now, since it has been suggested that the siesta could bring them higher profits, the practice cannot be understood simply as an interruption of produc-tion. Instead, it becomes part of the holistic process of profit making. The last stand of opposition to the siesta thus ceases to exist.

In comparison, the fluctuating attitudes towards the practice of napping in China and the West during the last two decades seem to show two views that take opposite directions. First, while the Chinese have moved from their tradition of taking naps to abolishing and downplaying it, Westerners have moved from disdaining it to respecting and emphasising it. Second, while for the Chinese whether or not to take a nap has become an individual choice, in the West it has become a concern of society and, therefore, of social policy. One factor that has contributed to these opposite views in China and in the West is, obviously, modernisation. For Westerners who have, for the most part, modernised their economy, their concern has begun to lean towards respecting higher human needs – many see the siesta as one of these needs. For the Chinese, on the other hand, still stumbling along their path towards modernisation, the abolition of nap-taking is one of the prices to pay for the ticket to modernity. The different orientation of the attitudes towards siesta in China and in the West, therefore, has epitomised the gap between the people in these two areas not only in terms of their cultures, but also in terms of the level of economic development.

One ground that both the people in China and those in the West share in common in their assessment of napping is the role of sleep in human activities. While people spend on average about one-third of their lifetime sleeping, what position should be assigned to it? Passive sleep is an interruption of active wakefulness, but at the same time it is also a major link in the entire chain of human activities that prepares one for the awakening. Both the Chinese and Westerners have an understanding of sleep's preparatory role in one way or another, but they diverge as far as the importance of this role is concerned. In her chapter in this volume, Brigitte Steger has shown how the monophasic sleep pattern emerged in nineteenth-century Japan accompanying the country's early industrialisation, only to lose its significance in the twentieth century. There is clearly an identifiable parallel between China and Japan, although in China such a transition from one sleep pattern to another came much later. It may be an exaggeration to claim that sleep patterns are indicators of the level of social and economic development, as Steger warns, but undoubtedly, as demonstrated in this study, the position where a society stands on the ladder of economic growth or modernisation underlies the diverging attitudes towards these patterns.

The lengthy discourse on the practice of mid-day naps has currently waned in China. Although no clear result can be seen as to whether the proponents of or opponents to the practice have won, one thing for certain is that the State Council's decision in 1985 to change the work schedule has never been reversed. It is probable that nobody will tell you whether or not you can take a nap, but the hastened pace in contemporary Chinese life has left little room for the practice to be continued. The twists and turns of the discourse since the late 1980s were a windsock of the political climate in China. They were indicative of the ups and downs in China's efforts to emulate the developed countries, and echoed the fluctuations in China–West relations. The reassessment of the value of napping corresponded to the Chinese efforts to develop a 'socialist market economy' which differs from Western economies, and the final orientation of the discourse, which depoliticised it, reflected the process of depoliticisation of the society as a whole. All these, therefore, clearly chart the path of modernisation in China. They indicate the Chinese people's awareness of where China came from, where it stands and where it is heading. As demonstrated in this discussion, two things are prominent in shaping this awareness. One is understanding China's desperate need for economic modernisation, a need that must be met at the expense of mid-day napping. The other is understanding that the mid-day nap has been ingrained into Chinese life and become a part of the working social system. Shaped by these two understandings, such awareness subsequently assigns a moral and political value to the practice of napping. The judgement of whether the practice is good or bad, right or wrong, therefore, remains specific only in a historical context. During the last two decades in China, the paramount task of economic modernisation clearly left its mark on the position assigned to the mid-day nap within the entire spectrum of human activities.

Bibliography

Books and articles

Borthwick, Mark (1998) *Pacific Century: the Emergence of Modern Pacific Asia*, 2nd edn. New York: Westview Press.

Bo Yang (1991) *The Ugly Chinaman and the Crisis of Chinese Culture*, trans. Don J. Cohen. Sydney: Allen & Unwin.

Chow, Tse-tsung (1981) *The May Fourth Movement: Intellectual Revolution in Modern China.* Cambridge, MA: Harvard University Press.

Hsu, Immanuel C. C. (1985) *Rise of Modern China.* Oxford: Oxford University Press.

Jin Ze and Chen Shejun (1985) 'Xiandai Shijian Guannian yu Xiandai Shenghuo Fangshi' (The modern concept of time and modern life-style), *Shanghai Shehui Kexueyuan Xuesu Jikan* (Academic Quarterly of the Shanghai Social Science Institute) 1: 146–159.

Li Zhisui (1996) *Private Life of Chairman Mao: the Memoirs of Mao's Personal Physician*, trans. Tai Hung-Chao. New York: Random House.

Lou Yongqu and Xue Yinxiang (1980) 'Xiandai Shijian Guannian' (Modern concept of time), Jingji Guanli (Economic Management) 1: 32–35.

Mao Mao (2000) *Wode Fuqin Deng Xiaoping* (My father Deng Xiaoping). Beijing: Zhongyong Wenxian Press.

Pei Feng (1987) 'Tan Shehui Zuyi Shenghuo Fangshi de jige Wenti' (Some questions on the socialist life-style), *Shehui Kexue Jikan* (Social Science Quarterly) 1: 29–35.

Peng Ding'an (1986a) 'Lishigan, Xiandai Yishi, yu Shijie Yishi' (Historical sense, modern and global consciousness), *Xuexi yu Tanso* (Study and Research) 1: 4–10.

Peng Ding'an (1986b) 'Xiandaihua yu Shehui Zuyi Shenghuo Fangshi' (Modernisation and the socialist life-style), *Shanghai Shehui Kexue* (Shanghai Social Science) 5: 43–47.

Schwarcz, Vera (1990) *The Chinese Enlightenment: Intellectuals and the Legacy of the May Fourth Movement of 1919.* Berkeley, CA: University of California Press.

Shen Jinhao (1995) 'Songdai Wenren de Wusui Zouqin jiqi Shenmei Xinli' (Mid-day nap of the Song literati and its aesthetic psychology), *Zhongguo Dianji ju Wenhua* (Chinese Classics and Culture) 3: 75–79.

Wittfogel, Karl A. (1957) *Oriental Despotism: A Comparative Study of Total Power.* New Haven, CT: Yale University Press.

Xin Xiangyang (1996) *Daguo Zhuhou: Zhongguo Zhongyang yu Difang Guanxi zhi Jie* (Regional government of the big country: the relations between central and local governments in China). Beijing: Zhongguo Shehui Press.

Xu Ben (1999) *Disenchanted Democracy: Chinese Cultural Criticism after 1989.* Ann Arbor, MI: University of Michigan Press.

Zheng Yongnian (1999) *Discovering Chinese Nationalism in China: Modernization, Identity, and International Relations.* Cambridge: Cambridge University Press.

Newspapers and magazines

Central European Times (lexis-nexis@prod.lexis-nexis.com)
Dazong Jiankang (Popular Health)
Dazong Yixue (Popular Medical Science)

Deutsche Presse-Agentur (lexis-nexis@prod.lexis-nexis.com)
Jiankang Bao (Health News)
Jingji Guanli (Economic Management)
Jinwan Bao (Evening News)
Kexue Shenghuo (Scientific Life)
Los Angeles Times
Meiri Qiaobao (The Bridge Daily)
National Post
New York Times
Renmin Ribao (People's Daily)
Toronto Star (lexis-nexis@prod.lexis-nexis.com)
Vancouver Sun (lexis-nexis@prod.lexis-nexis.com)
Zhongguo Shangye Bao (Chinese Commerce News)
Zhongguo Tiyu Bao (Chinese Sports News)

4 Negotiating sleep patterns in Japan

Brigitte Steger

The world has become chronically insomniac. Twenty-four-hour societies and globalisation have turned out to be greedy 'sleep thieves' (Coren 1996). The number of hours the Japanese sleep, for example, has decreased significantly over the past thirty years. On weekdays the cutback in sleeping time amounts to an average of thirty minutes per day for those over 10 years old. In October 2000, the average weekday sleeping time amounted to only seven hours and twenty-three minutes per day. This has been measured by time-use surveys conducted every five years by the Japanese Broadcasting Corporation (NHK) (Mitsuya and Nakano 2001: 19, 21).[1] Similar tendencies can be found in many other countries such as China, India, Korea, Germany, France, Spain and the United States (cf. Inoue 1996: 198–200; Garhammer 1999: 377). Sleep deficiency has its costs. To reduce these costs – drops in performance and increases in accidents – efforts in chrono-biological research and sleep research have intensified, leading to great gains in the understanding of human bodily rhythms and sleep mechanisms. Within this context, in contemporary Japan, books and television programmes on how to improve the quality of sleep, thereby decreasing the amount of time devoted to sleep, in order to enhance the quality of life and achieve greater success, are widespread and plentiful.

In this chapter, I examine Japanese how-to books on sleep that were published in the 1990s. In particular, I am interested in exploring the arguments on sleep management in post-modern societies: What kinds of sleeping behaviour do the authors favour? What arguments do they use and what is the background for their argumentation? I will show that in accordance with pre-modern writings, many of the authors put forward their opinions on time use and work ethics rather than on sleep itself, and they argue for a sleep pattern comparable with the one in pre-modern Japan. They do so, however, based on the latest biomedical knowledge and ways of thinking.

Fujimoto Kenkō, for example, a yogi and non-medical practitioner, titles one of his books *The ultra 'deep sleep short sleep' method that changes you (Anata o kaeru chō-'jukusui tanmin'-hō*, 1995). In the text he declares that there is no proof for the theory that eight hours of sleep per day are optimal and in general there is no such thing as an ideal sleeping time. According to sleep specialists, sleep depends more on individual life patterns; in other words, sleep is habitual. Referring to the results of the NHK time-use surveys, Fujimoto believes that in the twenty-first century the Japanese will arrive at a level where they require less than seven hours of sleep per day. He offers another unspecified statistic, according to which sleeping time in industrialised countries is, on average, shorter than in developing countries. 'As an industrialised country, it is logical that Japan is included in the short sleep group. It is a result of the relationship between the distribution of bright light and lamps and of sleeping time' (Fujimoto 1995: 21–22). Although some of Fujimoto's data and arguments are questionable, he is certainly correct in pointing out the habitual nature of sleep organisation. Looking at different societies from the perspective of how they organise sleep, and asking questions about the historical developments and socio-economical influences at stake, beg for further study.

Similar to Fujimoto, brain researcher Matsubara Eita presents a *Short-sleep-method that makes you smart (Atama o yoku suru tanmin-hō*, 1993) and suggests: 'only people who discard the "common sense" of the eight hour sleep can be successful'. He introduces a new perspective in which sleeping time should be thought of in twenty-four-hour units. Nocturnal sleep together with napping during commuting or breaks, or an afternoon nap, comprise what he calls 'patchwork sleep'. This concept of total sleep, he argues, is the sleep method that is most adequate for contemporary social obligations, in which the 'early to sleep and early to rise' pattern no longer makes sense. Today many people must stay up until late in the evening, but must also start work early the next day. When they get tired during the day, he argues, they should take a nap – on the train, at a meeting or whenever else their situation allows. These short naps are not just a means to compensate for a deficit, but they enhance energy and creativity and are an efficient tool to spur flashes of wit (Matsubara 1993: 3–4). Matsubara adds an important clue to our story. Socio-economic, cultural and other external conditions do not influence merely the length of sleep, but also sleep patterns. Whereas for earlier generations, an eight-hour, monophasic sleep might have been adequate, in post-industrial, globalised societies, people who strive for success cannot afford to spend so much time sleeping in bed at night. They are better off with short naps during the day.

Before I provide a detailed introduction and analysis of these new ideas for a polyphasic sleep model, I will first dig more deeply into the background. Many of the 'sociological' explanations in popular books are based on personal experience, stories that were handed down through unknown channels, common sense and speculation. Although they fight prejudices towards sleep, they generally do not see the historical and cultural determinedness of their own attitudes. Thus, before I turn to this discussion, I will examine the organisation of sleeping time throughout Japanese history in light of the arguments put forward in the popular debate. How can we qualify the notion that in pre-modern times and prior to widespread electricity, people naturally went to bed when it became dark and got up with the sun, and sleeping time in general was much longer than today? What is there to say about Fujimoto's hypothesis that the length of nocturnal sleep is related to a society's state of development? What is the relationship between work and other social obligations, leisure and amusement and sleep? Were there always regulations of sleeping time? When? And for whom? What did educational texts have to say about it? What about daytime sleep? Is it true that individual daytime napping is a result of today's economic system and that it is compensation for the lack of nocturnal sleep? Was there previously an institutionalised afternoon nap such as the siesta in the Spanish-speaking world or the *xiuxi* in China? Was daytime sleep tolerated in a more general sense or was it forbidden or simply non-existent, because people slept long hours at night?

Questions of sleep have always been included in a discussion of economic success and social advancement. Just like today, the pre-modern 'sleep economy' aimed at creating more time by reducing sleep. The view of how this time should be best used, however, has changed dramatically. Based on the typology of cultures of sleep organisation elaborated in the introduction to this volume, I will show that in Japan a napping culture has always been prevalent despite attempts starting at the end of the nineteenth century to propagate an eight-hour night-time sleep and abolish daytime sleep.[2] Control of nocturnal sleep and sleep reduction has always been 'compensated' by individual daytime sleep. Whereas in the past this was a matter taken for granted and did not involve any discussion, individual napping is now argued to be a sleep method contrasting the eight-hour sleep model. I am also interested in the continuity and changes in regulations and the moral advice on sleeping behaviour. These changes appear to put forward moral demands – such as controlling desires and/or feelings – that are only indirectly connected with sleeping and work ethics in general.

Nocturnal sleep in pre-modern Japan

In historical sources, the issue of sleep has seldom provoked systematic discussion; it is mostly described at the margins of fictional and non-fictional literature. Educational texts do not consider the topic of sleep as central to their concerns. The lack of discussion and huge amount of literature for review makes it difficult to evaluate sleeping behaviour in pre-modern Japan. Moreover, much of the educational writing appears to be a simple copy from Chinese sources (cf. Richter's contribution to this volume), and we do not know what portion of these writings reflects the daily lives of Japanese from various social backgrounds. For the time being our picture remains somewhat sketchy, but, nevertheless, certain tendencies are clear.

For ancient Japanese noble society (seventh to twelfth centuries), which is the only social group for whom we have descriptions of everyday (mostly night-) life, sleeping time seems to have been generally unregulated. 'There appears to have been no idea of a normal time, or even of a normal range of hours, at which to go to bed' (Morris 1969: 161). In fact, for ladies in waiting, one of their most important duties was to sit outside the emperor's bed chamber at night and keep vigil until the end of the hour of the ox (around 3 a.m.), which was announced by the night watchmen.

The zodiacal time system that was used was introduced from China in the seventh century. This had twelve equinoctial hours of two hours' Western time each, which were termed by the twelve Chinese zodiacs. They were calculated (and possibly also measured by means of a water-clock) by the astronomers at the yin–yang office (Saitō 1995: 236). Because of its astrological relevance, time consciousness was considerably high, but with the exception of the emperor and for ceremonial purposes, eating and sleeping were not among the activities regulated by this system. Daybreak was the one important caesura of time. In texts using the zodiacal time system, daybreak was determined by the switch from the hour of the ox to the hour of the tiger (i.e. 3 a.m.); but in belle-lettres we get the impression that the first crow of the rooster was more significant for the start of the day. It was believed that the first crow of the rooster would announce the return of the goddesses and gods to heaven (Tsujino 1978: 339) and the day would then begin. Therefore, this signal was important regardless of the objective zodiacal hour. It was the signal for lovers to separate; thus it was assumed that a noble man walking through the morning dew had had sex. For regulating sleep, however, the rooster's crow seems to have had little influence.

The literature of this time mostly deals with the nobility in the capital of Heian-kyō (today, Kyoto), and we know little about the great majority of the population, but from short remarks in novels we can assume that they started working when there was enough light to distinguish their environment, and they awoke shortly before that.[3] A recently discovered edict (848–851) tells us that peasants had to start working in the fields at the hour of the tiger (3 to 5 a.m.; Ishikawa-ken 2000: 8), which thus confirms the impression given by the belle-lettres. One social group with more regulated schedules were monks and nuns in the temples and monasteries. For liturgical purposes, they divided day and night into six units (cf. Pas 1986/87), and adjusted other activities to that rhythm and to their community. At around 10 p.m. it was considered sleeping time, but after about four Western hours the monks had to interrupt their sleep for two hours of meditation and prayers before they could return to their sleeping mats for two more hours.[4] The temple bell announced the hour so people in the vicinity could hear the signals and be aware of time. The temples measured time individually with the help of incense and the sun; thus, there must have actually been quite some divergence.

After the decline of imperial power by the end of the twelfth century, temples continued to announce hours. Zodiacal and liturgical time systems gradually merged and the time units became temporal, i.e. the length of hours was no longer drawn from the constellation of the stars, but from the position of the sun, which meant that the hours changed depending on the season. Texts of the following several centuries reveal hardly any concern with timing, but when the warlords in the second half of the sixteenth century tried to unify Japan and bring the country under their control as shogun, the observation of a common time gained importance. This did not imply any further change in the system itself. Therefore, when night-time sleep was set from the end of the twelfth century to the end of the nineteenth, it was done by fixing the hour when to go to bed and the hour when to get up, not by advising a certain amount of sleeping time. One such example is the family codex *Muro Kyūsō jikei jōmoku*, written by the Confucian scholar Muro Kyūsō (1658–1734) and published in the year of his death:

> In the morning get up at the hour of the rabbit,
> in the evening go to bed at the hour of the rat.
>   (Quoted in Kurokawa 2/1977: 22)

The hour of the rabbit equals two Western hours around sunrise, the hour of the rat around midnight. Several other texts suggest a somewhat earlier schedule, getting up at dawn. In the spring and autumn, from the middle of the hour of the rat to the middle of the hour of the rabbit, the suggested sleeping time would translate into about six hours, although people did not think of time as a quantity. Yet, in winter, night-hours are longer than day-hours, and in summer it is the other way around, which implies that sleeping time changed depending on the season. The example allows a range from a maximum of nine hours of sleep in winter to a minimum of four hours in summer. In fact, the seasonal sleeping rhythm analogous with nature was considered to be positive by authors who were concerned with health (cf. for example Kurokawa 12/1977: 24), borrowing from Chinese sources (cf. Richter in this volume). It is remarkable, though, that bedtime was to be around midnight (or around 9 to 11 p.m.), i.e. several hours after darkness had spread over the land, and that with six hours on average, nocturnal sleep was considerably shorter than the later alleged eight hours.

Muro Kyūsō's codex was addressed to the samurai class. During the so-called Edo period (1600–1867), a rather strict hierarchical class system was in effect, dividing the population into four classes: samurai, peasants, artisans and merchants, as well as some outcast groups, each with distinct cultures and social rules. Belonging to a certain social class did not necessarily say anything about a person's financial situation. However, since peasants who constituted the majority of the population were the only social group which had to pay taxes, most of them were poor. Nevertheless, not only the samurai but also peasants were to stay up long after the sun had set, even when they were not wealthy enough to afford perilla oil for lamps. In the *Keian ofuregaki*, an edict dated 1649, the shogunate commanded all inhabitants to get up early and work hard. Peasants were to work in the fields during the day and to then perform so-called night-work, *yonabe*, such as weaving straw, which they could do at home with hardly any light (cf. Linhart 1983: 359).

As long as work was accomplished, reducing sleep per se appears to have been hardly a moral injunction, as educational texts that speak in favour of sacrificing sleep are more the exception than the rule. One example, however, is the *Yōjōkun* (Teachings of health care) by the late neo-Confucian scholar Kaibara Ekiken (1630–1714) who writes that it is usually forgotten that not only the urge to eat and drink and the urge for sex shall be brought under control, but also the urge to sleep. Too much sleep, he writes, is contrary to health (Kaibara 1995: 26, 28, 38–39, 48). Similar attitudes are known in Buddhism as well. However, several authors of house codes and educational texts insist on not staying awake until late without having an important reason for doing so, in order to avoid wasting oil.

This was especially true of merchant families. Different to the nobility at the ancient court in Heian, outside of certain pleasure quarters such as the famous Yoshiwara in the city of Edo (present-day Tokyo), which was brightly illuminated and known as 'the city that never sleeps', there was a strong objection to spending time and money for amusement and reducing sleep. Whereas the night-work, *yonabe*, was commanded, talking until late at night, *yobanashi*, was discouraged through similar regulations (cf. Itō 1972: 154). If night-time amusement meant wasting money for lighting and sensual pleasures, it was discouraged even more so. There were, however, some occasions acceptable for people of all classes to stay awake late, including vigils – partly for religious purposes, partly for amusement – such as the *kōshin-machi* held every sixty days (cf. Iida 1994; Steger 1999).

There is one activity for which sleep reduction was widely recommended and the use of artificial light justified: studying. From the sixteenth century until the late nineteenth century, many private schools (*terakoya*), which were open to children of the lower classes, used the *Dōjikyō*, a collection of aphorisms written in classical Chinese, as a primer or first textbook. They therefore displayed Chinese, mostly Confucian and Buddhist, attitudes. The children (mostly boys) had to learn these sayings by heart. The aphorisms were extremely popular. Some examples related to sleep are:

> Rise early in the morning and wash your hands.
> Go to bed late and clean your feet.
> Cheerfully study literature by day and night.
> A drill in the groin keeps away sleep.
>   (Quoted in Kurokawa 9/1977: 11)

The last line implies that a student should hurt himself to avoid falling asleep when he should be studying. It goes back to the Chinese politician Su Qin who is said to have pierced his leg so that he would not fall asleep while studying at night (cf. Richter). Diligence and dedication to learning were thus expressed by reducing sleep in order to spend more time with the books. Girls were supposed to study equally hard. Early rising and reducing sleep were connected to moral demands and were meant to prepare them for their future roles as daughters-in-law, obedient and faithful to their new families. The *Onna jitsugokyō* was a textbook for them. The oldest known edition is from 1695; the content of classical moral teachings for girls and women is contained in the aphorisms:

> Avoid sleep and rehearse reading and writing.
> In the morning rise early, comb your hair and serve your in-laws.
> In the evening, go to sleep late, let the body rest and pray that your heart be upright.
>   (Quoted in Kurokawa 9/1977: 119, 125)

By rehearsing the texts from their books, young children internalised the virtue of reducing sleep for their moral and intellectual advancement. It was considered most virtuous when they made use of the moonlight being reflected by the snow rather than the light of a candle or lamp. There was no notion that (a certain amount of) sleep is a means of preparing students to memorise the texts more efficiently, and no contemplation of the idea that a lack of sleep might reduce concentration or a student's ability to memorise. Instead, as part of moral training they should learn to suppress their urge to sleep.

This was also the main purpose behind the most common demand made in terms of sleeping time: early rising. This demand can be found in educational texts for all social classes. An important reason for the command to rise early is, of course, that otherwise it would not be possible to accomplish daily tasks. By making use of the daylight, oil and candles could be saved. Yet, more importantly, controlling one's physical tendency towards laziness and sleeping late was thought to lead towards a life of virtue and was, in fact, a sign of a virtuous person. The crucial point of rising early was to suppress one's emotions and physical desires, and be morally strengthened. Rising early was considered a question of will and effort (cf. Steger 2001: 253–301).

Although rising early was also a virtue for example in medieval or industrial Europe and North America – and the implications for disciplining the body are evident everywhere – there is an important difference to point out. Sleep in premodern Japan was not considered a means to prepare for work, and there was no discussion in educational texts that a certain length of sleep would lead to optimal work performance. On the contrary, learning to overcome negative emotions such as laziness and weakness in the end leads to greater strength and success. To get out of bed early, even though it would be more pleasant to doze, was said to create energy (*genki*) (Yamamoto 1925: 4). It was considered a question of will and effort, rather than of physiology.

The sheer number of references that demand early rising, however, informs us clearly about the strong resistance to it. Yokoi Yayū (1787–1823), author of *Uzura goromo* (The quail dress), for example, laments that among all teachings – Buddhism, Shintoism and Confucianism – from the top rank of government functionary to the lowest rank of merchant, not even one includes the doctrine of taking a morning sleep (*asane*). In his opinion, dozing between dreaming and waking is the most enjoyable thing and – especially in the early summer, when nights are short – much better than having difficulties keeping one's eyes open during the day and stealing daytime by sleeping in the afternoon (Tsukamoto 1930: 578–579). In this essay Yokoi Yayū draws a direct relationship between early rising (especially in summer, when night-hours are short) and the need for an afternoon nap. This reference to daytime sleep seems to imply that napping was habitual. But how common was it? How was daytime sleep organised? Can we identify a relationship between the economic system and daytime sleep patterns?

Daytime sleep

In *The Pillow Book of Sei Shōnagon*, the English translation of the famous classical piece of literature *Makura no sōshi* (*c.* 1000) by Ivan Morris, court lady Sei Shōnagon lists the following occurrence under the chapter 'Depressing Things':

An elderly couple who have several grown-up children, and who may even have some grandchildren crawling about the house, are taking a nap in the daytime. The children who see them in this state are overcome by a forlorn feeling, and for other people it is all very depressing.

(Morris 1970: 43–44)

In a footnote to this paragraph, Morris remarks that 'there was a strong prejudice against taking naps in the daytime; the practice was considered especially undignified and non-aesthetic for elderly people' (1970: 282). Only a cursory familiarity with classical literature and life in ancient Japan is necessary to find this remark puzzling. The court life described – not least in the *Pillow Book* – usually takes place during the night. Moreover, many court people suffered from tedium rather than an unbearable workload. Thus it would be very surprising if a moral demand to avoid daytime naps had emerged. Upon re-examining the literature, I discovered that daytime sleep was in fact common. Napping is often mentioned incidentally, with hardly any moral commentary. Sometimes an author criticises an older person who has fallen asleep during a conversation, but mostly because he or she is annoyed by the snoring. The criticism is made regardless of whether it is during the day or night (cf. Formanek 1994: 131–133). Analysing the specific passages allowed me to resolve the contradiction; it was caused by Morris's mistranslation of the term *hirune*. *Hirune*, the word that today refers to daytime naps, had a sexual connotation during Sei Shōnagon's time. She did not rebuke the old couple for taking a rest in the afternoon, but for having sex in broad daylight despite their advanced age.

The attitude towards daytime sleep in the Edo period (1600–1867) was somewhat ambiguous. There are many indications that daytime sleep must have been common since many artisans, peasants and shopkeepers seemed to have taken a rest in the afternoon when their workloads allowed. Yet in general there is no evidence that Japanese society at large has ever acknowledged a set time for mid-day naps or a siesta, i.e. a time when social life comes to a rest. Daytime sleep has always been taken on an individual basis. Proverbs that originated at that time show diverse attitudes towards sleep after lunch. One says 'if you sleep (lie down) immediately after a meal, you get dull-witted', '*shokugo sugu neru to, don ni naru*'. Contrasting this, there is another proverb saying that 'a short nap after a meal is a universal remedy' (literally, cures ten thousand illnesses), '*shokugo no issui manbyōen*'. Thus, positive and negative effects of afternoon naps were known. The differences in attitudes could be interpreted by the existence of different ideological traditions as well as by looking closer at the terminology. In the first proverb the term used for sleep is '*neru*', which means to 'lie down' and only by implication also means to sleep (as well as to have sex, depending on the context). By contrast, '*issui*' in the second saying literally means 'one [piece or bit of] sleep' in the physiological sense. Thus the critique of afternoon napping might refer more to people 'lying around' than having a little shut-eye. This type of distinction is made in some texts, such as in the book *The story of health-care by the late Dōsan* (*Dōsan-ō yōjō monogatari*) by Imaōji Dōsan (1577–1626), the personal doctor of the emperor and shogun (cf. Kurokawa 12/1977: 10).

For an understanding of sleeping patterns it is useful to take a look at housing and bedding conditions. *Tatami* and futon, which are known as the traditional Japanese bedding, gradually came into use in the late sixteenth century, but only wealthy people and the pleasure quarters could afford them. Most people used daytime garments to cover themselves during sleep and peasants lay down on bundles of straw or other material left over from the field (Hanley 1997: 46–47). Bedding (mats, futon, quilts), where it existed, was only spread out for the night, usually for several people side by side, providing each other security, comfort and a feeling of belonging. In summer, people hung out a huge mosquito net, under which the whole family could find room. Being 'outside of the mosquito net' (*kaya no soto*) meant to be excluded from the community. In daytime, the bedding was put away in closets and little tables were brought out. These housing conditions and habits of the social and economic elite gradually spread into all strata of society. Rooms were multifunctional, whether the family living space was limited to one room or whether the rooms outnumbered the people living there.

I argue that these housing conditions had a strong influence on the development of daytime sleeping habits. When one room is used for waking activities as well as for sleeping by a number of people, this implies that resting and waking times have to be co-ordinated. A family turns its central room into a sleeping place when the time seems appropriate, and it has to make space available for daytime activities by putting away bedding in the morning. This, however, is only true for nocturnal sleep (or more correctly, sleep using bedding). During the day, people sit around low tables on the floor on cushions or mats. When they feel tired, they can just lean back and doze. Moreover, since children sleep more than adults, since Japanese women – as requested in the educational literature – generally have always woken up earlier than everybody else to prepare breakfast and since co-sleeping (sleeping together) was common, a tolerance towards sleep in the presence of persons who are awake has developed. People are accustomed to sleeping while others are going about the house. This holds true for those who sleep as well as for those who are awake. I should qualify that the attitude of being unable to sleep in another person's presence is the result of hard and difficult training in societies where children are meant to become independent by being put to sleep in their own rooms and where people find it improper to sleep in the presence of others. This training that starts in very early childhood causes a lot of tears (as many parents can attest to). In fact, many people in Japan and elsewhere sleep more comfortably when they are slightly aware of the presence of familiar persons (or types of persons), although this is now rapidly changing.

It is thus not surprising that, continuing from ancient literature, there are references to individual napping in the form of so-called *inemuri* (literally, to be present and sleep).[5] This is a socially distinct form of sleep whose main characteristic is that the sleeper is present in a situation meant for something other than sleep, such as falling asleep during work or at a party. The sleeper is not completely 'dead to the world', but only temporarily withdrawn, ready to get involved in the situation whenever it is necessary. Although potentially a threat to the fulfilment of social obligations and a sign of laziness, *inemuri* was obviously not a concern for authors of educational texts; it is only mentioned incidentally in belle-lettres and anecdotes. Usually, misfortune happening to an unwitting sleeper constitutes the material for a humorous anecdote. Playing tricks on people who have fallen asleep seems to have been popular and a source of laughter. 'If you snooze, you lose', is the overall tone. Little girls might bind the belts of their sleeping friends to a pillar, so that their robes would open unwittingly when they were called and stood to run away, as a print (around 1768) by Suzuki Harunobu shows (cf. Osumi *et al.* 2001: 15). Children would tickle the noses of sleeping salesmen (cf. *Taiyō* 1975: 16) or steal little rice cakes from old women who were caught off-guard. The sleeper, however, is not criticised (cf. Herring 2000: 36).

From all the references it is obvious that *inemuri* was widespread and considered natural. Large merchant houses only began to tell their clerks to be attentive when they began to compete with each other by improving their service in the early nineteenth century. In a family codex for the merchant Mizuguchiya in Nagoya, for instance, clerks are cautioned to help each other be attentive when a customer arrives. The customer must be greeted politely and served tea, and 'if one of you is napping ... the one next to him should wake him up' (quoted in Ramseyer 1979: 213). It is not the napping itself that is the object of criticism but, rather, the lack of attention to the customer. If this is not immediately necessary, a short in-between nap seems to have posed no real problem even at work.

In reviewing pre-modern sleep patterns, it becomes evident that nocturnal sleep periods of less than eight hours and individual nap-taking during the day are not exclusively elements of a post-modern sleep pattern and characteristic of busy societies, as suggested by the previously quoted authors, Matsubara and Fujimoto, but were also common in pre-modern Japan. The sleeping time of court nobility in ancient Japan was not regulated. In later centuries, the length of nocturnal sleep was determined by the hour to go to sleep and the hour to get up according to the flexible zodiacal time system. It therefore changed depending on the season. In general, however, nocturnal sleeping time was not strictly linked to darkness and was clearly less than eight hours. Although rising early was considered a virtue, and was thought to train people to suppress their inclinations towards laziness, the exact time of what was 'early' differs depending on the source. At the same time, it was common to work until long after the sun had set, even for people who could not afford artificial lighting. No concept of sleep as preparation for work and no idea of sleeping efficiently were known. Except for the purpose of studying, reducing sleep as such was hardly recommended. Wasting oil for amusement was strongly criticised and, if it was allowed at all, limited to pleasure quarters and certain events.

There is no evidence of regular mid-day naps or a kind of institutionalised social break in the afternoon such as the siesta, but it is obvious that many people took short naps when they were tired. Often they did so during work or play (*inemuri*), and that was not considered a problem as long as the work did not demand active contribution. The habit of *inemuri* seems to have been facilitated by the multifunctional nature of rooms, which allowed people to feel comfortable sleeping while others are awake. By categorising pre-modern Japanese culture within the typology of sleep organisation developed in the introduction to this volume, it becomes evident that a polyphasic sleep or napping culture was prevalent.

During most of the Edo period (1600–1867), Japan was a closed country, and contact with outside – mostly Chinese and Dutch – traders was strictly regulated and limited. Therefore, the modernisation which was promoted after the opening (1853) and the following Meiji restoration (1868), mostly implied Westernisation ('with a Japanese spirit'), which affected practically every aspect of Japanese social life. This modernisation also had an influence on the notions of sleep and on actual sleeping behaviour.

Modernising sleep patterns

In May 1874, the Japanese Ministry of Education of the new Meiji government (1868–1912), founded two years earlier and in charge of health affairs, published the encyclopaedia *Hyakka zensho*. In its chapter on health care it notes (abridged):

> Staying up at night and sleeping during the day damages health. That has thus to be avoided. The sleeping time of children is longer than that of adults; in winter it is longer than in summer, but 'as a guideline, the sleeping time of adults is set with eight hours. In contrast to this, many people adhere to the habit of sleeping (*gamin*) only six hours.'
>
> (Quoted in Kishino 1983: 5–6)

This short passage is remarkable in many respects. To the best of my knowledge it is the first official government publication in Japanese history that deals with sleeping time in terms of educating a healthy people. Health care and hygiene became central to the Meiji government's policy to build up a 'strong army and rich country'. The paragraph implies that the issue of recuperation has become an integral, although not very central, part of this concern. The notion of sleep as the necessary preparation for proper work performance was introduced here. Reflecting its importance, the Hygiene Section in charge of public health affairs was moved to the police department within the Ministry of Internal Affairs shortly after the publication of the *Hyakka zensho*. The Japanese adopted the notion of hygiene as public health as well as its administrative structure from the German (Prussian) model, which was similar in many European countries (see e.g. Nottingham in this volume). It is also from there that they copied the ideal of the eight-hour monophasic sleep. The statements that it would be unhealthy to sleep during the day, and that 'many people adhere to the habit of sleeping only six hours', indicate that daytime sleep had been previously common and night-time sleep was shorter than the new ideal, thereby confirming the picture drawn from pre-modern sources. The usage of the uncommon term '*gamin*' (sleeping in a prone position) reveals a distinction between 'proper' sleep in the sleeping place and sleep outside, which could have been in any position.

The eight-hour sleep ideal articulated here is interesting in another respect as well. The Gregorian calendar and the Western equinoctial system of timing day and night (i.e. with hours of constant length) were introduced on 1 January 1873. Time became a 'period of time' (*jikan*), a quantitative item that had a certain value. The concept of time as money was also introduced. This was opposed to the earlier (and still used) term for time, *toki*, which is a qualitative term originally meaning 'change' or 'season' (Nishimoto 1997: 244), important not only for co-ordinating activities, but also for astrological purposes. For the first time in Japanese history, sleeping time was measured by the number of hours rather than by the hour of retiring and rising – in which it was implied that sleeping time changed depending on the season. Obviously, eight hours meant that sleeping time had become comparably long; in that respect, modernisation for the Japanese seems to have implied more leisure than previously, although the advice of the encyclopaedia *Hyakka zensho* did not materialise for everybody in the country. Most importantly, however, with the introduction of a sleep ideal in terms of a certain length, sleeping time became a negotiable quantity, which is the basis for the discussion on the optimum duration of sleeping time, which I will introduce below.

In the process, the eight-hour monophasic sleep pattern became highly influential and increasingly important. It was prominently enforced in modern establishments such as military barracks and in some dormitories of the increasing number of state-run, industrial production places and schools. The first time-use surveys conducted by the NHK in 1941 reveal that workers and employees enjoyed longer and more regular sleeping hours than peasants and came close to the ideal (NHK 1990). An eight-hour, monophasic sleep is currently still a widespread ideal; and for some people it has become almost an obsession.

A trend towards more regulated and longer nocturnal sleep as shown in time-use surveys did not necessarily mean that workers in the industries got more sleep, but rather that there was a stricter distinction between sleep and waking activities, and a clearer attribution of sleep to the night. Industrial work makes individual napping and *inemuri* difficult, if not impossible. This reduction in daytime sleep was not fully compensated by longer nocturnal rest periods. Influenced by the international labour movement, social reformers advocated eight hours of work, eight hours of free time and eight hours of sleep per day. In the 1920s they conducted studies not only on the working conditions in factories, but also on working-class leisure. Gonda Yasunosuke writes in 1922 that 'the proletarians who are the main pillar of the people, and who have neither money nor leisure, are so exhausted in mind and body that they have no greater wish than to get a good satisfying (amount of) sleep' (Gonda 1989: 154–155).

By the 1930s, the voices of the reformers were hardly heard anymore. Reinforced in the pre-war and immediate post-war periods, working and studying hard were considered high virtues, for which sleep should be sacrificed if necessary. Correspondingly, leisure activities had a bad image. Because they were meant to work hard for their own income and social advancement as well as for the progress or reconstruction of the country, the majority of the population could not find the necessary or desired eight hours of nocturnal sleep. Thus, whenever they had a free period during the day, they could not help but fall asleep. Daytime sleep came to be seen as compensation for lack of rest at night. Lying around in the house and occasionally falling asleep (*gorone*) became the characteristic pastime, especially for people who could not afford other forms of recreation (Tada 1972: 47) – although it was common in all strata of society. In some vocational groups the habit of naps has persisted. Artisans, even today, try to find a quiet place after lunch to sleep for twenty minutes or so – on the grass, a bench or wherever possible (Inoue 1996: 66–69). For other people, an afternoon nap (*hirune*) does not have a positive image. Employees in the upper echelons of big companies do not get the opportunity to rest. A housewife should therefore keep her daytime naps to herself; otherwise she confirms the prejudice that she leads a leisurely and lazy life, while her husband sacrifices himself for the family. (In fact, Japanese women sleep about twenty minutes less per night than men.)

Office workers, however, most commonly practise *inemuri* when commuting or during other situations when nothing in particular needs to be done and they can use the time efficiently for sleep. For many people, commuting is included as part of their daily sleep budgets. At work, *inemuri* is generally not allowed. People are paid to work, and it would go against team spirit to burden colleagues with even more work while one sleeps. There are, however, situations that provide some opportunity to rest. The most noticeable occasions are meetings, lectures and conferences. In international conferences, Japanese are known for the three 'S's', which stand for 'smile, sleep and silence'. When active contribution is not required, sleep may be overlooked, although it is an ambivalent affair. The degree to which *inemuri* is accepted is also determined by social hierarchy. It is likely that the sleep of a department head would be kindly overlooked. Young employees, however, need to make a good impression on their superiors, and should not doze off too visibly. Yet everybody would find it outrageous if someone were fired for falling asleep at the computer.

Generations of high school students, known to be under a great deal of pressure to perform well in university entrance exams, apparently follow the traditional method of studying both day and night. Confucian and Buddhist attitudes are still recognisable. '*Yontō goraku*' (four [hours of sleep means] to pass, five to fail) has long been a widespread motto. Only in two exceptional cases during my fieldwork was I told that children were sent off to bed at a certain time to enable their concentration at school the next day, although they had indicated that they still must or want to study. Children typically attend private intensive study schools in the late afternoon, often falling asleep immediately thereafter. After dinner they might rest for a while and watch television or play computer games before studying again until late at night. Alternatively, they might go to sleep early, and be woken by their mother serving them a pot of tea and a few snacks before she goes to sleep herself. Then the children study for a few hours during the night when it is silent in the house with no one to disturb them. Understandably, they often fall asleep during class, especially during those classes that they do not need for entrance examinations. Most teachers do not care much. Since they have to teach more than forty students in one class, they prefer students' *inemuri* to their chatting, and consider it a student's own responsibility to understand what is going on in class. Moreover, they are aware that many children are up half the night studying, so they pity them and let them sleep. In that way, *inemuri* even becomes a kind of subtle proof that the child had been working hard all night. This works despite the fact that, at the same time, teachers are well aware that the description above reveals the image rather than the reality and that the average student spends a large part of his or her waking hours watching television, making use of free Internet access or staying out (cf. Ayukawa's chapter).

From the 1970s onwards, the general attitude towards leisure activities gradually changed, which also had an influence on sleep. Beginning in the 1970s, based on the politico-economic theories that had become popular at the time, the amount of time and money spent on leisure and services was introduced as an indicator of wealth. The higher the percentage of the service sector of the GNP, the more advanced a society (cf. Linhart 1988: 274–275). These kinds of theories have long played a decisive role in the Japanese government's so-called leisure development policy. Since Japan has always wanted to succeed in becoming the number one state in the world, it has aimed at increasing time and money spent on leisure activities during the past forty years. After the oil shock in 1973, a high priority was given to increasing consumption within Japan in order to secure a market for the leisure industry. Japan also needed to react to the empowered labour movement and thus increased productivity (Masugata 1993: 17). A five-day workweek was gradually introduced so that people could find free time for weekend trips. Spending time and money on active leisure and consumption has steadily acquired a positive image. People were discouraged from just lying around and watching television in their free time. Instead, they were encouraged to use this time actively, to find new hobbies and improve the quality of their lives.

In the process, active leisure performance gained ground. Figures for time and money spent on leisure activities rose impressively. Yet, in contrast to expectations, working time did not diminish. Especially during the so-called bubble economy with its peak in the late 1980s, time spent at both work and active leisure increased, as can be seen in the NHK time-use surveys. 'Work like a president, enjoy yourself like a king', was the guiding motto. Two figures, however, decreased: hours spent watching television (which is not included in the leisure category) and, above all, sleeping, i.e. nocturnal sleep (Japan Broadcasting Corporation 1996). Even during the recession that has lasted since the early 1990s, the time spent sleeping continues to decrease (Mitsuya and Nakano 2001).

NHK figures clearly show that regardless of other trends, average sleeping time has dropped steadily since the beginning of the leisure development policy. This statistical correlation does not necessarily imply a causative relation, but my interviews and argumentation in advice books on sleep suggest that one exists. The change in leisure behaviour is not an isolated phenomenon. It came together in a package with greater competition on the job market, globalisation, global tendencies towards diversification of working schedules and life-styles, and the twenty-four-hour service industry. All developments contribute to the feeling that people are becoming continuously busier and simply do not have the desirable eight hours to sleep at night. Moreover, sleep-related problems are on the rise. This situation has led to an intensification of sleep research and growth in the markets for paperback self-help and advice books and television programmes on how to cope with the situation. As indicated earlier, the topic of individual daytime sleep is prominent in the discussion. It is nonetheless worth noting that medical doctors, sleep researchers and chrono-biologists are not the only ones who explain how to organise sleep. A number of authors are retired businessmen who want to share their experience with the younger generation. (None of the thirty-odd books on the topic that I have found was written by a woman.)

'The short-sleep method that makes you smart'

A prime aim of sleep research efforts is to make sleep more efficient. 'Quality rather than quantity' is the guiding motto. It goes without saying that this intention matches many people's needs. Feeling more recuperated with less time invested in sleep will attract most people in our busy cultures. Chrono-biologists and sleep researchers try to reduce the time needed to fall asleep and to minimise insomnia and other sleep-related problems. In this respect, Japanese research interests do not differ from those of most other places in the world. Advice ranges from considerations of eating habits, bedding and adhering to regular sleep–wake patterns, to the use of pre-sleep rituals. Books describe the approximately ninety-minute sleep cycle and explain the different states of non-REM and REM sleep within one cycle as well as the latest understanding of each of their functions.[6] Researchers explain that most deep sleep (non-REM states III and IV) occurs within the first three or four cycles; thus recuperation is ensured after four and a half or six hours. After this, the sleeper remains mostly in superficial and REM sleep (which is a superficial state of sleep as far as brain waves are concerned, but important for mental and psychological recuperation); some authors imply or state that superficial sleep is unnecessary and idle time. It has become evident in sleep research that there are individual differences in the time necessary for recuperation. Like Matsubara, quoted at the beginning of this chapter, most authors deduce from these research results that it is a matter of individual will and knowledge that allows people to keep their sleep short and efficient. They say that the ideal of an eight-hour sleep is nonsense, that sleeping time is habitual and the 'long sleep' which had some justification in earlier times is now obsolete. The reasoning is: sleeping long hours increases the percentage of superficial sleep. Sleep becomes inefficient. Therefore you should sleep less. If you are really tired, sleep comes more quickly.

With little nocturnal sleep, however, most people get sleepy during the day. In fact, there is one particular prominent issue in the Japanese discussion: napping. The president of the Asian Sleep Research Society, Inoue Shōjirō, regards sleepiness as a mechanism of the body to protect against the brain short-circuiting and suggests taking a nap if one feels tired, for sleep is the only complete mode of recuperation for the brain and body (Inoue 1996: 74–77). A nap – whether a siesta or *inemuri*[7] – should not last longer than twenty minutes, which is about the time after which you fall into a deep sleep. If you are woken from a deep sleep, you feel even worse than before the nap. If you sleep only a few minutes, you wake up and feel perfectly refreshed. His colleague Torii Shizuo argues in a similar way: 'The basic difference between superficial sleep and deep sleep is that deep sleep is for resting the body, superficial sleep for resting the mind.' Short daytime naps characteristically take place in a state of shallow sleep. When you sleep for only a few hours at night, the body gets sufficient rest, but does not sufficiently reduce stress. Catching up can be done by *inemuri* (here, microsleep) (Torii 1995: 89–90). The difference between their arguments is that while Inoue suggests taking a proper nap of about fifteen minutes and using *inemuri* as an 'emergency measure', Torii hails *inemuri* as the original, natural form of human sleep (Torii 1995: 14). Furthermore, he emphasises the actual advantages of *inemuri*; for example, obtaining flashes of wit or insight at the workplace. He explains thus: The human brain has two parts, of which the left side works analytically and the right sees pictures. Especially desk workers generally tend to make use only of the logical left half of their brains. Yet, in order to be creative, they need to make use of the 'gestalt' or designing half as well. It has become evident through computer tomography tests that immediately after one falls asleep, this right half becomes active. In that way, a solution for a problem long dealt with in the logical part can be seen clearly as a picture in the right part – a flash of insight. If sleep is prolonged, however, this picture is long forgotten by the time one wakes. Therefore, sleep should last for only a few minutes (Torii 1995: 45–46).

Several authors take up these arguments and arrange them to fit into their worldviews. They emphasise the benefits of daytime naps, especially for the effect of feeling clear and refreshed and obtaining flashes of wit. Thus you can become smarter by making use of short naps. Yet, if you sleep idly during the night, for instance seven or eight hours, you will not be able to fall asleep during the day, and cannot experience the merits of this superb means for improving your intelligence. Thus, Matsubara refers to the habit of *inemuri* as a characteristic of successful businesspeople and politicians (Matsubara 1993: 43). The benefit is twofold: first, by reducing sleep one gains additional time to enjoy all kinds of pleasures as well as time for additional studies leading to worldly advancement; second, short naps increase intelligence, so studying (and work) proceeds easier and with less effort. Thus the eight-hour monophasic sleep pattern, which has never fully materialised, is being challenged, even as an ideal. With the extended nights of twenty-four-hour illuminated cities, the monophasic sleep pattern should be replaced by 'short-sleep' or even 'ultra-short-sleep' periods throughout the day and night (Matsubara 1993: 26–29). Matsubara refers to the gradual 'colonisation' of the night over the past thirty years, and regards short nocturnal sleeping periods as characteristic of post-modern societies. Yet, as I have stated previously, polyphasic sleep patterns are not a new phenomenon, for they appear to have been common before the introduction of the eight-hour sleep ideal in the late nineteenth century.

Many of the books on sleep, especially the ones written by authors without medical training, are actually about saving time rather than about sleep. Not unlike the advice found in pre-modern educational texts, many authors provide readers with the simple equation 'less time for sleep = more time to be active'. Fujimoto invites readers to imagine how their lives would change if they had five (*sic!*) more hours at their disposal each day: everything would become possible. By reducing sleep by five hours per day, you gain five hours of entirely free time to add to your present time budget. In a month that would amount to an additional 150 hours or about a week, and in one year it is possible to gain seventy full days! Not everybody, Fujimoto admits, is able to reduce sleep by five hours overnight, but for a start, one hour would be relatively easy (Fujimoto 1995: 4–5). Just like other authors of similar publications, he neglects the view that sleep deprivation can endanger health and concentration. On the contrary, in the tradition of Confucian and Buddhist views of self-cultivation, and in line with most other authors, he stresses that by controlling inclinations towards laziness and sleepiness, it is possible to attain positive energy. As Sakai Hiroshi, a 70-year-old retired businessman and the author of the best- and long-selling *The four-hour sleep method to get smart* (*Atama no yoku naru yojikan suimin-hō*), explains: when you adhere to the four-hour sleep method, you will be attacked by the 'sleep demons' every once in a while. Thus you must not lose your attention for a moment. In this way, the short-sleep method becomes permanent mental training (Sakai 1992: 211). Reducing sleep makes people active and even increases their intelligence (because of the *inemuri* effect). In a way different from earlier texts, reducing sleep is currently being pushed with the backing of the latest medical knowledge (or, in the case of Sakai, his own theory), which argues against the eight-hour monophasic sleep ideal. Sleep has become a quantitative and negotiable item.

Moreover, the reasons, or arguments, for why sleep should be reduced have changed. In pre-modern times (and until the period following the Second World War), spending evenings and nights on amusement was rather strictly rejected, even more so when spending money was involved. Nowadays, however, consumption and the enjoyment of leisure activities are strongly encouraged. A group of businesspeople, lawyers, journalists and office workers in their book *The way of life-style which uses the morning wisely* (*Asa no chiteki seikatsujutsu*), argue (abridged):

> For everyone, a day has twenty-four hours and a year 365 days. But how much of this time can you (the reader) really enjoy and do whatever you like? This question will shock you, because you are always in a hurry and

have no time to enjoy and fulfil your dreams. The only time of the day that is not yet full of stress is the morning. Therefore, you should consider this time carefully and use it properly.

(Gendai jōhō kōgaku kenkyūkai 1994: 3–6)

Getting up earlier will not only create more – entirely free – time:

Performing leisure activities in the morning brings additional merit: one can save money on electricity (air-conditioning and lighting) and whiskey, and start the day with something pleasurable. By doing so, one goes to work in a cheerful mood. Leisure is no longer 'left-over or spare time' after work, when one is weary, as the Japanese term *yoka* suggests. It is a newly created free time.

(cf. Gendai jōhō kōgaku kenkyūkai 1994: 130–135)

This argument refers to the discussion surrounding the leisure development policy, in which it has often been said that the Japanese, due to their culture, are unable to enjoy free time and do not value amusement highly, which is clearly shown in their language. Whereas the English term leisure (also used in Japanese as a borrowed term) stands on its own, the Japanese term *yoka* is the 'left-over spare time'. Thus, the research group argues that by reducing sleep (through early rising) the quality of leisure and enjoyment will improve. However, this should not be at the expense of work and performance. Instead, recreational activities should put people in a positive and energetic mood for their work, and thereby support the economy. Sleep reduction is no longer propagated by means of reducing or controlling pleasure, but by enhancing and promoting it. But also evident is that this implies a change of argument rather than a change of attitude in the elderly authors. Nevertheless, as can be learned from the chapter by Ayukawa, young people indeed take these promising arguments seriously.

Conclusion

Japanese sleep patterns as well as the rationale for them display both continuities and ruptures. Despite attempts in modern Japan to establish an eight-hour monophasic sleep regime, Japan can be categorised as a polyphasic sleep or napping culture. Polyphasic sleep patterns appear to be the patterns of choice in ancient and pre-modern societies as well as in present-day, twenty-four-hour economies. Sleep patterns cannot be regarded as indicators of a certain level of economic or social development. The eight-hour sleep must likewise be seen as a particular sleep pattern, reflecting industrial, monochronic scheduling, which emerged, yet has lost its significance.

Sleeping time was not regulated for the Heian-era nobility, and their lives (and work) mostly took place at night. The duration of commoners' night-time sleep was adjusted to darkness to a certain degree, which is why its length varied depending on the season until well into the twentieth century. Yet, in pre-modern Japan, even people with no money for artificial lighting stayed awake at night when the workload demanded. There was no notion of a certain amount of time necessary for sleep, but, rather, young students in particular should learn to 'forget sleep' and study instead. Staying up late for amusement, by contrast, was strictly regulated and discouraged.

Under the influence of the West in the second half of the nineteenth century, time in general and sleep in particular in Japan are now thought of in terms of negotiable quantities. For optimal efficiency and health, sleep should last a certain number of hours. Hygienists in modern Japan were interested in promoting strong and healthy people. They therefore encouraged them to rejuvenate fully, for which they suggested sleeping eight hours at night, which appears to be more than what people had enjoyed earlier. At the same time, doctors and educators tried to abolish daytime sleep.

Sleep reduction was long considered an ideal way to make available additional time for work and study. In the past few decades, making time for leisure and enjoyment has gained a positive image. This does not imply that working hours have decreased and lives have become more relaxed, but rather it led to a gradual decrease of sleeping time. As an answer to the conflict between pressures to reduce sleeping time further and the body's desire for rejuvenation, sleep research has recognised that there are individual differences, and, as a whole, tries to discover ways of improving the quality of sleep, thereby still reducing its quantity. Some authors have begun to reconsider sleeping patterns. Based on findings that the human body's physiological rhythm demands a mid-day rest, they advise distributing sleeping periods over both night and day.

Inemuri, being present in a social situation and sleeping, was common in pre-modern times and has never been completely abolished despite its negative image. In the past few years a re-evaluation of the habit has taken place. Until recently (and still now, to some extent), *inemuri* has been tolerated, respecting people's exhaustion, and it has been overlooked as much as possible, although it was generally not seen as positive behaviour. In recent years, however, more and more people – medical doctors as well as businessmen – are promoting taking short daytime naps on a regular basis, and they promise that this habit will boost your intelligence and ability to succeed.

Notes

1   Since survey methods have changed, absolute numbers need to be analysed more carefully, which would go beyond the frame of this article. For more detailed information, please refer to the NHK survey publications or Steger (2001: 106–112, 162–178).

2   My typology categorises cultures into: (1) monophasic sleep cultures with one period of nocturnal sleep of usually about eight hours, (2) biphasic sleep or siesta cultures with a socially fixed period in the early afternoon for resting and napping in addition to a somewhat shorter period of nocturnal sleep, and (3) polyphasic sleep or napping cultures with individual daytime naps in addition to a shorter night-time sleep.

3   Japan's population around 1000 is estimated to have been roughly 5 million people, out of which only 1 per cent lived in the capital. Around 10 per cent of these belonged to the nobility (Morris 1969: 93).
4   It remains unclear whether this system of six time units (*rokuji*) and the sleep rhythm was observed by all the temples and all the schools of Buddhism, since there are only rare hints on time.
5   I provide a sociological interpretation in the introduction to this volume.
6   REM stands for 'rapid eye movement', referring to the eyeball's flickering during this state. Dreams usually occur during REM sleep, and it is said to be important for mental and psychological recuperation. The period of sleep without eyeball movement is called non-REM sleep. One can distinguish four non-REM states by the heights of the brain waves. During states I (sleep onset phase) and II, sleep is shallow and it is easy to wake up. After about twenty minutes a healthy sleeper enters states III and then IV; both are important for physical recuperation. It is difficult to wake up sleepers during one of these states, and they will take some time to clear their heads. As far as brain waves are concerned, REM sleep is superficial, but it is even more difficult to wake someone during this state.
7   The authors (reflecting common language use) are rather vague as far as the usage of *inemuri* is concerned. They often use it as a term to describe superficial or short sleep or sleep in between, but it always has the connotation of sleep in a social situation that is meant for something other than sleep.

Bibliography

Coren, Stanley (1996) *Sleep Thieves. An Eye-Opening Exploration into the Science and Mysteries of Sleep*. New York: The Free Press.

Formanek, Susanne (1994) *Denn dem Alter kann keiner entfliehen. Altern und Alter im Japan der Nara- und Heian-Zeit* (For none can escape age. Aging and old age in Japan of the Nara and Heian eras). Vienna: Verlag der Österreichischen Akademie der Wissenschaften.

Fujimoto Kenkō (1995) *Anata o kaeru chō-'jukusui tanmin'-hō* (The ultra 'deep sleep short sleep' method that changes you). Tōkyō: Mikage Shobō.

Garhammer, Manfred (1999) *Wie Europäer ihre Zeit nutzen. Zeitstrukturen und Zeitkulturen im Zeitalter der Globalisierung* (How Europeans use their time. Time structures and time cultures in times of globalisation). Berlin: Edition Sigma.

Gendai jōhō kōgaku kenkyūkai (1994) *Asa no chiteki seikatsujutsu* (The way of life-style which uses the morning wisely). Tōkyō: Kōdansha.

Gonda Yasunosuke (1989 [1922]) *Minshū goraku to kichō* (Popular culture and basic studies), newly ed. Ishikawa Hiroyoshi. Tōkyō: Ōzorosha (Yoka, goraku kenkyūkisō bunkenshū 1).

Hanley, Susan B. (1997) *Everyday Things in Premodern Japan. The Hidden Legacy of Material Culture*. Berkeley, CA: University of California Press.

Herring, Ann (2000) *The Dawn of Wisdom. Selections from the Japanese Collection of the Cotsen Children's Library*, ed. Don J. Cohn. Los Angeles: Cotsen Occasional Press.

Iida Michio (1994) *Himachi, tsukimachi, kōshinmachi* ((The vigils) Himachi, Tsukimachi, Kōshin-machi). Kyōto: Jinbun Shoin.

Inoue Shōjirō (1996) *Hirune no susume. Tanjikan suimin no fushigi* (Recommendation of afternoon naps. The curious thing about short sleep). Tōkyō: Ie no Kōkyōkai.

Ishikawa-ken (maizō bunka-zai sentā) (2000) 'Saishin hakkutsu jōhō 2000' (Information of recent discoveries 2000). Available online: <http://www.ishikawa-maibun.or.jp> (accessed 9 September 2000).

Itō Oshirō (1972) *Fukuoka-ken shi-shiryō. Dai 6-shū* (Historical sources of the Fukuoka prefecture, Vol. 6). Tōkyō: Meicho Shuppan.

Japan Broadcasting Corporation (1996) *Japanese time use in 1995*. Tōkyō: Public Opinion Research Division, Broadcasting Culture Research Institute.

Kaibara Ekiken (1995 [1965]) *Yōjōkun. Wazoku dōjikun* (Teachings of health care. Common sense teachings for Japanese children), ed. and annot. Ishikawa Ken. Tōkyō: Iwanami Shoten.

Kishino Yūzō (ed.) (1983) *Kindai taiiku bunken shūsei. Vol. 2/29 Hoken, Eisei VI* (Collection of writings on modern physical training. Vol 2/29 Social security, hygiene VI). Tōkyō: Nihon Tosho Sentā.

Kurokawa Masamichi (2/1977) *Kunkai-hen, jō* (Admonition, part 1) (*Nihon kyōiku bunkō* 2 (Japanese educational library 2)). Tōkyō: Nihon Tosho Sentā.

Kurokawa Masamichi (9/1977) *Kyōkasho-hen* (Textbooks, school books) (*Nihon kyōiku bunkō* 9 (Japanese educational library 9)). Tōkyō: Nihon Tosho Sentā.

Kurokawa Masamichi (12/1977) *Eisei oyobi yūgi-hen* (Hygiene and amusement) (*Nihon kyōiku bunkō* 12 (Japanese educational library 12)). Tōkyō: Nihon Tosho Sentā.

Linhart, Sepp (1983) 'Japan', in Otto Ladstätter and Sepp Linhart *China und Japan*. Vienna: Böhlau.

Linhart, Sepp (1988) 'From Industrial to Postindustrial Society. Changes in Japanese Leisure-Related Values and Behavior', *Journal of Japanese Studies* 14(2): 271–307.

Masugata Toshiko (1993) 'Yoka no genzai' (Leisure today), *Kokumin seikatsu kenkyū* 32(4): 15–32.

Matsubara Eita (1993) *Atama o yoku suru tanmin-hō* (The short-sleep method that makes you smart). Tōkyō: Mikage Shobō.

Mitsuya Keiko and Nakano Sachiko (2001) 'Fukyōshita de zōka shita yūshokusha no shigoto jikan. 2000nen kokumin seikatsu jikan chōsa no kekka kara' (Under the recession, working hours have increased for job-holders. From the results of the 2000 year time-use survey of the population), *Hōsō kenkyū to chōsa* 51(4): 2–25.

Morris, Ivan (1969) *The World of the Shining Prince*. Harmondsworth: Penguin Books.

Morris, Ivan (transl. and ed.) (1970) *The Pillow Book of Sei Shōnagon*. Harmondsworth: Penguin Books.

NHK (Nihon Hōsō Kyōkai and Suzuki Yutaka) (1990) *Kokumin seikatsu jikan chōsa (shōwa 16-nen chōsa) 6. Ippan chōsa hōkoku* (1941 time-use surveys of the Japanese population), 8 vols. Tōkyō: Ōzorasha.

Nishimoto Ikuko (1997) 'The "Civilization" of Time. Japan and the Adoption of the Western Time System', *Time & Society* 6(2–3): 237–259.

Osumi Takeshige *et al.* (eds) (2001) *Shokōkai. Suisu, Baua-korekushon. Ukiyoe bi no kiwami, zuroku* (The First Ukiyo-e Exhibition from the Baur Collection, Switzerland, 'Essence of Beauty'), Exhibition catalogue. Tōkyō: Sun Office.

Pas, Julian F. (1986/87) 'Six Daily Periods of Worship: Symbolic Meaning in Buddhist Liturgy and Eschatology', *Monumenta Serica* 37: 49–82.

Ramseyer, J. Mark (1979) 'Thrift and Diligence: House Codes of Tokugawa Merchant Families', *Monumenta Nipponica* 34(2): 209–230.

Sakai Hiroshi (1992) *Atama no yoku naru yojikan suimin-hō* (The four-hour sleep method to get smart). Tōkyō: KK Ronguserāsu.

Saitō Kuniji (1995) *Nihon, Ch goku, Chōsen. Kodai no jikoku seido. Ko-tenmongaku ni yoru kenshū* (Japan, China, Korea. Time systems in ancient times. A study based on traditional astronomy). Tōkyō: Yūsankaku.

Steger, Brigitte (1999) 'Warten auf Kōshin. Theorie und Praxis des Kōshin-machi' (Waiting for Kōshin. Theory and praxis of the Kōshin-machi), *Informationen des Akademischen Arbeitskreises Japan. Minikomi* 4: 5–9.

Steger, Brigitte (2001) '(Keine) Zeit zum Schlafen? Eine japanologisch-anthropologische Studie' ((No) time to sleep? A study on sleep in Japan from the perspective of social and cultural sciences), Doctoral dissertation, University of Vienna.

Tada Michitarō (1972) *Shigusa no Nihon bunka* (The culture of gesture in Japan). Tōkyō: Chikuma Shobō.

Taiyō (1975) *Nihon kodomo asobi-shū* (Collection of Japanese children's games) (Taiyō, The Sun, monthly deluxe 140), January.

Torii Shizuo (1995) *Inemuri nifun de genki nijikan. Desuku de utatane dekiru sarariiman hodo shigoto ga dekiru* (Two hours fit with two minutes nap. The salarymen who sleep at their desks can work like this). Tōkyō: Goma Shobō.

Tsujino Kanji (1978) *Manyōjidai no seikatsu* (Life during the time of the Manyōshū). Tōkyō: Tanka Shinbunsha.

Tsukamoto Tetsuzō (1930) *Fūzoku monzen. Wakan bunsō. Usura goromo* (The writings of a selection of folklore texts, Japanese-Chinese literary talent and the quail dress). Tōkyō: Tanka Shinbunsha.

Yamamoto Ryūnosuke (1925) *Hayaoki* (Early rising). Tōkyō: Kibōsha.

5 Sleep without a home

The embedment of sleep in the lives of the rough-sleeping homeless in Amsterdam

Peter Rensen

Sleep and homelessness: ethnographic research

In *You Owe Yourself a Drunk*, anthropologist James Spradley demonstrates that sleep is an act embodying numerous facets of homelessness. In his opinion, sleep should form a major focus of research on the homeless 'because it provides insight into many facets of culture, as well as an understanding of relations with the police and factors important for the survival of urban nomads' (Spradley 1970: 98). Spradley's outstanding work and recommendations have had little impact on subsequent research. Although some social scientists have pointed out the importance of sleep in the lives of the homeless (Cohen and Sokolovsky 1989: 77–78; Liebow 1995: 27–29; Dordick 1997), their treatment of this theme is mainly limited to descriptions of the problems the homeless face and some of their solutions. The integration of the relationship between sleep and homelessness as promoted by Spradley is rare within a general view of homelessness.

To the best of my knowledge, sociologist Mitchell Duneier is the only contributor to current research who has devoted extensive attention to the relationship between sleep and homelessness. In *Sidewalk* (2000: 157–173), he describes the life of a group of homeless individuals who buy and sell second-hand books and magazines in New York's Greenwich Village. Certain group members sleep near newsstands on the street, expressly for the purpose of keeping those spots occupied, or to guard their belongings. They feel at ease there, safe among their friends. By engaging in commerce, these individuals have gained a social network, a livelihood and an identity. According to Duneier, sleeping outside is the logical consequence of the pivotal role that work plays in the lives of these individuals (Duneier 2000: 162, 169). Duneier's methodology for studying homelessness and sleep is very similar to Spradley's. Duneier also uses sleep to determine themes central in the lives of the homeless and emphasizes the fact that a complex of arguments influences the choice of a sleeping place. In his contemplations on sleep and homelessness, Duneier aptly states: 'To understand the act of sleeping on the sidewalks … it is always useful to consider a person's overall logic' (2000: 162).

Spradley and Duneier both use sleep as a theme to shed light on the 'overall logic' in the lives of the homeless. In this chapter I look at the present, homeless rough sleepers in Amsterdam, for whom I find Duneier and Spradley's convictions also valid. One aim of this chapter is to enrich this argument with empirical proof from Amsterdam as a case study. To detect these themes, I use a method rather similar to Duneier's. I ask: 'Why do rough sleepers in Amsterdam sleep outside?' In attempting to answer this question, I uncover the themes that are important in the lives of the rough-sleeping homeless under study. For Spradley's urban nomads the relationship with the police and justice is an important element in their lives. For Duneier's book and magazine sellers work is the important element. This chapter also largely concentrates on those elements that might present reasons for sleeping outside. First, I point out the influence of personal attributes such as addiction or mental disease on sleeping habits. Second, I take into consideration the opportunities for autonomy that the urban environment offers homeless individuals. Third, I look at the rules established in the care organizations for the homeless in Amsterdam. By applying the necessary sociological creativity, it is possible to see these three elements functioning at the micro, meso and macro levels. To put these elements in context I also look at the themes that might form a reason for the homeless *not* to sleep outside, such as weather conditions, police intervention or the lack of security.

Like Spradley and Duneier, I do not address the question of why people become homeless. What causes an individual to become (and remain) homeless is not necessarily what prompts him or her to sleep outside. I examine homeless individuals and focus on situations in which sleeping outside has become an actual choice. Life on the streets has its consequences for the rough sleeper. These consequences are part of the overall logic of rough sleepers. However interesting it may be, I will not address sexuality. For people who sleep outside, sleep and sex are not as clearly related as they are for those people whose sleeping place is one of their most intimate havens. Although both sleep and sex are endangered by lack of privacy, the consideration of sex alone does not have a great impact on the decision to sleep rough. Before exploring why the homeless sleep outside, I will first offer a few notes on how I collected the information for this chapter.

Research and methods

Since the winter of 1999/2000, I have mingled with outside sleepers in Amsterdam to collect material for my doctoral thesis. The current text draws greatly on my field notes. Amsterdam's homeless form a continuum that shifts from indoors to outdoors. Some homeless individuals have access to residential accommodation. They get a key from a friend, relative or acquaintance and can use all of the indoor facilities – usually on a temporary basis. A large number are housed in institutions, boarding houses, sheltered accommodation programmes or cheap hotels. Many go to night-shelters, which offer accommodation on most days of the month. In addition, an extensive network of walk-in shelters and day occupation projects offer the homeless shelter *during the day*. The majority of Amsterdam's homeless are certainly not always outside. Only a small group of individuals spend a relatively large proportion of their time outdoors. Outside sleepers, on whom my research focuses, account for a relatively small percentage of the homeless in Amsterdam. Since 1995, outside sleepers in Amsterdam have been counted and interviewed every other year (Deben and Korf 1995; Deben and van Gestel 1995; Korf *et al.* 1997; 1999; Gemeente Amsterdam (Amsterdam Municipal Authorities) 1999; Deben and Rensen 2001). In 1999, the estimate came to almost 200 individuals (Korf *et al.* 1999: 8) with a decrease of rough sleepers in the city centre between 1997 and 2001 (Deben and Rensen 2001).

To find respondents among the rough sleepers, I went into the city between 1 and 4 a.m. This provided the assurance that I was really talking to the homeless who are sleeping outside. After two months I selected five rough sleepers who were able to reflect not only on their own situation but also on homelessness in Amsterdam in general. These five individuals developed into key informants. I met regularly and talked with twenty-five rough sleepers, but not as intensively as with the nucleus group of five persons.

My study was explorative. The key informants were free to bring up the themes and I tried to let their insider's perspective prevail as much as possible. Initially, I did not carry out structural interviews. I observed and listened to the conversations between them and other homeless or non-homeless, sometimes asking a question, in part to legitimate my presence. After a while I began to interview them in the most casual way and sometimes I created a more official atmosphere to pose straightforward questions. I tried to visit my respondents at all times of the day including the night. Every now and then I stayed with them at their spots the whole night. This gave me the opportunity to see what happens during the night; whether they sleep, how and under what circumstances. I could then reflect on these observations with the key informants. Most of the field notes I use here are either direct observations or reflections on these observations.

Why don't the homeless sleep outside?

The reasons why homeless individuals avoid sleeping outside are numerous. Two of these are very basic: weather conditions and lack of safety. Outside sleepers can, when necessary, ward off the cold, damp and rain. Their clothing, sleeping gear and sleeping spot can mitigate the effects of the weather. Controlling their social environment, however, is a more difficult task. Very decisive in the lives of rough sleepers is the fact that they have to sleep in public spaces. They lack walls to protect them from other people. Sleep makes them vulnerable and undermines their ability to defend themselves properly. Even the most seasoned veterans among them never lose the fear of sleeping outside at night.

> 'Just huddle up to sleep there in the doorway,' said Gerard, an old hand on the streets, pointing me to his sleeping spot across the road. 'Then you'll feel what it's like.'
>
> 'What will I feel?', I asked.
>
> 'The fear, of course. The fear that someone'll get you', he snapped back slightly irritated by such ignorance.

That fear is not unfounded. Various outside sleepers have told me that strangers had urinated on them. Others related stories of being attacked for no reason by groups of young people. One of these individuals was defenceless as his arms and legs were zipped up inside a hooded sleeping bag. Outside sleepers can also fall victim to acts of random violence. One individual told me that he had barely escaped suffocation when some young people set a waste container on fire in the enclosed space where he was sleeping. All of these incidents happened at night; thus fear of being attacked or otherwise injured is one reason for rough sleepers to sleep during the day. In addition to these basic problems are others more specifically related to conditions in Amsterdam. The most significant examples include: a city ordinance against sleeping outside, police intervention and conflicts between outside sleepers and other street people. According to Gerard, who spent his first night outside in Amsterdam a decade ago, 'You could lay down anywhere you liked. People were friendly and cops never bothered you.' Things have changed drastically in the last ten years. Today, Gerard is in a continual process of negotiation with local residents, police officers and authorities to keep his regular sleeping place.

In the late 1980s and early 1990s, Amsterdam witnessed a rise in its population of homeless people and outside sleepers. Increasingly, city residents and regular visitors began to feel inconvenienced by them. They urged the municipal authorities to take action. Since then, supervision of outside sleepers has intensified. A general local by-law was passed, allowing Amsterdam police officers to bar people from sleeping outside. Despite the fact that sleeping outside is officially not tolerated, the police often leave outside sleepers in peace for humanitarian reasons. However, this tolerance only extends to individuals who cause no problems. It is difficult for people to prove that they are *not* creating a public nuisance. One individual, Sara, referred to this problem as a 'reverse burden of proof'. Nowhere in Amsterdam's current urban environment can outside sleepers rest assured that they can stay indefinitely. In recent years they have been almost entirely purged from the city's centre. Only a few odd diehards, like Gerard, have managed to rekindle tolerance of their presence time and again.

The problems that outside sleepers face from fellow outside sleepers or other homeless people have seldom been discussed in the academic literature. The outside sleepers in Amsterdam have been very hard hit by this particular problem. During my fieldwork I encountered numerous incidents where the offender was a fellow outside sleeper. Outside sleepers steal from one another. They come to quiet sleeping spots and cause a commotion. They regularly resort to violence in their relations with each other in order to protect their own interests. One of my key informants, Richard, was almost murdered in his sleeping spot by an outside sleeper whom he had thought was a friend. During my fieldwork under a bridge at the Amstel River, I witnessed a number of fights. One individual hit several others during their sleep. Another threw a female drug addict into the freezing Amstel. A sleeping area in northern Amsterdam has been the scene of a long series of violent incidents between outside sleepers. Sara, the woman who has lived there the longest, was stabbed in the back by a psychotic man. Fights and stabbings break out on a regular basis in the summer and during my fieldwork there were two cases of arson. Such incidents created a public nuisance for neighbours, who threatened to have the sleepers removed by the police.

For those people who are not homeless, sleep and the time around it is a pleasant experience. For most outside sleepers it is a gruelling task. Those able to remain asleep for long, uninterrupted stretches are few and far between. In light of the sleeping difficulties, the question of why people would sleep outside becomes all the more pertinent.

Sleeping rough, addiction and mental illness

There is an ongoing discussion in the academic literature on homelessness concerning the reasons why people are and stay homeless. A vast amount of literature based mostly on medical, psychological and psychiatric studies exists in which personal characteristics are regarded as the root cause of homelessness. On the other hand, there is a vast amount of literature based on sociological and anthropological studies which regards social structures as the root of homelessness. Rough sleepers in Amsterdam are in no way representative of the population of Holland or Amsterdam. There is a higher concentration of addiction and psychiatric problems. There have not yet been studies to determine how many rough sleepers are drug addicts. However, survey data offers an indication that almost half of the outside sleepers in central Amsterdam have been categorized as having an addiction problem (Korf *et al.* 1999: 18) and almost all of those in the south-eastern part of the city, the Bijlmermeer, fall into the addict category (Gemeente Amsterdam 1999: 13). Thus, we can conclude with a certain measure of certainty that at least half of Amsterdam's outside sleepers are addicted to hard drugs. Drug addiction and outside sleeping are intricately linked in Amsterdam. Additionally, a group of alcoholics exists among the rough sleepers. Based on my fieldwork, I would estimate the number of heavy drinkers among outside sleepers at 15 per cent. The number of rough sleepers suffering from psychiatric disorders has yet to be researched. As far as I can tell, the group is smaller than is often assumed.

The concentration of addiction and mental illness may easily lead to speculation on the correlation between personal characteristics and homelessness. As a sociologist I am not qualified to judge the personal characteristics which might lie behind addiction or mental disease, but I can address the influence that these 'personal' attributes have on the lives of rough sleepers. I will confine myself here almost exclusively to addiction, beginning with the example of Wouter, whose drug addiction deeply influences his sleeping behaviour.

For half a year, I spotted Wouter at irregular intervals, sleeping or resting in different odd spots throughout the city. These included doorways, walk-in shelters and, when possible, night-shelters or a friend's house. The last time I saw him, he had acquired a permanent 'sleeping spot' in Westerpark, on the outskirts of the city centre. He had found a thicket where he could roll out a mattress wrapped in a sheet of plastic. Using the frame of a table he had found near a waste dump, he 'levelled out' the incline he slept on, so that he could stretch out completely. Although he got drenched in the rain, he claimed that he did not mind. I had met Wouter for the first time on 29 October 1999. Later I realized that this encounter was typical of his way of living during the half-year period in which we had contact.

It was 6:30 and a cold winter morning descended on Amsterdam's deserted Dam Square. A man rummaged about aimlessly before ducking into an alley. I found him tucked halfway into a doorway, clutching a McDonald's straw and a scrap of silverfoil. He had just snorted the last of his base coke. He was thin. Despite the cold, he was wearing a pair of plastic flip-flops. His toes were black with street grime.

'Aren't you cold?' I asked pointing at his feet.

'Doesn't bother me,' he answered dully.

Before I even had a chance to ask, he started filling me in on his thoughts in jerks and jolts of speech. 'I'm sick of this,' he said. 'You know, I started out for the fun of it. I began by playing guitar on the street. I really liked it at first.' He fell silent. 'I've got to get out of here,' he started up again suddenly. 'Out of this place. Away from the streets.' He talked about his life over the past few weeks. It had been one long cycle of begging, drug use, begging, drug use and an occasional catnap. Talking about it with no cocaine or money left, the despair suddenly became overwhelming. A tear dropped on his coat sleeve, leaving a stream of dissolved grime. He looked at it as though it were a raindrop.

Ten minutes later, the pauses between my questions and Wouter's answers grew increasingly longer. Slowly he fell over, his eyes shut, only to shoot back up in a sitting position as though a wasp had stung him. 'Did you see that?' he asked laughing ironically. 'I fell over. Usually, I think I can get back up again, but sometimes you just pass a point of no return. There's no way you can get back up then.' He stood up and shook himself off. 'I've really got to crash,' he said, stretching. We walked to the corner of Dam Square and Kalverstraat.

'It's chilly here,' he said dryly, catching a gust of morning air. 'I thought I'd be okay with some cardboard, but it doesn't do any good in this damp air.'

'Where are you going to sleep?' I asked.

'Oh, I usually check out a few spots,' he said nonchalantly. One block further up, the answer became more concrete. 'I think I'll sleep in the tram.'

Wouter's case is far from exceptional. Some drug addicts, such as Wouter, go on binges of short or long stretches of uninterrupted drug use. They stay awake day and night. Often, dealers disappear from the streets by four in the morning. By obtaining a small supply at that hour, however, outside walkers can keep going until the early morning, when they can try to earn some money for the next fix. It is not unusual for these individuals to go without sleep for three or four days at a time.

Once they run out of drugs and the means of hustling for them, sleep becomes a real option. If, when and where these individuals sleep depends largely on where and when the binge grinds to a halt. Their decision to sleep outside is, both short and long term, very much influenced by their drug use. The need for rest has to compete with the drug addiction. Strictly speaking, one can say that addiction can lead a homeless person to sleep outside. The same might be true for mental diseases or general character defects. These traits can dominate to a great extent the way rough sleepers act as far as sleep is concerned. Moira Bokstijn, a care worker with an organization that provides assistance to the homeless from a van that drives around the city, visits outside sleepers at their sleeping spots. She addresses the relationship with rough sleepers whom she defines as psychiatric patients thus: 'Those still sleeping out there on the streets are convinced that we want to poison them, burn them or manipulate them. They want nothing to do with us.'

Addiction and mental diseases can lead to conduct that perpetuates outside sleeping. Does that mean that addiction is the reason for its continuation? From a sociological point of view two arguments are crucial. First, individual character-istics are rooted in social frameworks. The lives of drug addicts depend for example very much on government policy. The illegal nature of hard drugs is one of the greatest influences on the lives of drug-addicted outside sleepers. Hard drugs are expensive because they are illegal. Usually outside sleepers who engage in crime do so to support their habit. Often, the income these individuals receive in social benefits is not enough to support their drug addiction. Almost 50 per cent of outside sleepers receive no social benefits (Deben and Rensen 2001). That, in turn, forces many to resort to some means of hustling for money. The rhythms of their lives, when and where they sleep, are determined in part by their hustling ventures. Social frameworks play a role in these individuals' choice to sleep outside. This also applies to alcoholics and those with psychiatric disorders, and also to a great extent to illegal aliens. The way drug use and other personal characteristics influence sleeping conduct cannot be separated from the wider social framework.

Second, personal characteristics do not conclusively explain why anyone would sleep outside. In most cases, drug addiction, alcoholism and psychiatric disorders do not, in themselves, drive the individual to a life on the street. Only a fraction of Amsterdam's addicts and psychiatric patients sleep on the streets. The question is therefore: why do some people choose to sleep inside and others outside? The discussion below examines further considerations that play a role in this choice.

Obstacles of the welfare state

Gøsta Esping-Andersen in *The Three Worlds of Welfare Capitalism* (1990) measures the welfare state according to its degree of de-commodification. The term refers to the extent to which a society's social security provisions enable individuals to withdraw from bare market conditions. According to Esping-Andersen (1990:

74), the Dutch welfare state features many traits of a de-commodified social democratic model. This model places the individual less at the mercy of market forces than does the market model (e.g. in North America) or the corporate model (e.g. in Germany). This immediately gives rise to the question of why homeless people in the Netherlands sleep outside. Everyone in the Netherlands is entitled to social benefits. These benefits enable individuals to rent living accommodation in the country's internationally acclaimed, state-run rental housing sector. All Dutch nationals are entitled to independent living accommodation. A wide range of supplementary provisions have been established in connection with that right, including rent subsidies for those whose rent exceeds what they can afford with their social benefits.

Aside from provisions made by the welfare state, various separate institutions and government programmes have been established for the homeless. These institutions and programmes play a significant role in the choices homeless individuals make. The institutions in Amsterdam do more than just provide the traditional 'bed, bath and breakfast'. They also form a link between the homeless and the general structures of the welfare state. Often, housing and benefits are only available to the homeless through institutions such as the Salvation Army. Another type of institution focuses on providing health care to the homeless. This includes organizations that provide care for drug users. This form of care consists primarily of providing free methadone, a substitute for heroin and cocaine. To an extent, these care organizations are subject to regulations laid down by the welfare state; however, they have also developed their own official, or semi-official dynamics based on their own set of rules. In this respect, the care sector for the homeless functions as a miniature welfare state. And the rules of that miniature welfare state play a role in some individuals' decisions to sleep indoors or, conversely, to sleep or remain outdoors.

During the 1990s various authors noted that homelessness is partially a product of obstacles created by the welfare state. Frans Spierings (1991) pointed to the exclusion mechanisms of modern society, where individualism, professionalism and consumerism require a capacity for responsibility from the homeless that some do not have. Spierings (1997) also noted that increasing differentiation in regulations has excluded homeless individuals with multiple problems. According to Léon Deben *et al.* (1992: 98), those who become homeless – unlike the picture Spierings paints – do not sever their ties to our complex society. Rather, they enter into a fierce confrontation with it. Desiree van den Bogaard introduced the term *guided transience* (1993: 19–22). This refers to homeless people's need for a schedule to keep track of all their appointments and for a wallet full of passes and cards to use what are supposedly easy-access care facilities.

It is useful to identify the exclusion mechanisms in care provision by pointing out guided transience and modernization. But even when the homeless are very well equipped to be consumers of care in a modernized society, some will nonetheless be excluded. Most homeless cannot register with regular housing agencies. To obtain a residence, they must participate in a supervised living programme run by an appointed care organization. These programmes are time consuming and make demands on participants, aimed at their social rehabilitation. Some of the homeless do not meet the requirements necessary to gain admission to night-shelters or sheltered accommodation programmes (cf. Rensen 1999). The care sector for the homeless offers a differentiated network of sleeping possibilities. An important division can be made between the places where the homeless can stay night and day and the places where they have to arrive late in the evening (around 10 p.m.) and leave in the morning (around 8 a.m.). In sheltered accommodation programmes, where the homeless can stay day and night, like social pensions, entry is bound to a specific set of rules. Different pensions have different target groups like younger vagrants or mentally ill homeless. Before entry, a homeless person must be personally assigned to the place. Because of this differentiated set of rules, places in day and night care are scarce. Day and night care costs approximately 450 euro per person per month. This amount covers food, bathing facilities and a few additional provisions. Outside sleepers who receive no social benefits are usually unable to afford admission to these programmes. They are only eligible for inexpensive or free night-shelters.

Night-shelters are either free or inexpensive and intended for all homeless. No assignment is needed. Although a minimum set of rules should guarantee a low threshold, in practice these rules exclude a large group. In night-shelters the use of drugs and alcohol is forbidden. Once inside in the evening no one is allowed to leave until the morning. Those who nonetheless leave are not allowed back in. Some outside sleepers are unable or unwilling to adhere to these rules. They are too dependent on drugs to do without from evening to morning, and some would become dope-sick and be unable to sleep anyway.

Strictly speaking, illegal aliens are also banned from sheltered accommodation programmes and night-shelters. Ineligible for social benefits, they are unable to afford admission to these programmes. Everyone entering a night-shelter must show ID at the door. Individuals without a Dutch passport are not permitted. Although night-shelters may occasionally admit illegal aliens, these individuals are definitely turned away in other instances. The admission of illegal aliens to night-shelters is a nebulous and politically charged grey area in which existing policies or regulations are partly replaced by a broad range of ever-changing rules that vary with the organization or institution. About 60 per cent of outside sleepers claim they do not turn to social welfare institutions; a quarter cited the 'house rules' as the reason. Fifteen per cent avoid these institutions because of their 'atmosphere' and 10 per cent because of 'other visitors' (Korf *et al.* 1999: 33). A small percentage have been banned from these institutions, as sheltered accommodation programmes and night-shelters can ban individuals for certain periods if they have violated the rules (Korf *et al.* 1999: 36).

Those who do not avail themselves of the care provisions *may* lose their social benefits as a result, since all applicants for benefits must have an official residence or living accommodation. The homeless can apply for a mail address at a relevant social welfare institution in order to meet that qualification. However, these institutions do not grant all requests from individuals who make no use of their services. Over half of all outside sleepers receive no salary or social benefits

(Korf *et al.* 1999: 28). Some individuals have consequently become completely absorbed into a street-based life-style. Somewhere along the line they turned their backs once and for all on homeless shelters.

Obstacles to shelter in practice: Richard, a case in point

Some outside sleepers avoid homeless shelters because of the 'house rules', the 'atmosphere' and 'other visitors'. The story of Richard illustrates these dynamics. He is one of the outside sleepers I encountered frequently in 1999/2000. I met him during a time when he was sleeping under the parking garage of a large chain store on the edge of the old section of the city. After barely escaping a murder attempt by a fellow outside sleeper, Richard decided to register for a residence. He was placed in De Kroon, a sheltered accommodation programme for night and day. Many homeless people participate or participated in phase one of this supervised living programme. Richard refers to his stay at De Kroon as 'an ordeal'. For him, one of the disadvantages of De Kroon was the lack of money. He receives social benefits of 640 euro per month. On the streets, that entire amount was his to spend. The sheltered accommodation programme cost him 450 euro per month for room and board. He was also charged an additional amount at the end of the month for coffee and administrative fees. That left him with at most 190 euro a month from his benefits. He received 23 euro of that as a weekly allowance. He was also permitted to make additional weekly withdrawals from the remaining 98 euro. Richard found it very difficult to make ends meet. Whenever he ran out of money, he fell prey to boredom.

Richard is a heroin and cocaine addict with a fair amount of control over his addiction. For the last eight years, he has received methadone ampoules from the Municipal Health Services. He does not need drugs to ward off dope-sickness. Nonetheless, his addiction does play a role. When he has money, he spends an average of 5 euro per day on soft drugs in order to feel good. That habit alone absorbed three-quarters of his monthly income. Consequently, he often spent his allowance before the end of the week.

The second disadvantage was more fundamental. De Kroon is an easy-access facility for the homeless. The residents can stay inside day and night. Almost all of them are addicts whose lives lie on the balance between indoors and outdoors. Richard found it exceedingly difficult to live under one roof with these people – especially since the management made no effort to maintain order. Richard shared a room with five others. Dirk was a friend. Randy was a mate. He had no problems with them. The other three were drug users he did not trust. One of them, a con artist, was constantly on the prowl for money and possessions. The second was a thief who took things from the room every now and again. The third was also a thief who tended to live at night and sleep during the day. Richard, Dirk and Randy established rules for their room. No stealing or loud noises. According to Richard, there was only one way to enforce the rules: controlled violence. Violent conduct, however, was among the grounds for removal from the sheltered accommodation programme. And removal would preclude the possibility of obtaining an individual home. Richard's life at De Kroon involved maintaining a delicate balance between safeguarding order in communal living areas and ensuring his continued residence there. As soon as he moved in, one of his roommates stole 15 euro from him. 'I bounced that guy all around the room,' Richard recounted. A few weeks later, he stole something else from Richard, only to receive another beating. Another few weeks passed when Richard caught a second roommate trying to steal three of his T-shirts. Richard recalled the incident:

> 'I woke him up and asked how those three T-shirts had landed next to his bed? "I don't know," he said, "and don't start accusing me, eh." So I dragged him downstairs. All the supervisors were there. So right there in front of all of them I said, "How come my T-shirts are next to his bed?" Everybody understood that I was accusing him of stealing. They all looked the other way. So I said, "Well what do you know, the staff are turning a blind eye. What kind of snooty joint is this, a nursery?" And I left.'

Richard's difficulties in sharing living quarters were not limited to his room-mates. There were tensions – to put it mildly – between him and some other housemates:

> 'There was also this Surinamese guy,' he recalled. 'A real son-of-a-bitch. Recently, I bought fried rice with Dirk. We heated it in the microwave. We were eating when he comes along: "So, needle queens." That's what he always called us. He stood at the table and spat on our food. The guy on duty just stood there and watched. I said, "you're standing there watching him spit in our food and you're doing nothing about it. Do you want me to beat him up? You want me to cross that line?" "That's not nice," he said, "that's not nice." I told him, "That's not nice? Go to hell!" I flipped my plate over on the table and walked away. If somebody pulled that with me outside, I'd have stuck my fork through his throat.'

An addict for twenty-five years, Richard is a seasoned veteran at homeless-ness. He has lived in boarding houses, sheltered accommodation programmes and on the streets in the Netherlands and Germany. His housemates' conduct did not surprise him. He knew most of them from the circle of fellow addicts. When he slept on the streets, he was able to avoid the worst among them. In the sheltered accommodation programme, incidents and fights were unavoidable. Gradually, he fell more and more into bickering. During his stay, and even after he was assured admittance to phase two, Richard had to suppress his urge to return to the streets. In many ways, life outside was more pleasant than it was indoors. Problems there could usually be avoided with a threat of violence. Aside from that, life in the sheltered accommodation programme was extremely perilous for Richard as compared with life on the streets. To keep indoor life somewhat bearable, he struggled with a delicate balance with his drug use, a balance he achieved using methadone ampoules. At the same time, he was convinced that his options were limited to long-term residence in sheltered accommodation programmes. During one of our talks I asked him:

> 'But haven't you considered maintaining a friendship with a care worker, letting him get a place for you to live and sleeping outside in the meantime?'
>
> 'That's the problem,' Richard responded. 'That's not how it works. Believe me. They won't admit you to phase two. Phase one is that sheltered accommodation programme. If you're sleeping outside, no one's going to help you.'

Many outside sleepers avoid these institutions because of their 'rules' and 'atmosphere', abstract terms that refer to very practical daily problems. It is impossible for Richard to maintain his street life-style in the sheltered accommodation programme. His status, in relation to that of other homeless individuals and addicts, is drastically different in the programme. At the same time, his poverty limits his freedom of movement. Many outside sleepers share Richard's objections to life in sheltered accommodation programmes or boarding houses. Those who have managed to keep their pride intact on the streets find it hard to 'swallow humiliations for a bed inside', as Richard put it.

The magnetic appeal of sleeping outside: social ties in the urban environment

In the Netherlands, explanations as to why homeless individuals sleep on the streets almost always point out the obstacles created by the welfare state. My explanation above does the same. During the 1990s, the theory of exclusion gained ground over the poverty theory. Far less attention has been devoted to the appeal of the streets. Sleeping in public areas can *also* have its advantages. Some outside sleepers have ties to certain settings in the city, to a social scene. Contacts with other homeless individuals and outside sleepers are extremely important. Although their homeless partners sometimes turn into a threat, as I stated previously, most homeless must continue to rely on each other because they have no alternative. They need other homeless to fulfil their social and material needs. To some extent outside sleepers help each other and seek each other's company for that reason. This dynamic is a focal subject in the academic literature on the homeless. Dordick explains it succinctly:

> Homelessness encourages a process in which personal relationships are mobilized in the production of what the physical environment fails to provide: a safe and secure place to live.
>
> (Dordick 1997: 193)

Outside sleepers also have contact with city residents who are not homeless. That contact can be with an individual or with numerous local residents. These relationships play a key role in their choice to sleep in the city's public areas. Gerard's case, which is outlined below, is a clear example.

I first met Gerard in November 1999. He has lived on the streets off and on since he was 14, using heroin and occasionally dabbling in cocaine. According to his own account, he had spent *every single* night outside since 1996. In the last few years, he has kept permanent quarters behind the prestigious Magna Plaza shopping centre in the heart of Amsterdam. Using bags full of belongings, Gerard has completely walled in the landing to the stairs leading to the emergency exit. Two Coca Cola parasols serve as his roof. Gerard 'built' this structure gradually, continually returning to the scene after the police sent him away. Little by little, he has furnished it to meet his needs. Gerard sees this spot as just the solution for him. The space is small, with only enough room for one. That gives him the perfect excuse to keep other street people at bay, especially addicts looking for a secluded spot to use drugs. His sleeping spot is elevated. He left an open slit on one side of his 'shack', which gives him an excellent view of his surroundings. 'The traffic here goes one way,' he told me. 'I can see everyone coming, including the police. In the morning, I look through here to see whether the light's on in the café across the street. They often give me coffee.'

Gerard built his 'shack' around an emergency exit now no longer in use. The crack under the glass door allows warm air to seep through, making things more comfortable in the winter. He also feels the transparent door gives his abode a more spacious feel. The waitress across the street, who faithfully serves him coffee, calls his sleeping quarters a 'filthy pile of trash'. Indeed it does look like a chaotic mess and the landing reeks with a rancid human odour, but Gerard describes it as 'the most beautiful sleeping spot I ever had outside'.

The police and other authorities came to tolerate Gerard's presence after a long period of acquaintance. This tolerance is largely due to his social contacts among the locals. Gerard has an amazing network of friends and acquaintances in the city centre. In some streets, he knows almost all of the shopkeepers and neighbourhood employees. As one café owner put it: 'He doesn't do anything weird. He doesn't cause problems.' No one complains about Gerard. As a result, the police have increasingly left him in peace. Gerard's urban environment and relationships with city residents have secured him the freedom he desires. He sleeps where he feels most at home: in his own neighbourhood. His status as a fellow neighbour is due in part to his outdoor sleeping spot in the neighbourhood. Neighbourhood residents support him with money, food and clothing because he sleeps on the streets. According to Gerard, their goodwill towards him is largely due to his prevention of two night-time burglaries. Gerard's presence at night gives the neighbourhood residents, shopkeepers and restaurant owners a greater sense of security. He has no need for the welfare state or homeless shelters. Years ago, he spent the occasional night or time period in night-shelters. Today, his opinions about them are unyielding. Homeless shelters deprive him of the freedom the streets offer. His willingness to talk about them is limited to curt one-liners such as: 'If you want a shower, you can't have one; when you don't want one, you're forced to have one.'

In *Sidewalk*, Duneier's ethnography of a group of homeless book and magazine sellers in New York's Greenwich Village, one of the most important informants called himself a 'public character' (Duneier 2000: 8), a term borrowed from sociologist Jane Jacobs, who wrote about Greenwich Village in her 1961 classic, *Death and Life of Great American Cities*. According to Jacobs' definition, a public character is based in a neighbourhood, has many social contacts there and spends a good deal of time on the streets. Jacobs' book focuses on local shop-keepers and residents who not only live in, but also perform some sort of public service for, the neighbourhood. Duneier describes the book and magazine salesmen as the new public characters in a changing Greenwich Village. He does so even though he is well aware that these African American men, some of whom are crack addicts, hold a different place in the neighbourhood than did Jacobs' white tradespeople four decades earlier. According to Duneier's concept, Gerard is among the new public characters of Amsterdam. To quote Jacobs, he is 'the eye upon the street'. However, Gerard is an exception among outside sleepers. Few are so well established in a neighbourhood, have as many contacts and really participate in the local community. Nonetheless, a significant number of outside sleepers with permanent sleeping spots do maintain contact with people in their immediate environment. These are people who have something to offer them, be it material or social. One group of outside sleepers sleeps near their acquaintances, friends or family. Others sleep in close proximity to care organizations. Yet another group has established friendly relationships with night guards, gate-keepers and other employees of businesses and public facilities, such as railway stations. The nature of their sleeping spot plays a role. The closer they stay to residential complexes, the more contact they have with the residents. Occasionally, individuals are tolerated in their regular sleeping spots because they keep away other – less familiar – homeless people.

To call this category of outside sleepers 'public characters' would be stretching Duneier's use of the term. All the same, other users of the same public space see them as the 'eyes upon the street'. A few who do odd jobs for businesses or individual residents can be labelled 'neighbourhood vagrants'. Neighbourhood vagrants are a mixed lot. They can include alcoholics and drug addicts or those suffering from psychiatric disorders. Ties between other users of the same public space and these vagrants vary with each individual. Of those who suffer from psychiatric disorders some have a fairly good grip on street life. They approach local residents and fellow public space users actively with a view to achieving their goal: maintaining a permanent sleeping spot. Others are extremely withdrawn and prefer minimal contact with the neighbourhood. Maria has been a neighbourhood vagrant in Amsterdam's city centre for the past twenty years. All the locals know her but no one has any idea what has driven this woman to roam the streets. Neighbourhood vagrants suffering from psychiatric disorders often prompt 'the neighbourhood' to have mercy on them. Local residents and fellow public space users see their psychiatric disorders as a reason to 'avoid disturbing' their sleeping spots. The neighbourhood expects little of the sleeper who, in turn, expects little of the neighbourhood. Over the course of time, both sides develop a mutually satisfactory code of conduct. Neighbourhood vagrants refrain from crime at least in their own neighbourhoods and they are well aware that the neighbourhood would turn against them if they were to be arrested for criminal activity there.

Finding some shelter inside can have an enormous effect on the daily lives of these outside sleepers – public characters and neighbourhood vagrants alike. The more frequently they stay away, the more they lose contact with the neighbourhood. Their role as the 'eye upon the street' would diminish, giving the neighbourhood less reason to tolerate them. They would also miss out on the gifts they would normally receive at their regular haunts. Their relationships with the locals would dwindle. If Gerard were to leave 'his' neighbourhood, he would relinquish an enormous portion of his livelihood. Although this is less true of most neighbourhood vagrants, the importance of this group's ties to their neighbourhoods should not be underestimated. From a social standpoint, these contacts form a bridge to ordinary urban life, regardless of how useless that bridge may be at times. Besides, it is difficult for those with permanent sleeping spots to use night-shelters. There they would be unable to keep an eye on their outside spots. Their mattresses or other belongings could be stolen. Another homeless person might sleep in their spot and cause local residents or the authorities to take action.

Between fatigue and 'half-sleep'

Sleep is a rare privilege for the majority of outside sleepers. Even resting is scarcely possible. Outside sleepers and walkers alike suffer from bouts of chronic fatigue. In the course of my research, I actually saw individuals that I was 'following' break down mentally and physically. Occasionally, they were incapable of keeping their eyes open. They talked with their eyes shut or fell asleep for short stretches of time. A few times I heard individuals uttering gibberish, talking as they dreamed or crying softly. One of the most touching moments during my research occurred when Meta, a Surinamese addict, fell asleep against me in broad daylight following what had been at least a three-day binge. When she awoke, she thanked me for staying there and watching her belongings.

It is obvious that bad weather conditions, police control or the lack of security may keep the rough sleeper from sleeping. The roles played by the magnetic appeal of the street, the rules of social care and personal attributes such as drug addiction are less obvious. The cycle of day and night also plays a key role. The diverging elements that keep the rough sleeper from sleep lead to a sleeping practice I call 'half-sleep': trying to rest or sleep without giving the impression that you are sleeping. In my opinion, the practice of half-sleep is the way rough sleepers try to fight exhaustion.

Lodewijk Brunt (1996: 70–85) has pointed out how little attention social scientists have devoted to life at night. This is certainly true of research on the homeless. Their choice of sleeping spots, however, is closely related to the cycle of day and night. At night, the streets have a different appeal than they do during the day. Quite a few homeless decide to stay awake at night. When they need rest, they have to find a sleeping place in the day. Shelters for the homeless in Amsterdam offer sleeping accommodation, but only at night. This rule that requires the homeless to sleep at night has always been in place. This is reflected for example in Carl Cohen and Jay Sokolovsky's American study of older home-less individuals on the Bowery in New York. In it, a weary vagrant bemoans the rule: 'They tell you, bedtime is midnight' (Cohen and Sokolovsky 1989: 77–78). Outside sleepers who stay awake or 'work' at night are not allowed to use night-shelters. They sleep during the day or not at all. Daytime sleepers have to make their own sleeping arrangements, because the shelters provide no beds during the day. Most outside sleepers who prefer to stay awake at night are drug users. The option of buying and using drugs at night may be preferable for them. At night, they have less intervention to fear from the police or other authorities and fewer addicts roam the streets during those hours.

For outside sleepers who engage in crime, the night is a good time to be active. Bicycle thieves and burglars work well in the shelter of the dark, where they run less risk of being caught. The drug users who sleep outside include a few individuals who work as runners; they negotiate between dealers and other drug users. Another small group of outside sleepers engage in legal 'work' at night. Günther, a German heroin addict, is a prime example. He plays the flute every night in front of the casino on Rembrandtplein, one of Amsterdam's famous squares. The last stragglers leave around 3:30 a.m. Many have had good nights at the tables and feel quite generous. A few outside sleepers go begging late at night around Dam Square, Central Station and convenience stores or night shops. A few have regular haunts, which they frequent almost every night. Some hunt through waste bins at night in search of food and useful articles. Statue mimes, some of whom live on the streets, also work late at night and sleep in the early morning or during the day. Outside sleepers thus participate in the ever-growing, twenty-four-hour economy thriving in Amsterdam. The night is a time of reduced competition.

The largest group of outside sleepers frequently awake at night are the home-less drug addicts on a binge who are not willing or able to stay inside the night-shelter for ten hours in succession without using drugs as the rules prescribe. This group of homeless people who frequent the night has to find an alternative to sleep. Lots of them try to get some rest or sleep at daytime 'walk-in centres', ten of which are spread across Amsterdam's inner city, although sleeping in these shelters is formally forbidden. Ron's agonizing experience illus-trates the effects of this:

> 7 March 2000, 11 a.m. Things were quiet in the activity centre of a major help-for-the-homeless organization. A number of homeless people were painting and hammering on the first floor. The activity hall upstairs serves as the 'walk-in' area. That morning, a handful of homeless people were sitting at the familiar Formica tables. 'Is the coffee ready yet?' one of the young men called out to a care worker. Everyone else was silent.

I sat at a table with Carlos and Ron, both addicts in their thirties. Ron was in bad shape. His hands were soiled and covered in scrapes and sores. His face and neck were spotted with ulcers. Tears dripped from his eyes. His clothes were filthy. A cup of tea with milk and sugar stood on the table in front of him, but he never got around to drinking it. He kept falling asleep. Sleeping was against the rules at that walk-in shelter. Pauline, the care worker on duty, left Ron in peace for a few moments. But once his chin dropped onto his chest and he began snoring, she took action. 'Ron, Ron!' she called, walking up to him and giving his shoulder a gentle push. Ron woke, mumbling unintelligibly. He sipped some tea, only to doze off again. Every time Ron actually fell asleep, Pauline tried to wake him. When she was busy making coffee, one of the young homeless people took over the task spontaneously. Standing next to Ron, he clapped his hands together, yelling at the top of his lungs, 'Hey man, wake up!' Then he sat down again and announced triumphantly, 'See, that's the way to do it.' But even that method had lost any effect on Ron. His head lay on a comic book, which he pretended to read every time someone woke him. The crumpled booklet was drenched in spit and coffee. Occasionally, he woke spontaneously, shot up straight only to drift away into a deep sleep ten minutes later. He fell over twice, banging his head hard against a chair during one of the falls. Every so often, he mumbled inarticulate apologies.

As Carlos and I talked, Ron sank down further and further. Although he wanted to sit up straight and drink some tea, he was simply unable. From time to time, he made jerky movements.

'What did you do, man?' Carlos asked.

'Opium,' Ron mumbled.

'Yeah, opium'll send you off to a different world,' Carlos commented.

Time and again, Ron shifted positions, rubbed his face and sank back into a slumber. Ron kept placing his tea directly in front of him and put his arm around it. After a ten-minute struggle, he finally managed to get his fingers around the plastic cup, only to drop it anyway. For Pauline, that was the last straw. She asked him to leave. Before he stood up, he mumbled, 'My fingernails are loose.' Trying to reassure him, I looked at his nails and said, 'Oh, they're not in that bad a shape.' But Ron was insistent. 'No, they're dropping off.'

Ron's expulsion from the shelter was no exceptional incident. Dozens of homeless individuals and outside sleepers are sent away from shelters for falling asleep. Not all walk-in shelters in Amsterdam enforce the ban on sleeping as strictly. In practice, care workers apply the rule to keep 'the atmosphere inside' under control. Those who manage to pretend they are reading, thinking or daydreaming stand a chance of being left in peace. The ban on sleeping does not apply to resting. The line between sleep and rest is fluid. However, anyone with their head thrown back is very likely to be sent away, regardless of whether they have an open mouth or, even worse, are dribbling or snoring. Dribbling is dirty. Snoring is irritating. Such are the fairly arbitrary criteria by which care workers determine who may or may not sleep.

This practice of sending homeless people away seems to conflict with the purpose most shelters intend to serve: to offer the homeless a place to 'recover', as care workers call it. In order to recover, Ron first needed to rest. Also, sending him out on the streets was not without dangers. Carlos, a seasoned drug user himself, was surprised at Ron's state. Ron was also suffering from delusions with no connection to reality. Despite all of this, the care worker allowed the rule that restricts sleep to the night to prevail over the shelter's overall objective. Two aims of the care sector conflict here: on the one hand, to offer refuge; on the other hand, to (re)activate the homeless. During the day, activity prevails over refuge, all the more because a sleeping homeless person in a day activity shelter demotivates the others.

As Ron's case also illustrates, the concept of half-sleep is inextricably tied to the use of alcohol, drugs and medicines, which is common among outside sleepers. Individuals can experience a heightened or dulled sense of consciousness when stoned or drunk. Ron was too heavily under the influence and too tired to pretend to be awake. For that reason, his efforts to remain in a state of half-sleep were doomed to fail. In other cases, however, narcotics and stimulants make it easier to engage in half-sleep. They bring about the kind of altered state of mind needed to rest without sleeping. In that sense, being stoned or drunk are forms of half-sleep.

One form of half-sleep, which is intricately tied to life on the streets, should not go unmentioned here. When outside sleepers use hard drugs for long, continual stretches, they enter an altered state of mind in which drug use becomes an increasing fixation. As they smoke or inject drugs, their thoughts wander to the next fix of cocaine or heroin.

That fixation can become so overpowering that it distorts their perceptions of their immediate environment. Such binges can end in what one homeless addict ironically termed 'digging for treasure'. He was referring to the act of searching every object within reach for drugs. During one of my nightly treks I watched as an outside sleeper, an addict, spent forty-five minutes meticulously searching the cracks between ten paving stones with a spoke of a bicycle wheel. He was looking for a fix of cocaine or heroin, both of which are sold in miniscule pill-sized bags on the streets. On another occasion, an outside sleeper began digging barehanded in a flowerpot because in the glow of the street lamps, the little white granules there looked like cocaine to him. Occasionally, drug users are aware of their aberrant behaviour. Most, however, are completely absorbed in their state of mind. As Wouter, the outside sleeper I mentioned before, explained, 'As long as you're stoned, you're sure you'll find something. It's hard to even describe the disappointment that hits when the high is gone.' Despite the degradation that follows the high, at times these searching rituals are steeped in a sense of serenity. The resting period usually sets in between 4 a.m. and 6 a.m. when the dealers go home, the noise from cars and other city traffic dies down and almost all residents are asleep. Outside sleepers may not sleep during this period, but they do rest.

Many outside sleepers with a drug addiction are used to concealing sleep or to resting without sleeping due to their frequent use of narcotics. 'Digging for treasure' is the ultimate example of that. In a certain sense, the half-sleep that their environment forces them to engage in is an extension of life on the streets. Half-sleep is the poignant by-product of the interplay between individual attributes, like addiction, and outside influences, such as the attraction of the street and the shelter rules.

Conclusion

Sleeping outside is almost always a compromise. The homeless must not be reduced to their sleeping habits. To understand the act of sleeping outside other important elements in their lives have to be taken into account. Duneier's plea to consider the 'overall logic' of the homeless is entirely valid.

The Amsterdam example acknowledges the empirically based insights of Duneier. Rough sleepers not only sleep, but have to live their lives asleep and awake. Rough sleepers must protect themselves against bad weather; they need to ensure that the social environment does not endanger, but, rather, protects them. They need to build social relationships with people in the neighbourhood, the police and other authorities. Those rough sleepers who use social care must also ensure their position in these institutions. At the same time, they have to earn an income. If eligible they can fulfil this need within the social security system. In practice, half of the rough sleepers in Amsterdam do not have social security. This group has to earn a living in other ways. Of those who receive social security, a large percentage must earn extra money because social security is not sufficient for them to support their life-styles. This holds especially true for those rough sleepers who gamble or use drugs. Although very important, sleep is just a small part of the rough-sleeping experience.

In general, rough sleepers are ambivalent about the meaning of sleep and rest. Rest, at a given time, is both important and unimportant. Because it is so difficult to obtain, sleep is a central theme in their lives. To prevent exhaustion they have to take their chances in order to get rest. They often wonder where and when they will sleep. But other aspects of their lives, such as earning money, are also important. Because of that, sleep becomes something to take as it comes, to postpone. A lot of rough sleepers are exhausted at times but try not to think about it. The logic of homelessness thus implies a certain indifference towards rest.

The act of sleeping must always be seen from within the 'overall logic'. In this respect, rough sleepers are no different from the non-homeless. For the latter, sleep is a realm defined by the distribution of work and free time, family life and the accompanying cycle of day and night. For them, sleep is as much embedded in life as a whole as it is for rough sleepers.

Although the embedment within the context of life as a whole is the same for the homeless and non-homeless, the outcome is very different. Outside sleepers have their own particular approach to sleep, in terms of both their actual sleeping habits and the significance they attach to it. The word 'logic' in Duneier's quotation is crucial. It implies viewing social conditions from the homeless person's logic or perspective. What differentiates rough sleepers and society in general are the social conditions under which they must live. In society in general, people have a stable sleeping place. They can go to bed where and when they want. The non-homeless can fulfil the primary need of rest without worrying about rain and cold or other people; they don't have to find sleeping equipment or a sleeping place. The certainty of a sleeping room within a home makes it possible to separate sleep to a certain extent from other parts of life such as working and social life. That is the main difference between the homeless and non-homeless, a crucial difference which makes the homeless who sleep inside social care institutions much more similar to the non-homeless than to rough sleepers, a fact underestimated in the literature on the 'homeless'. Rough sleepers face a specific set of social conditions that makes it difficult if not impossible to separate rest and sleep from other basic necessities. This makes the content of their 'overall logic' and their sleeping habits profoundly different from that of the general population.

Bibliography

Bogaard, Desiree van den (1993) 'Begeleid zwerven' (Guided transience), *Passage* 2(1): 19–22.

Braam, Stella (2000) 'Het verborgen leven op Schiphol' (The hidden life of Schiphol airport), *FNV-Magazine* 28 September: 14–17.

Brunt, Lodewijk (1996) *Stad* (City). Amsterdam: Boom.

Cloward, Richard A. and Lloyd E. Ohlin (1960) *Delinquency and Opportunity. A Theory of Delinquent Gangs.* New York: The Free Press.

Cohen, Carl I. and Jay Sokolovsky (1989) *Old Men of the Bowery. Strategies for Survival Among the Homeless.* New York and London: The Guilford Press.

Deben, Léon and Barbra van Gestel (1995) *Inventarisatie bergingen hoogbouw Bijlmermeer* (Inventory of highrise buildings in Bijlmermeer). Amsterdam: Housing Association New Amsterdam and University of Amsterdam.

Deben, Léon and Dirk Korf (1995) 'Intern verslag tel/consumentenonderzoek' (Internal report counting/consumer research). Unpublished.

Deben, Léon and Peter Rensen (2001) *Uitgeteld! Buitenslapers in Amsterdam 1995–2001* (Counted out! Rough sleepers in Amsterdam). Amsterdam: Aksant.

Deben, Léon, Jan Godschalk and Coos Huijsman (1992) *Dak-en thuislozen in Amsterdam en elders in de Randstad* (Homeless in Amsterdam and elsewhere in the Randstad). Amsterdam: Centre for Urban Studies and University of Amsterdam.

Doorn, Lia van (2002) *Een tijd op straat* (A time on the street). Utrecht: NIZW.

Dordick, Gwendolyn A. (1997) *Something Left to Lose. Personal Relationships and Survival among New York's Homeless.* Philadelphia: Temple University Press.

Duneier, Mitchell (2000) *Sidewalk.* New York: Farrar, Straus and Giroux.

Esping-Andersen, Gøsta (1990) *The Three Worlds of Welfare Capitalism.* Cambridge: Polity Press.

Gemeente Amsterdam/Eysink Smeets & Etman (1999) 'Dakloze verslaafden in Amsterdam-Zuidoost' (Homeless drug addicts in Amsterdam-Zuidoost). Unpublished.

Greshof, Dorien (1996) 'Wie we zijn is waar we slapen 's nachts' (Who we are is where we sleep at night), *Passage* 5(2): 55–62.

Korf, Dirk *et al.* (1997) *Dak-en thuislozen in Amsterdam. Tel en consumentenonderzoek* (Homeless in Amsterdam. Counting- and consumer research). Amsterdam: University of Amsterdam/Office for Research and Statistics Amsterdam.

Korf, Dirk *et al.* (1999) *Een sleutel voor de toekomst. Tel en consumentenonderzoek onder daklozen in Amsterdam* (A key to the future. Counting- and consumer research among the homeless in Amsterdam). Amsterdam: Thela Thesis.

Liebow, Elliot (1995) *Tell Them Who I Am.* New York: Penguin Books.

Rensen, Peter (1999) 'Daklozenbeleid in Amsterdam' (Homeless policy in Amsterdam). Unpublished.

Spierings, Frans (1991) 'Relationele onbekwaamheid van thuislozen. De moderniserings-theorie' (Relational incompetence of the homeless. The modernization theory), *Sociologische Gids* 4: 414–423.

Spierings, Frans (1997) 'Een wereld zonder thuis. Dak en thuislozen, niet-gebruik van voorzieningen en het toeschouwersperspectief' (A world without a home. Homeless, non-use of welfare-arrangements and the perspective of the spectator), *Sociologische Gids* 4: 311–323.

Spradley, James A. (1970) *You Owe Yourself a Drunk. An Ethnography of Urban Nomads.* Boston: Little, Brown.

6   Sleep and night-time combat in contemporary armed forces

Technology, knowledge and the enhancement of the soldier's body

Eyal Ben-Ari

In this chapter I examine the ideas and practices related to sleep and night-time combat as they have been evolving in the militaries of the industrial democracies over the past two decades. One needs no more than a cursory familiarity with the military to understand how sleep has always been an issue confronted by both soldiers and commanders. While practical rules and regulations have been propagated in regard to sleep for decades, it is only in the past few years that the organisational aspects of sleep have begun to be regularly incorporated into the planning and execution of military operations. In other words, while in the past knowledge about sleep was usually part of military 'common sense' or the specialised expertise held by physicians and behavioural scientists, it is now becoming an integral element in the set of explicit rules and procedures on the basis of which the armed forces operate. The reasons for these developments are related to the many technological innovations that now allow military forces to remain active around the clock – to partake in 'continuous operations' – and to be rapidly deployed a few time zones away from their bases.

These innovations have led the military establishments of the industrial democracies to ask increasingly about the means by which units should handle sleep and rest given the need for restoring the fighting capabilities of their troops. It is only in the past few years that one finds the use of such military terms as 'sleep management strategies', 'unit sleep plans', 'sleep discipline' or 'sleep management systems' (Welch 1995; WRAIR 1997).

In this chapter I examine such sleep management systems and the strategies used to implement them. I do this by exploring the discursive and behavioural practices related to the military's effort to interpret and control the 'bodily' and 'mindful' states of soldiers so that they are useful to the organisation. My argument is that the sleep management systems now being developed in various military establishments around the world are part of the wider organisational 'logic' of these forces. These systems work not only on the basis of the military recruiting or disciplining of individual soldiers in order to utilise fully their physical and mental abilities. Rather, these systems (and the military in general) work on the basis of blurring the line between the body and its environment and by enhancing the very bodily and mental capacities of soldiers. Along these lines, I suggest that an examination of sleep in the military may allow us a unique theo-retical vantage point from which to examine the relations between technology, bodies and machines in complex organisations. In other words, an investigation of sleep (and sleep-related activities) as an intersection of organisational arrange-ments, embodied experience and technological means may clarify the discursive and behavioural practices (and their limits) by which militaries variously recruit, use and alter the very bodies of soldiers.

A note on methodology

To the best of my knowledge, there exists no extended ethnography of sleep in the military. What one does find are occasional hints and observations rather than sustained descriptions. Along these lines, as a basis for my analysis I have used a variety of texts published by and about contemporary armed forces: both formal texts – rooted for example in organisation studies or military science – and primary and secondary literature written by scholars and ex-soldiers. Thus, for instance, I have made use of works on war and killing, personal commen-taries of commanders and soldiers, academic studies of the military that mention sleep, and organisational primers and handbooks devoted to the actual 'work' of soldiering.

Since so much of this literature is focused on US forces my stress has been on the US Navy and US Army. Moreover, because so much of the data is of recent origin, I have also made extensive use of the Internet and the electronic archives of the US military. An added reason for this focus is that US forces are very much the models from which other military establishments learn and thus can be seen as harbingers of future developments. While my emphasis in this chapter is on combat, it should be mentioned that problems related to sleep deprivation also arise in various other kinds of deployment and in military shift work (cf. Castro and Adler 1999; Rhem 2000; Stafford 1998).

The night, technology and continuous operations

Owing to the advent and the lowering of the cost of a host of new technological means, combat has been transformed into an operation lasting twenty-four hours a day (Fowler 1998). These technological means include night-vision binoculars, weapon sighting systems, riflescopes, illuminators, laser range-finders, image intensification systems, thermal imaging systems and supplemental lighting (Fowler 1999; SAS 1999). They also include many defensive measures such as technologies for reducing electromagnetic emissions and 'thermal signatures', erecting 'light-proofing' shelters, using filtered lights and eliminating all but essential noise. Along these lines, for example, the US Army's primary attack helicopter, the Apache, is designed to fight and survive during day and night and allows the crew to navigate and conduct precision attacks in all kinds of weather (Apache 1999).

Closely related to these technologies are training and simulation 'packages' such as the product called 'Paint the Night' which is a thermal-scene (infrared), electro-optic simulation for military exercises, or the US Navy's Night Combat Test Laboratory allowing the study of night-enhancement devices, located in a light-tight aircraft hanger. The idea behind such packages is to 'insure that pilots and crew are compatible with night-vision devices under specified mission conditions' (Bogie 1998). The US Army, for its part, has developed a window-less night-fighter instruction classroom where soldiers receive instruction in night-vision goggles, thermal devices, laser pointers and illuminators, infrared munitions and night-sky orientation (Night Stalker 1999). It also built the 'Nightfighter' programme for night vision and marksmanship, leader training and small-unit proficiency (IFRU 1999). In fact, the terms 'continuous operations' and 'sustained combat operations' currently in vogue in many military circles clearly express this move towards utilising the destructive potential of the military around the clock. As McManners (1994: 158) concludes, 'on the modern battlefield, night has become the same as day', and as Holmes (1985: 123) suggests, in the future night attacks may become the rule rather than the exception. Against this background we are able to understand why commanders, and some scholars, have begun to deal with the special problems posed by such day and night operations for the human beings staffing the combat units of the armed forces.

As the editors suggest in the introduction to their present volume, sleep is probably *the* mechanism of release from individual pressures. People are released not only from external pressures such as social ties and demands (roles), but also from the internal pressures of individual psychological forces. Sleep, in other words, allows us to retreat from everything that is 'objectively' and 'subjectively' social (Schwartz 1973: 20). Like hunger and thirst, for example, sleep deprivation is directly related to a diminishing ability to carry out tasks. But unlike hunger or thirst, sleep itself involves a much more direct relinquishment of individual and organisational control over reality because, from a social point of view, the regular mechanisms of social control are either absent or altered. If sleep is, thus, 'the' tension release phenomenon that has a restorative function for humans then it would seem to be of central importance in combat, the ultimate tension- and stress-filled situation.

Sleep and night-time combat

Sleep and sleep deprivation pose problems on multiple levels for military organisations. From an organisational point of view, the key problem centres on the individual soldier who needs psychological and physical rest in order to perform his (more rarely, her) role. Individual lack of sleep, to make this point explicit, may hinder the military's necessary ability to maintain the demands of readiness and effectiveness (measures of how well prepared units are for combat).

First, a large amount of accumulated evidence about actual combat shows that continuous fighting is characterised by brief, fragmented sleep (Shay 1995:

173–174), and that extended sleep deprivation leads to such symptoms as blurring of vision and hallucinations (Ellis 1980: 234–238; Lieblich 1989: 73). In addition, lack of sleep in combat training has led to what soldiers call 'droning' (a condition in which troops can put one foot in front of the other and respond if challenged, but have trouble shifting from one cognitive framework to another) and periods of 'microsleep' into which someone standing upright with eyes wide open may slip while droning (Shay 1998).

Second, a steady stream of academic studies has shown that lack of sleep can lead to sleepiness, attention lapses, irritability, susceptibility to accidents and decreased attention to self-care (Borbély and Tononi 1998). Thus, for example, American researchers have found that while sleep deprivation does not impair physical strength, endurance or co-ordination, it is decision-making, logic and the 'higher' mental functions that are the most degraded by sleep deprivation (WRAIR 1997). Concretely, sleep deprivation has been linked both to the need for greater amounts of time to make the correct decision to avert catastrophe (Moore 1996) and to the occurrence of mistakes such as firing on friendly forces (Shay 1998).

Third, these problems are compounded by jet lag, which is an outcome of the logistical possibilities now in place to move thousands of soldiers and their equipment rapidly by aircraft (Calow 1997; Spindweber *et al.* 1986). Similarly, communications make commanders (especially since the war in Vietnam) much more accessible to their superiors a few time zones away.

The weariness that soldiers experience, however, is not the simple outcome of sleep deprivation, but related to circadian desynchronisation and consequent fatigue (Williams *et al.* 1998). This fatigue is related to the gradual readjustment of various physiological rhythms such as urine excretion (a day or two), steady tempo of the heart (four to eight days) or adrenal cortisol production (five to ten days) brought on by sleep deprivation. Murray Melbin (1987: 105–107) concludes that overall it may take two weeks before all of these functions have stabilised.

For all of this, however, such problems are not untypical of many 'incessant' organisations such as hospitals, or fire and police departments. What distinguishes military organisations is the environment they are supposed to function in, and are trained to perform in, namely combat. At the risk of stating the obvious, let me emphasise that the focal environment at the level of field units is combat and not war in general. What interests soldiers most is the localised, violent encounter of two armed forces (Boene 1990: 29; Ben-Ari 1998). What kind of experience is combat? Depictions of combat typical of any modern army present a scene of the actual firefight marked by utmost chaos and confusion. In this situation the soldier not only confronts the imminent danger of loss of life and limb; he also witnesses injury and death suffered by others (Gal 1988; Moskos 1988: 5). In addition, there is a constant and gnawing sense of uncertainty about the unfolding 'action' on the battlefield (often termed the 'fog' of battle) (Keegan 1976: 47). In such a situation an overwhelming totality of sounds, smells and sights come together in a form that individuals find very hard to analyse in any meaningful way (Shalit 1988: 147). Closely related to this experience are more 'routine' stresses: the weight of the pack and the equipment, the lack of food and water, and difficult weather conditions. This situation implies that the effects of sleep deprivation on the body are heightened and reinforced by the pressures of battle (Dinter 1985; Holmes 1985: 125).

It is in this respect that the special qualities of night-time fighting are important. Because of the impairment of vision, the intensification of sounds and the potential for surprise associated with darkness, night-time combat is often perceived by soldiers to be even more threatening than daytime battles (Ellis 1980: 65, 96; Shay 1995: 59–60). Among the problems reported by soldiers – even in more recent wars – are disorientation, feelings of being alone, problems with navigation and lowered visibility (McManners 1994: 164–165). Night-time is still very frightening because of the loss of control associated with it, and because it still seems to resonate with popular depictions of this period as full of chaos and danger, and therefore threat (Melbin 1987: 43; Maver in this volume). As one military commentator has noted, despite all of the night-vision devices it still gets dark at night and 'a fuzzy telescope stuck to your face does not daytime make' (Bolger 1999: 121). Thus continuous operations, because they involve the still qualitatively different aspects of waging battle during the night, carry additional stresses and pressures.

Why not enough sleep?

Understanding combat as involving individual and organisational stresses and tensions that are compounded in the context of continuous operations would seem to underscore the importance of sleep and rest. As previously noted, if, indeed, sleep is the phenomenon of release from pressure and of restorative potential then it would seem crucial that combat troops receive the maximal amount of rest possible. At the same time, there is ample evidence to show that soldiers – and most importantly commanders – do not get enough sleep whether in combat or in training geared towards combat (DiGiovanni 2000; Grossman 1995: 71; Garamone 1999; Holmes 1985: 124; WRAIR 1997). The reasons for this situation bear upon both organisational and wider cultural themes.

The first reason is related to the amount and diversity of demands on the time and attention of soldiers and commanders. Moreover, the sheer quantity and quality of information processing and decision-making that they must carry out under conditions of severe pressure are extraordinary (Kamena 1999). It is no surprise, then, that for soldiers, and again especially for commanders, sleep loses out to other considerations (Shay 1998; Kamena 1999). As Melbin (1987: 17) succinctly puts it, meeting a deadline means staying awake.

A second explanation for lack of sleep is 'cultural' in the sense of the historical (often religious) identification of sleep – and other 'bodily' functions such as eating and drinking – with self-indulgence, and conversely the positively valued aspects of self-denial (Shay 1998). Speaking in an American context, Shay (1998) calls this theme 'our love affair with stoic self-denial', while in the Israeli Army these behaviours are termed part of the 'cult of suffering' (Zev Lehrer, personal communication). Melbin (1987: 36–37) and Chris Nottingham (in this volume) contend that because surveillance declines at night, there is more toleration of alternative, 'deviant' behaviour. Alternatively, however, one could make the case that it is precisely this lack of surveillance that entails even more self-discipline with regard to night-time behaviour and sleep. Concretely, these cultural themes are expressed in behaviour such as commanders eating after their troops have done so and, in a like manner, sleeping less than the soldiers under their command.

Third, this behaviour, in turn, is closely related to the idea that field commanders often serve as role models for troops (Shamir and Ben-Ari 1999). A typical admonition by a military physician underscores this line of reasoning: you 'have an obligation to set a good example for those you lead. If you ignore your own sleep requirements, those whom you lead may ignore theirs' (DiGiovanni 2000). Similarly, a US Army document (WRAIR 1997) states: 'Effective sleep management starts with command emphasis; leaders must set the example for their units.'

A fourth and closely related reason centres on images of the exemplary masculinity in the military (Connel 1995: 214). Images of becoming a man through military service and participation in combat have long been associated with the figure of the hero. Concretely, the link between masculinity and military service centres on the idea of a series of tests and trials in which individuals overcome various obstacles (Ben-Ari 2001; Arkin and Dubrofsky 1978). A central aspect of these situations involves control over and overcoming the 'limits' of the body. In this respect again, forgoing sleep is seen as one test of an individual (Shay 1998).

It is all of these attitudes, in turn, which underlie the fifth reason for lack of sleep: the resentment, or possible resentment, felt by individuals who are awake towards those soldiers who are sleeping (and therefore being 'self-indulgent'). Thus, for example, in an article on aircrew rest, Welch (1995) explains that 'resentment results from the perception that crew rest somehow exempts aviators from the rigours of military duty' and from the fact that 'crew rest policies have been abused to avoid undesirable missions'. But he is well aware of the background factors and thus says, 'crew rest is not a dirty word' (Welch 1995). In this sense, then, the 'cult of self-denial' is reinforced through the group dynamics found in military organisations.

'Sleep logistics'

In the past two decades or so, military establishments around the world have begun to react explicitly to, and plan for, problems related to continuous operations and sleep. Let me provide two extended examples – one from the US Navy and one from the US Army (the ground forces) – and then go on to explore their implications. I should explain that both systems are now out of the purely experimental stage and are being slowly implemented in various types of training.

Moreover, given the restrictions on the data being released by the US military establishment, I have rather limited information about the actual experiences of the troops who are subject to these systems.

The Sleep Management Manual

First, consider the *Sleep Management Manual* developed by the US Naval Health Research Center (Kelly *et al.* 1994). This booklet was written on the basis of a large research project on 'sleep logistics', based on 'scientific knowledge of how sleep loss influences human performance, and provid[ing] techniques to assure that every member of a group receives sufficient sleep at appropriate times so that serious sleep loss does not interfere with mission completion' (Naitoh *et al.* 1990: 1). The logic at the base of this research thus links sleep to 'force effectiveness' and the very 'survival' of naval units and ships. The data for this project was derived from sleep logs (record books kept by individuals about their actual sleeping routines), which have been used within and outside the military to develop 'optimal sleep/wake schedules [for maximal organisational efficiency] in a sustained military operation' (Naitoh *et al.* 1990: 1).

The manual is very much a prescriptive, 'how-to' handbook – like many instruction booklets prepared by and for military forces around the world – its purpose being to provide naval personnel (including Marines) with basic facts about sleep and to teach them specific sleep management techniques. The sections covered in the manual begin with explanations about 'sleep need' and about averages and individual differences. Echoing wider themes, the manual stresses that the need for more sleep than average (eight hours) should not be seen as 'a sign of weakness, laziness, or lack of motivation. The amount of sleep you need and your response to sleep loss is a biological characteristic.' The next section talks about sleep timing with clarification about 'morning' and 'evening' types and stressing that timing, unlike amount of sleep, can be adjusted. Then there is a section on the effects of sleep loss such as impaired vigilance, faulty short-term memory, problems in communication, and after two days without sleep the possibility of illusions or hallucinations.

The subsequent section is devoted to the need to get a good sleep and then the basics of the circadian rhythms with the warning that industrial and vehicular accidents tend to occur during the circadian low period. A segment on shift work follows a section on jet lag and ways to overcome it. Next come a few sections on countermeasures such as providing bright light and naps as useful preventative measures for jet lag. Here another admonition appears: 'sleeping at the scheduled time must be considered an important duty. Personnel instructed to sleep should not feel guilty about sleeping when others work. Personnel who are working should not resent those who are sleeping.' The following chapter is devoted to medications and the states when physicians may prescribe stimulants such as amphetamines during some operations. The penultimate section is on other strategies such as confirming comprehension with tired personnel by repeating orders, knowing everyone's sleeping needs, and awareness of symptoms such as irritability. Finally, the conclusion encapsulates many of the issues dealt with in the manual:

> Sleep is a vital physical need. Without sleep, humans have degraded performance and alertness. This is not a sign of weakness or low motivation. The best countermeasures for sleep deprivation is sleep. … Planning and allocating time for personnel to sleep is a critical but often ignored factor in military logistics. Human sleep requirements should be managed like other mission assets for successful operations. Often the personnel most critical to the operation get the least sleep. A commander feels his constant presence is required, so he does not sleep and thereby puts the mission at risk. … Utilize multiple strategies to promote performance and alertness during operations.
>
> (Kelly *et al.* 1994: 24)

The 'Sleep Management System'

A much more elaborate 'Sleep Management System' has been developed since the mid-1990s within the US Army Medical Research and Material Command (WRAIR 1997). It is based on research carried out at the Walter Reed Army Institute and observations from the Army's training centres and the Gulf War. The system is designed to maximise individual and unit performance during continuous operations and is to be implemented at the level of field units. Concretely, it includes hardware, software (a quantitative Sleep/Performance Model), a wrist-worn 'Personnel Status Monitor', pharmacological agents to assist in the sleep/wake cycle, and an appropriate doctrine in and around the 'insertion' of troops into combat.

Let me explain each of these elements. The use of the wrist-worn microprocessor is designed to overcome the unreliability of self-reports of sleep logs. Weighing less than 100 grams and forming part of the soldier's personal status monitor, it works by measuring arm movements to estimate sleep duration and timing. The software, located with command elements, periodically interrogates the sleep/activity monitor of each individual soldier via a local area radio frequency network (Elsemore *et al.* 1993). The system then generates reports on sleep obtained and predicts effects on performance for individuals and units. These predictions are based on previous research and the assumption that six hours of sleep are needed to 'sustain performance indefinitely'. The computer model predicts individuals' cognitive performance as a function of their 'sleep history' (hours of sleep in each twenty-four-hour period over the previous five to ten days).

The system also includes a 'sleep-induction/rapid-reawakening' procedure consisting of two pills taken orally: the first to induce sleep, the second as an antidote to the sleep-inducer to restore full alertness. Once in combat, commanders may elect to administer another stimulant to enhance the alertness of personnel. This procedure is based on the Army's experimentation with sleep-inducing drugs such as Triazolam, Zolpidem and with stimulants such as

Flumazenil, although it found that coffee is a good stimulant in that it does not impair performance (WRAIR 1997; Bonnet *et al.* 1995).

What is interesting in this system – as in the Navy's scheme – is that it does not posit a 'universal' pattern of sleep and rest but rather takes into account individual differences by integrating data about particular habits into the unit's overall sleep management strategies. Individual variation in terms of performance and sleep is considered important because it allows a better prediction of unit performance. Indeed, the texts accompanying the system all stress that commanders need to know who is at risk, when and for how long (WRAIR 1997).

Timetables, predictability and individual 'differences'

What is at the base of these two systems? Combat units are trained to operate in brutal, threatening and chaotic environments. In order to perform under such circumstances, these units – and the personnel constituting them – are expected to combine two sets of characteristics. On the one hand, the performance of combat units is based on maximal co-ordination, regulation and intentionality. This kind of emphasis on order and planning is necessary in order to handle the chaotic conditions of combat. On the other hand, these units are expected to be highly flexible, and able to scour and react actively to their environments (Ben-Ari 1998). This emphasis arises from the fact that battles and firefights have their own constantly changing and transforming rhythms. In fact, a line of scholars has suggested that especially on the battlefields of the future, more initiative and innovation on the part of soldiers and commanders will be needed (Gray 1997: 202). It is for this reason that the cognitive capacities of soldiers and commanders stand at the core of analyses of sleep deprivation because they are most needed in terms of the reactive capacity of the military's field units. To take one example from a handbook disseminated by the US Naval Medical Center: 'What is effected by sleep debt is the ability of the brain to perform its higher functions, such as learning new information, recalling previously learned information, reacting to information, and analyzing information and making decisions' (DiGiovanni 2000).

But what are the concrete implications of these understandings for the practices and arrangements made in regard to sleep? My argument is that in order to handle the uncertainty entailed by the highly volatile environment of combat, military units undertake various arrangements and measures. Consider the plethora of timetables and rosters used in the military. The way that the armed forces approach problems related to sleep and sleep deprivation centres first of all on the control and management of time. The most distinctive organisational mechanisms for creating order are timetables, essentially time–space organising devices. Members of an organisation have to know the 'time' most of the time in order for the co-ordination and synchronisation of people and resources to take place (Hassard 1996: 583). Melbin (1987) suggests that incessant organisations face three core problems with regard to timetables: coverage, referring to how projects will be staffed with the personnel to carry them out; continuity, involving the maintenance of a course of action in a habitual, coherent way; and control, which concerns the supervision of the organisation and how its decisions will be made.

From this point of view, sleep management entails, first of all, the assignment of personnel – the allocation of teams with the right combination of skills to carry out functions, substituting them regularly over time. In addition, with each new relay of troops the unit must also assure that there is a proper transfer of information from one to the next. Thus the sleep management systems devised by US forces should be seen alongside firing tables, task assignment programmes, unit combat readiness and location tables, and definitions of missions and forces. The point to note in regard to all these kinds of lists and tables is the assumption that underlies their use: we expect military units to operate in routine, efficient, reliable and (therefore) predictable ways.

What both the Navy and Army systems do is precisely this kind of scheduling with regard to sleep. The primary aim of both systems is to reach an 'optimal' sleep schedule for all members of a given unit. This particular stress offers a direct contrast to the case of the homeless depicted by Peter Rensen (in this volume) who have to adjust their individual inclinations to one overall insti- tutional timetable. Take the assumptions on which the two schemes are based: Hassard (1996: 584) suggests that 'technological determinism dominates modern perceptions of time, so correct arithmetical equations are seen as the solutions to time problems: there are finite limits and optimal solutions to temporal structuring'. This is the idea behind the stress on the software provided by the Army's system and the sleep logs found in the Navy's project. Both the manual and the computer model stress times for sleep and rest and dosing schedules for drugs in ways that facilitate the efficient use of resources according to the set of priorities set by the military unit in what is assumed to be a clear and quantifiable manner. If we look at the language used in the overview of the US Army's 'Sleep Management System', we learn that the wrist-worn monitor 'measures and records arm movements, and analyzes these data', that the experts designing the system are 'refining and validating a quan- titative Sleep/Performance Model', that the software developed will 'accurately, objectively, and unobtrusively measure sleep in operational settings', and that the computer model thus generated will be able to 'predict present and future performance'. The overview then goes on to explain that findings about the effects of Triazolam were 'statistically significant'.

The most acute problems, however, appear in the 'upper echelons' of the unit. When commanders go to sleep the unit enters a phase in which top deci- sion-makers are absent. To follow Schwartz (1973: 32), the commander, an individual temporarily 'taking leave' of the world by going to sleep, relinquishes control of the organisation. Moreover, the military unit is most vulnerable when commanders suffer from sleep deprivation because of their role in information processing, planning and decision-making. Military organisations usually solve these problems by issuing contingency plans, by assigning deputies to temporary decision-making roles and by setting the discretion they will have when the boss is unavailable. Thus, for instance, the text accompanying the Army's system explains: 'Delegation of appropriate duties and responsibilities to key staff members, liaison officers and other Tactical Operations Center (TOC) personnel is crucial.' It is for this reason that the emphasis in both sleep management systems is very much on commanders and their actions and on the cognitive capacities of 'ordinary' soldiers.

Interestingly, making special provisions for the sleep of commanders involves another dimension. A point frequently found in accounts of the military (Shay 1998) is the apprehension that lower-echelon soldiers have of waking commanders. On top of the usual idea that the sleeper has the right to be insulated from the ordinary claims of society, when the sleeper is the boss, the reluctance to wake him or her is even more intense (Melbin 1987: 92). Thus the usual rules that surround the sleeping person (e.g. where and when to sleep, or by whom and how one can be disturbed) are different and usually more strictly enforced in the case of commanders.

Bodies, minds and machines

Yet both sleep management systems work on the basis of another set of assumptions that are crucial to my argument. One assumption is that it is the individual soldier's body that is the 'instrument' through which the various practices are effected (Frank 1991: 51). Here it would do well to underscore the assumed link between the 'efficient' and 'effective' performance of soldiers and the idea that sleep itself is recuperative. Before the onset of modernisation this assumed relation is not found in other societies – such as Japan or China. It should thus be seen as a construct that developed historically in tandem with certain notions about the body and about work and that continues to have an effect on systems such as those I am examining here.

The logic here is very simple: from an organisational point of view, the problem is how to control the internal 'bodily' and 'mindful' states of the soldiers in order to be able to 'work' on the threatening environment. But as we have seen, sleep is problematic because of both the uncertainty engendered by the individual body and the total relinquishment of control involved in sleep. To return to a point made earlier, the physiological bases of body rhythms and the fact that one cannot accumulate sleep (Melbin 1987: 62–63) imply strict limits on the ways in which soldiers can be 'totally' engaged by the armed forces. The English phrase for deep sleep – to be 'dead to the world' – captures this point well. To be sure, in various ways the military reaches inside soldiers' bodies and unsettles them and soldiers are often pushed to perform to the very limits of their physical and mental abilities. What is important, however, is the manner in which the military relates to the bodies of soldiers.

My suggestion is that we understand military systems as peculiar schemes termed 'cyborgs' – cybernetic mechanisms – those hybrid machines and organisms that fuse the organic and the technical (within a particular historical and cultural context) (Haraway 1991; 1997). As Hayles (in Landow 2000) observes, cyborgs already exist in the technical sense as in the case of people with pace-makers, artificial joints, drug implant systems, implanted corneal lenses and artificial skin. Indeed, Steven Hawking using a computer to communicate is prob-ably the world's most famous cyborg. In another essay, Chris Gray (1997) suggests that we understand militaries as cyborgs, as peculiar systems integrating humans and machines through technology (knowledge and techniques). Encapsulated perhaps in such military terms as 'human engineering', 'psychotechnology', 'human quality control', 'man/weapon systems' (Gray 1989: 59) or 'humanware', the guiding imagery is of human–machine extensions within larger systems of military power. Soldiering, according to this view, is the juncture of ideals, metals, chemicals and people that makes weapons of computers and computers of weapons and soldiers.

But it is a distinctive kind of juncture, of integration, that we find in the mili-tary. In general, cyborg technologies can be 'restorative' (restoring lost limbs, for instance), 'normalising' (taking such medication as anti-depressants), 'reconfig-uring' (possible future genetic alterations of human creatures) and 'enhancing' (Gray, Mentor and Figueroa-Sarriera in Landow 2000). It is this last kind of rela-tion that most characterises the military (and industry) where technology is aimed primarily at increasing, improving, adding to, augmenting or boosting the perfor-mance of soldiers and units. In fact, one of the foremost military commentators of our time, Robert Leonhard (1999: 134–135), chooses to call technological improvements and initiatives in the US Army 'enhancements'.

Two examples from my data illuminate the point I am trying to make. The first is part of the Army's project and involves the use of artificial neural networks (WRH 2000): collections of mathematical models that emulate some of the observed properties of biological nervous systems and that draw on the analogies of adaptive biological learning. The key element of these collections is the novel structure of the information processing system that is composed of a large number of interconnected elements that are analogous to neurons and tied together with weighted connections analogous to synapses. The Walter Reed Hospital research staff report that in order to monitor alertness in operational settings the research centre began to experiment with one such artificial network linking heart rates with sleep. They then state that this artificial network success-fully discriminated rested from sleep-deprived EEG. The report then goes on to say that the Army is now evaluating other devices for monitoring alertness such as eye-tracking, pupilometry or computer-based facial expression analysis. Indeed, these experiments are an excellent example of how the corporeal body is integrated into a wider system through the concrete use of measuring machines and computers and the link between all three elements via information. What is important, of course, is that these systems are all ultimately designed to enhance soldiers' performance. What we see in such schemes is that the line between machines and bodies has never been so vague (Gray 1997), and that the 'vague' lines are the outcome of the processes characterising such military integration: they are based on patterns of self-regulation and feedback loops. In other words, these processes flow not only within human subjects but also between them and their environment.

The second example, also taken from the scheme developed by the US Army, exemplifies this last point. We are told that the 'Sleep Management System is being designed for integration into the hardware and software of the Personnel Status Monitor/Soldier Computer. It will be a modular component of the Personnel Status Monitor/Soldier Computer and will add less than 100 grams to the soldier's load' (WRAIR 1997). What is significant in regard to these monitors is not only the fact that they are 'extensions' of the body, which are controlled by the military. No less importantly, these monitors are the concrete manifestations of the link between bodies and bodily states and the larger loops of information transmission and reaction found in the military. Through the transmission of information, these monitors link corporeal states to software packages in computers in ways that allow the military organisation both to scrutinise these states and to issue orders for their transformation.

It is precisely in these terms that the use of drugs in sleep management systems should be seen. The use of stimulants has a history in military establishments. For example, the German armed forces used various stimulants during the Second World War and it is reported that between 1966 and 1969 the US military consumed more amphetamines than the entire British and US forces in the Second World War. Indeed, during the Vietnam War and in various training stints the US and Soviet militaries used a variety of drugs such as amphetamines and depressants (Gray 1989: 61), and related research included a variety of themes from controlling fear to improving night vision (Gray 1997: 166). This trend has continued into the 1990s through the continued use of amphetamines by pilots during the Gulf War (Kelly *et al.* 1995), and US Navy experiments with the effects of such drugs as Pemoline.

The programming of soldiers' bodies through the use of drugs in the context of sleep programmes can be seen as part of both the control and the 'enhancement' of their bodies. To reiterate, while anyone programmed to resist disease or drugged to think or feel differently (psychopharmacology) is technically a cyborg, what is a central point here is the specific direction that this programming takes: the enhancement of soldiers' physical and mental capacities. For example, while the Navy carried out a number of experiments designed to 'define the limits of human endurance in SUSOP [sustained operations]', drugs are specifically designed to add to, to go beyond, these limits through technology (Naitoh 1988). Or, to take another example from a research project on the effects of using amino acids to reduce jet lag among US Marines, the report on this project includes mention of the use of medilogs – analogue mood scales, the Stanford Sleepiness Scale and the Profile of Mood States – and concludes: 'improving sleep by psychopharmacological means is associated with enhanced performance the next day' (Spindweber *et al.* 1986). Finally, large-scale research projects such as 'Project Endure' of the US Army's Human Resources Office (HUMRO) have been specifically designed to help understand how humans can fight twenty-four hours a day. Among other things it includes the development of night goggles and scopes but also attempts to modify the human eye itself for night vision. This is done by applying Atropine and Benactyzine to dilate pupils. Accordingly, in the two systems I have been examining, problems are reduced to psychological, organisational or biotechnological techniques with the aim of creating the 'optimal soldier' through enhancing his or her given physiological and cognitive aptitudes.

Let me add a further twist to the argument. If we understand that part of the reason for the fact that soldiers and commanders do not get enough sleep is related to the cult of 'self-denial' and images of masculinity centred on being 'tough guys', then it would seem that the individuals freely participate in the taking of drugs. Indeed, it may well be (and here I am speculating) that many soldiers view the enhancement brought about by the use of drugs in a very positive light (like athletes). In this sense there is no contradiction between 'being a man' and the needs of the military machine to go on working in its own rational manner because being a man and taking drugs may fit both with self-perceptions and with organisational requirements. From a wider perspective, while the taking of stimulants to offset the effects of sleep deprivation may be experienced as an individual action voluntarily undertaken, the action's origin and aim are organisational.

To get back to the main line of my argument, it seems that we have a curious set of links here. 'Advances' in military technology have made continuous operations possible. These kinds of operations, in turn, necessitate increasingly powerful regulation of rest and sleep. But sleep and rest themselves are important especially for the soldiers' cognitive functions, i.e. for operating the very technologies that make continuous fighting possible. My general point is that the sleep management systems belong to the very same 'family' of cyborgs to which night-vision devices belong – whether contraptions such as goggles or drugs for dilating the pupils – in the sense of enhancing human capabilities through technological means. The personnel monitor, the drugs and night-vision equipment, to give concrete examples, belong to the group of 'situational awareness technologies': combinations of combat units with onboard computers, position-location devices and digital communication capabilities (Leonhard 1999). These technologies allow soldiers and commanders to know where and in what kind of situation they, their friendly forces and the enemy are.

Thus the sleep management systems devised by military organisations should be seen as part of a wider set of military creations that seek to combine, or merge into, unified systems: soldiers' bodies and brains, the concrete military machines they operate and the information systems to which they belong. To follow Gray (1997: 200), through systems analysis, social psychology, physiology, psychopharmacology, behavioural sociology, personnel management and computer-mediated systems, the individual soldier becomes part of a formal weapons system.

Killing and the limits of the body

The aim of the sleep management systems I have been examining is to create 'optimal effectiveness' at the individual and unit levels. Yet technology cannot govern individuals perfectly. For example, take the case of drugs, which reach the limit of their effectiveness precisely in and around the very core of military expertise: violence. In contrast to popular imagery, one of the major problems all military forces face is motivating soldiers to kill (Grossman 1995). Thus the many training programmes of armed forces around the world are aimed at inculcating an 'un-natural' ability to take the life of another human being. What is interesting in this respect, however, is the relation between killing and sleep. Bourke (1999: 252), for example, found that the major factors reducing the tolerance to the psychological price of killing in twentieth-century wars were sleep deprivation and general exhaustion. Grossman (1995: 72) directly links lack of sleep to higher rates of psychological casualties in all wars. Thus the limits of the body in the military are unlike those of other organisations. The reaction to killing is visceral, with the whole body often responding to such actions. Along these lines, much of military psychotherapy is focused on the debilitating effects of combat. Indeed, shell shock or battle fatigue is expressed in terms of lack of action or as lack of control over one's body and its appendages and therefore as an impediment to carrying out one's military role. The very terms 'combat reactions', 'battle fatigue' and 'functional debilitation' (Gabriel 1987: 48, 74; Shalit 1988: 103; Gal 1988) capture the notion of the soldier's involuntary response to the firefight in terms of inability to contribute to the military effort.

It thus seems that sleep deprivation may 'weaken' the acquired abilities to kill. The programmes for sleep and rest that we have been exploring here, however, do not address the limits posed by killing. Indeed, the texts accompanying the two systems reflect the tendency for militaries to sanitise their work: for example, to talk about 'servicing the targets' rather than 'killing the enemy' (Downs 1987). For instance, while occasional reference is made to 'hostile environments' or 'fighting', these texts centre on notions of 'performance' as though participation in battle is some form of extended theatrical presentation. The transcript accompanying the US Army's system (WRAIR 1997) reports on research into the effects of sleep on the 'productivity' and 'throughput' measures of artillery batteries' 'performance'. This productivity, of course, is a measure of the number and accuracy of shells fired by a unit of weaponry, but in using such terms as 'productivity' or 'performance' the preoccupation of the military with violence is obfuscated.

While drugs – and the whole technological paraphernalia of sleep management systems – may 'enhance' the very limits of soldiers' bodies for a limited period, they may also ultimately damage them. Thus the uncertainties of battles not only have to do with the enemy, the weather or physical difficulties. For front-line soldiers the uncertainty has to do with their very bodies perpetrating and being victims of violence. Later, the realities of battle – of killing and of death – may pursue soldiers into their sleep and dreams. In fact, a large scholarly literature about the long-term effects of participation in firefights underscores how these experiences are related to problems related to sleep (Solomon 1993; Turner 1996: 67–93).

Again, however, things are more complex. One may make the argument that night combat may actually contribute to the creation of a distance that may 'aid' in killing. Grossman (1995: 169) and Gray (1989: 57) suggest that night-vision devices now available for almost all soldiers provide a 'superb form of psychological distance by converting the target into an inhuman green blob'. The complete integration of night-vision equipment into the modern battlefield may further lead to expansion of what was called 'Nintendo warfare' during the Gulf War, to what Grossman (1995: 172) calls 'an incredibly sterile kind of killing'.

Conclusion

In this chapter I have examined the place of sleep in combat units of the armed forces of the industrial democracies. The military is the epitome of what Melbin (1987) terms the ever vigilant, 'incessant organisation' tasked with being perpetually ready for battle. Yet this incessant organisation depends on individuals. Along the lines suggested by the editors in their introduction to this volume, an examination of the treatment of sleep in the military, as in any group or institution, illuminates some of the problems of 'managing' the very bodies and brains of these troops. More concretely, the intensely technological character of modern military establishments – and especially given the host of innovations characterising armed forces over the past few decades – raises the theoretical question of the relations between the body and technology. Technology, the practical application of knowledge and the use of techniques in social activities, is a social product involving both the 'hardware' of human artefacts such as tools and machines and the knowledge and ideas involved in different activities (Jary and Jary 1991: 651–652). In this respect, an examination of sleep in the military exposes some of the links between bodies, machines and knowledge in the context of highly complex organisations.

My argument has been that one can only understand sleep management systems as part of the wider logic of contemporary military organisations. Thus it is not only a matter of the military recruiting or disciplining the individual body and brain (or its cognitive capacities) as Michel Foucault would have it. It is a matter of how this recruitment and disciplining takes shape. The sleep management systems and the wider military work on the basis of blurring the line between the body and its environment and specifically by enhancing the very bodily and mental capacities of soldiers. Seen in this light, we begin to understand that sleep is not related just to social conventions and rules, to individual experiences, or the corporeal body. As I have tried to show, the social regulation of sleep should be understood as part of a wider system of brains/bodies/machines/knowledge. The sleep of soldiers, then, is but part of a much wider set of systems that seek to blur the lines between soldiers and their environment by enhancing their bodies in ways that link them to the work of the armed forces, to the machines they operate and to the new technologies that make the destructive potential of the military a concern lasting twenty-four hours a day.

Acknowledgements

I would like to thank Efrat Ben-Ze'ev, Nurit Stadler and Brigitte Steger for excellent comments on an earlier version of this chapter.

Bibliography

Apache (1999) *AH-Apache*. Available online: <http://www.military.com/Resources/EquipmentDetails> (accessed 2001).

Arkin, William and Lynne R. Dubrofsky (1978) 'Military Socialization and Masculinity', *Journal of Social Issues* 34(1): 151–168.

Ben-Ari, Eyal (1998) *Mastering Soldiers: Conflict, Emotions and the Enemy in an Israeli Military Battalion*. New York: Berghahn Books.

Ben-Ari, Eyal, with the assistance of Galeet Dardashti (2001) 'Tests of Soldierhood: Trials of Manhood: Military Service and Male Ideals in Israel', in Daniel Maman, Zeev Rosenhek and Eyal Ben-Ari (eds) *War, Politics and Society in Israel: Theoretical and Comparative Perspectives*. New Brunswick, NJ: Transaction, 239–268.

Boene, Bernard (1990) 'How Unique Should the Military Be? A Review of Representative Literature and Outline of Synthetic Formulation', *Archives Européen de Sociologie* 31(1): 3–59.

Bogie, B. J. (1998) *Night Combat Fact Sheet*. Available online: <http://www.nawcad.navy.mil/nawcad/factsheets/nctl.pdf> (accessed 2001).

Bolger, Daniel P. (1999) 'The Electric Pawn: Prospects for Light Forces on the Digitized Battlefield', in Robert L. Bateman III (ed.) *Digital War: A View From the Front Lines*. Novato, CA: Presido Press, 113–130.

Bonnet, M. H., S. Gomez, O. Wirth and D. L. Arand (1995) 'The Use of Caffeine Versus Prophylactic Naps in Sustained Performance', *Sleep* 18(2): 97–104.

Borbély, Alexander A. and Guilio Tononi (1998) 'The Quest for the Essence of Sleep', *Daedalus* 127(2): 167–198.

Bourke, Joanna (1999) *An Intimate History of Killing: Face-to-Face Killing in Twentieth-Century Warfare*. London: Granta Books.

Calow, Stan (1997) *Going Overseas for Overseas Deployment Training (ODT)?*. Available online: <http://call.army.mil/call/nftf/sepoct97/overseas.htm> (accessed 2001).

Castro, Carl A. and Amy B. Adler (1999) 'OPTEMPO [Operations Tempo]: Effects on Soldier and Unit Readiness', *Parameters* Autumn: 86–95.

Connel, R. W. (1995) *Masculinities*. London: Polity Press.

DiGiovanni, Clete (2000) *Sleep and Sleep Deprivation*. Bethesda, MD: Naval Medical Center. Available online: <http://www.mcu.usmc.mil/TbsNew/SleepDep.htm> (accessed 2001).

Dinter, Elmar (1985) *Hero or Coward: Pressures Facing the Soldier in Battle*. London: Frank Cass.

Downs, Fred (1987) 'Death and the Dark Side of Command', *Washington Post* 16 August.

Dyer, Gwyn (1985) *War*. New York: Crown.

Ellis, John (1980) *The Sharp End: The Fighting Man in World War II*. London: Pimlico.

Elsemore, T. F., P. Naitoh and S. Linnville (1993) *Performance Assessment in Sustained Operations Using a Computer-based Synthetic Work Task*. San Diego, CA: Naval Health Research Center. Available online: <http://www.nhrc.navy.mil/Pubs/abstract/92/30.html> (accessed 2001).

Fowler, Will (1998) *Night Vision: The Night Has a Thousand Eyes*. Available online: <http://www.combat-online.com/nightvis.htm> (accessed 2001).

Fowler, Will (1999) *Evading TI* [Thermal Imaging]. Available online: <http://www.combat-online.com/thermal.htm> (accessed 2001).

Frank, Arthur W. (1991) 'For a Sociology of the Body', in Mike Featherstone, Mike Hepworth and Bryan Turner (eds) *The Body: Social Process and Cultural Theory*. London: Sage, 36–102.

Gabriel, Richard (1987) *No More Heroes: Madness & Psychiatry in War*. New York: Hill and Wang.

Gal, Reuven (1988) *Stressful Combat Situations: Causes, Reactions and Coping*. Zichron Ya'akov: The Israel Institute for Military Studies.

Garamone, Jim (1999) 'Rite of Passage: Making Basic Training Tougher', American Forces Press Service. Available online: <http://www.defenselink.mil/news/Jan1999> (accessed 2001).

Gray, Chris H. (1989) 'The Cyborg Soldier: The US Military and the Post-Modern Warrior', in Les Levidow and Kevin Robins (eds) *Cyborg Worlds: The Military Information Society*. London: Free Association Books, 43–72.

Gray, Chris H. (1997) *Postmodern War: The New Politics of Conflict*. New York: Routledge.

Grossman, Dave (1995) *On Killing: The Psychological Cost of Learning to Kill in War and Society*. Boston: Little Brown.

Haraway, Donna (1991) *Simians, Cyborgs, and Women: The Reinvention of Nature*. London: Routledge.

Haraway, Donna (1997) *Modest_Witness@Second_Millenium. _FemaleMan@_Meets_OncoMouse: Feminism and Technoscience*. New York: Routledge.

Hassard, John (1996) 'Images of Time in Work and Organizations', in Stewart R. Clegg, Cynthia Hardy and Walter R. Nord (eds) *Handbook of Organization Studies*. London: Sage, 581–598.

Holmes, Richard (1985) *Acts of War: The Behavior of Men in Battle*. New York: The Free Press.

IFRU (1999) *Infantry Forces Research Unit: Current Research Topics*. Fort Benning, GA: Infantry Forces Research Unit.

Jary, David and Julia Jary (1991) *Collins Dictionary of Sociology*. Glasgow: HarperCollins.

Kamena, Gene C. (1999) *The Dying Art of Battle Rhythm*. Available online: <http://call.army.mil/products/trngqtr/tq3–99/kamena.htm> (accessed 2001).

Keegan, John (1976) *The Face of Battle*. New York: Vintage Books.

Kelly, Tamsin Lisa, Mark R. Rosekind and Paul Naitoh (1994) *Sleep Management Manual* (Technical Document No. 94–5E). San Diego, CA: Naval Health Research Center.

Kelly, Tamsin Lisa, S. A. Gomez, K. Schlangen and T. Elsmore (1995) 'The Effects of Pemoline on Performance and Mood During Sleep Deprivation', *Military Psychology* 9(3): 213–255.

Landow, George P. (2000) *Cyborg: Some Definitions, Descriptions, and Exemplifications*. Available online: <http://landow.stg.brown.edu/cpace/cyborg/definition.html> (accessed 2001).

Leonhard, Robert R. (1999) 'A Culture of Velocity', in Robert L. Bateman III (ed.) *Digital War: A View From the Front Lines*. Novato, CA: Presido Press, 131–152.

Lieblich, Amia (1989) *Transition to Adulthood Through Military Service: The Israeli Case*. Albany, NY: State University of New York Press.

McManners, Hugh (1994) *The Scars of War*. London: HarperCollins.

Melbin, Murray (1987) *Night as Frontier: Colonizing the World After Dark*. New York: The Free Press.

Mitchell, William J. (1995) *City of Bits: Space, Place, and the Infobahn*. Cambridge, MA: MIT Press.

126 *Eyal Ben-Ari*

Moore, Alan (1996) *Sleep to Survive*. Available online: <http://www.dtic.mil/soldiers/august96/text/sleep.htm> (accessed 2001).

Moskos, Charles C. (1988) *Soldiers and Sociology*, United States Army Research Institute for the Behavioral and Social Sciences. Washington, DC: Government Publishing House.

Naitoh, P. (1988) *Sustained Operations: Research Results* (Report No. A191–794). San Diego, CA: Naval Health Research Center.

Naitoh, P., G. Banta, T. Kelly, J. Bower and R. Burr (1990) *Sleep Logs: Measurement of Individual and Operational Efficiency* (Report No. 90–29). San Diego, CA: Naval Health Research Center.

Night Stalker (1999) *Special Operations Specialties: Night Fighting*. Available online: <http://www.specialoperations.com/specialities/nitefite.html> (accessed 2001).

Radine, Lawrence (1977) *The Taming of the Troops: Social Control in the United States*. Westport, CT: Greenwood Press.

Rhem, Kathleen T. (2000) 'Health Officials Battle Combat Stress', American Forces Press Service. Available online: <http://www.defenselin.mil/news/Feb2000> (accessed 2001).

SAS (1999) *SAS Weapons and Kit*. Available online: <http://www.combat-online.com/saskit.htm> (accessed 2001).

Schwartz, Barry (1973) 'Notes on the Sociology of Sleep', in Arnold Birenbaum and Edward Sagarin (eds) *People in Places: The Sociology of the Familiar*. London: Nelson, 18–34.

Shalit, Ben (1988) *The Psychology of Conflict and Combat*. New York: Praeger.

Shamir, Boas and Eyal Ben-Ari (1999) 'Challenges of Military Leadership in Changing Armies', *Journal of Political and Military Sociology* 28(1): 43–59.

Shay, Jonathan (1995) *Achilles in Vietnam: Combat Trauma and the Undoing of Character*. New York: Touchstone Books.

Shay, Jonathan (1998) 'Ethical Standing for Commander Self-Care: The Need for Sleep', *Parameters* Summer: 93–105.

Solomon, Zehava (1993) *Combat Stress Reactions: The Enduring Toll of War*. New York: Plenum Press.

Spindweber, C. L., S. C. Webb and J. C. Gillin (1986) *Jet Lag in Military Operations: Field Trial of L-tryptophan in Reducing Sleep-loss Effects*. San Diego, CA: Naval Health Research Center. Available online: <http://www.nhrc.navy.mil/Pubs/abstract/86/15.html> (accessed 2001).

Stafford, Lisa E. (1998) 'Daytime Dozing: Something to Wake Up About'. Available online: <http://www.dtic.mil/afps/news/9804155.html> (accessed 2001).

Turner, Fred (1996) *Echoes of Combat: The Vietnam War in American Memory*. New York: Anchor Books.

Welch, Douglas A. (1995) *Crew Rest is not a Dirty Word*. Available online: <http://call.army.mil/call/ctc_bull/aviation/marapr95/crwrst.htm> (accessed 2001).

Williams, D., J. Streeter and Tamsin Kelly (1998) *Fatigue in Naval Tactical Aviators* (Technical Document No. 98–20). San Diego, CA: Naval Health Research Center.

WRAIR (1997) *Sleep, Sleep Deprivation, and Human Performance*. Washington, DC: Walter Reed Army Institute of Research. Available online: <http://wrair-www.army.mil/depts/beahviobio> (accessed 2001).

WRH (2000) *On-Line, Real-Time Alertness and Performance Monitoring*. Washington, DC: Walter Reed Hospital. Available online: <http://wrair-www.army.mil/depts/beahviobio/rtma.htm> (accessed 2001).

7 'The Mirk Shades O'Nicht'

Nocturnal representations of urban Scotland in the nineteenth century

Irene Maver

> Then hie thee awa' through the mirk shades o' nicht,
> Nor seek thou the banquet to share …
> Oh! rather lay thy heid in the puir man's beild,
> And be thankfu' whate'er may betide,
> Than hanker for the wine-cups in yon ha' o' sin,
> Where the malisons o' Heaven maun abide![1]
> (From 'The Midnight Revel of Mugdock', in Macdonald 1854: 299–300)

The 'mirk shades o' nicht' is the Scots vernacular version of the 'dark shades of night'. The phrase and its poetic overtones give a specific sense of identity to this exploration of urban Scotland during the nineteenth century. There are a number of reasons for contributing such a perspective to night-time analyses. First, the Scottish dimension is seldom referred to in historical or sociological investigations of nocturnal imagery or behaviour, yet the literary and scientific output of Scots like Robert Louis Stevenson and William Murdoch has played a significant part in shaping modern perceptions of the night. A misleading Anglocentric approach also has been evident; for instance, Wolfgang Schivelbusch's otherwise insightful history of artificial light in the nineteenth century is devalued by its blanket reference to 'English industrial pioneers', including Murdoch, who did so much to popularize the use of gas lighting (Schivelbusch 1995: 20). In the British urban context, the night-time experience of London has attracted the lion's share of attention. While Scotland's cities cannot match the magnitude of the metropolitan example, they offer scope for comparison and contrast through an eclectic range of primary material, especially the copious but hitherto underrated literary and journalistic sources which are used to illustrate this essay. By focusing on Edinburgh and Glasgow, in particular, it is hoped to even out the research emphasis, and add a distinctive case study to the historiography of the night.

As for the thematic purpose, the object is to explain how far cultural continuities underlay representations of the night, and recurred throughout the century, despite the pace of social and technological change. Edinburgh and Glasgow are particularly useful examples to draw upon, as both cities were recognized as modern and progressive centres respectively of intellectual achievement and entrepreneurial initiative. Yet, as commentators at the time were often uncomfortably aware, the cities' enlightenment qualities had the paradoxical effect of more sharply displaying the urban dark side and intensifying the threat of nocturnal danger. Night, which is regarded throughout this essay as conterminous with hours of darkness, became a metaphor for uncertainty, challenging prevailing assumptions about scientific determinism. Not surprisingly, night, as a metaphysical construct, also had the power to subvert accepted moral standards. In a society like Scotland where religious influence was deeply ingrained, the nocturnal domain could even symbolize the antithesis of godliness. Control of the night, or more specifically, night-time behaviour, thus suggested much about contemporary concern to harness technology and create security and order in the increasingly complex social entity of the city. These points will be elaborated in the course of this essay; what should be stressed from the outset is that night has multiple meanings that go beyond straightforward temporal definitions. The projection of contemporary values onto the night makes it a mirror of society, and in nineteenth-century Scotland the nocturnal reflection was profoundly ambiguous.

Edinburgh: duality and the shadow

In 1819 the journalist and writer John Gibson Lockhart paid effusive tribute to the physical appearance of Edinburgh. In prose that abounded in superlatives such as 'majestic' and 'sublime', he described the city impressionistically, according to the effects of changing light on the landscape. Night and the glow of moonlight had especial resonance for Lockhart:

> Wherever I spend the evening, I must always walk homewards by the long line of Prince's-Street; and along all that spacious line, the midnight shadows of Castle-rock for ever spread themselves forth, and wrap the ground on which I tread in their broad repose of blackness. It is not possible to imagine a more majestic accompaniment to the deep repose of that hour. … How soft, yet how awful, the beauty and the silence of the hour of spirits.
>
> (Lockhart 1977: 61–62)

Edinburgh at night was identified with 'the eternal rock sleeping in the stillness of nature'; a pristine, almost primeval image, which implied that nocturnal human activity was both intrusive and unnatural. As one critic has pointed out, Lockhart deliberately imbued the city with a romantically idealized quality, where elemental forces represented the abiding spirit of place (Noble 1985: 81–82). Yet there was also a dichotomy in Lockhart's approach. The achievement of the New Town, conceived in the 1750s as one of the most ambitious civic planning projects in Europe, was intended to thrust Edinburgh to the forefront of modernity. Thus, alongside the looming geological landmark of the Castle Rock, Lockhart could not resist contrasting the prestigious commercial thoroughfare of Prince's Street. Another duality he did not acknowledge was the continuing presence of the Old Town, the historic heart of Edinburgh, which also represented the volatile dark side, as living conditions steadily deteriorated in districts like the Canongate, the Grassmarket and the West Port.

Ambiguous shadows from the past seemed to haunt the Old Town, an impression that was eloquently reinforced when Robert Chambers' *Traditions of Edinburgh* first appeared in 1824. A member of a prosperous Edinburgh publishing family, Chambers shrewdly understood the impact of nostalgia as a literary selling point. Edinburgh, after all, was inextricably associated with the career of Walter Scott, the internationally acclaimed poet and novelist who specialized in historical romances. Using Scott as a role model, Chambers fed popular taste for the picturesque and mysterious, and in *Traditions of Edinburgh* he depicted a city that was the antithesis of the gleaming New Town. In striking contrast with Prince's Street, the West Bow was described as 'a curious, angular, whimsical looking street, of great steepness and narrowness', which seemed 'eminently a place of old grandmother's tales, and sure at all times to maintain a ghost or two in its community' (Chambers 1846: 28–29). Chambers then went on to relate the story of the West Bow's most notorious inhabitant, the seventeenth-century necromancer, Major Thomas Weir. The Major was a former military man who had given all the appearance of being a devout Presbyterian and upright Edinburgh citizen. However, his conscience ultimately got the better of him, and in a crisis of remorse he confessed his devotion to the black arts. He was executed in 1670, one of many Scots who suffered the ultimate penalty of the law for allegedly practising witchcraft. Needless to say, his West Bow residence soon acquired the reputation of being haunted, and for decades thereafter the Major's apparition reputedly appeared at night, 'like a black and silent shadow about the street' (Chambers 1846: 38).

Chambers was perpetuating the legend first elaborated in George Sinclair's lurid treatise on the occult, *Satan's Invisible World Discovered*, published in 1685. Sinclair's account of the Major's career placed particular emphasis on the testimony of contemporary witnesses to the uncanny midnight activities in the West Bow (Sinclair 1808: 143–154). The story is intriguing, both for its longevity and because it was an early example of the egregious dualism which recurred repeatedly in representations of the Scottish city. Not only did the Major's corrupted inner self belie his outward persona of respectability, but his pact with Satan symbolized a conscious spiritual inversion of the Calvinist ideal of God's Covenant. Repudiating godliness inevitably meant embracing the sinister 'lord of darkness', and fear of succumbing to Satan's beguiling temptations remained deeply embedded in the popular imagination. According to one chronicler of the 'darker superstitions of Scotland', Satan was regarded as ubiquitous; 'the arch-enemy of mankind, ever ready in finding instruments to wreak his vengeance on them' (Dalyell 1835: 7).

While the Scottish Enlightenment went a long way towards mellowing attitudes about the supernatural, Presbyterianism, as the dominant Christian faith from 1690, remained strongly influenced by the rhetoric of polarities. For instance, although the references were allegorical, the diabolical (and explicitly female) imagery of one eminent Enlightenment divine, William Leechman, was intended to make a strong moral impact: 'Pleasure is a Demonness of a very malignant kind, that haunts, infests and fascinates, particularly those places of the earth which have carried their improvements and refinements highest' (quoted in Kennedy 1995: 67). The shadow lurked even in the era of progress, rationalism and urbanization, and vigilance was urged to control tendencies that led to self-debasement.

Of course, there was nothing distinctively Scottish about the theme of duality or how darkness and night could represent a powerful expression of inverted values. Within the European context, the urban night had universal qualities that transcended the differences between cities. In his comparative investigation of Paris, Berlin and London over the period 1840 to 1930, Joachim Schlör makes immediate reference to the nocturnal associations and images common to the cities and how these contributed to 'an overarching unity that allows us to speak of *night in the big city*' (Schlör 1998: 9–10). He argues that a blend of fear and fascination aroused emotive responses from a range of contemporary commentators and that nocturnal activity was often categorized, especially in popular literature, according to contrasting word-pairs: 'light and shadow, dream and nightmare, wealth and poverty'. The modern and the primitive were further contradictory characteristics, as urban technology, especially street lighting, was developed in order to overcome the constraints and dangers of darkness. The recurring use of opposites suggests that perceptions, emotions and experiences had peculiar intensity at night, although, paradoxically, they also could be elusive and equivocal. Behaviour was less inhibited, and consequently less predictable, not least because opportunities for entertainment and indulgence, the consumer dimension of the night, were heightened. The Demonness of Pleasure stalked streets well beyond Scotland, and there was similar anxiety from the urban authorities to stem her malign influence.

Yet if generalizations can be made about past attitudes to the urban night, there was also considerable diversity of experience between and within communities. History, culture, economy and environment could shape nocturnal behaviour, as becomes evident comparing the chapters collected in this volume. Reference has already been made to the religious associations of the urban dark side, and how these related to Scotland. Perceptions were compounded by the northerly location of Scottish cities, and the prolonged hours of darkness in winter. For Robert Louis Stevenson, writing in 1878, the Edinburgh winter represented 'gloom and depression':

> The days are so short that a man does much of his business, and certainly all of his pleasure, by the haggard glare of gas lamps. ... And meantime the wind whistles through the town as if it were an open meadow; and if you lie awake all night you hear it shrieking and raving overhead with a noise of shipwrecks and of falling houses.
>
> (Stevenson 1900: 146–147)

The impact of weather and the seasons inevitably affected the life-style of the inhabitants, and it is scarcely surprising that Edinburgh was known as 'Auld Reikie', because of the permanent pall of smoke that emanated from fires burning in the Old Town. The smoky sobriquet symbolized the nether side to the self-promoted image of Edinburgh as the 'Athens of the North', a further indication of the duality that characterized the city. In addition to smoke was the intrusion of 'haar', cold, damp sea-fog that was (and remains) a distinguishing elemental feature of Edinburgh. Nor did the prevailing Old Town architecture lend itself to liberating the city from the oppressive effects of the environment. The original proposals for inaugurating New Town developments, made in 1752, were explicit about the problems:

> ... the houses stand more crowded than in any other town in *Europe*, and are built to a height that is almost incredible. Hence necessarily follows a great want of free air, light, cleanliness and every other comfortable accommodation. Hence also many families, sometimes no less than ten or a dozen, are obliged to live overhead of each other in the same building; where, to all the other inconveniences, is added that of a common stair, which is no other in effect that an upright street, constantly dark and dirty.
>
> (Quoted in Youngson 1988: 5–6)

However, the proposed transformation of Edinburgh related to more than the built environment. Life in the Old Town may have been cramped and incommodious, but it also had a boisterous momentum that could display disturbing qualities. For those in authority these became all too evident at night. At the start of the eighteenth century magistrates were so concerned about the antisocial impact of late hours that they reinforced local laws imposing a ten o'clock curfew. The restrictions had evolved as far back as the fifteenth century, when fear of conflagration provided one of the main reasons for civic action: too many hazardous fires and lights were thought to be burning at night (Marwick 1865: 152–155). The curfew was an intriguing early example of what Schlör calls 'prohibited time', and from the 1700s was intended to be rigorously enforced (Schlör 1998: 103). To quell the incidence of 'abounding drunkenness, uncleanness, night revellings, and other immoralities and disorders', the Town Guard patrolled the city, while bells and the tattoo of the ten o'clock drum provided a cautionary reminder to citizens to return to their homes (Arnot 1998: 108). As was indicated in Robert Fergusson's exuberant poem of 1773, 'Auld Reikie', citizens latterly ignored the strictures:

> Now some to porter, some to punch,
> Some to their wife, and some their wench,
> Retire, while noisy ten-hours' drum
> Gars a' your trades gae dandring hame.
> Now mony a club, jocose and free,
> Gie a' to merriment and glee.[2]
>
> (Fergusson 2000: 105)

Despite official disapproval, Edinburgh's thriving clubs and taverns, and the prodigious drinking habits of the patrons, became a defining feature of the Old Town during the eighteenth century. In this context, the spacious and salubrious New Town was an attempt to reverse what were seen as the Old Town's disconcerting night-time qualities. Taking stylistic inspiration from European exemplars such as London and Berlin, civic leaders were determined to embrace progress and give tangible expression to their quest for order.

It is revealing that in *Traditions of Edinburgh*, Chambers identified tavern life as belonging to the unrefined, pre-New Town past:

> When the worship of Bacchus held such sway in our city, his peculiar temples – the taverns – must, one would suppose, have been places of some importance. ... The truth was, however, that a coarse and darksome snugness was courted by the worshippers. Large, well-lighted rooms, with a look-out to a street, would not have suited them.
>
> (Chambers 1846: 152)

The contrast of light and darkness emphasizes how far social preferences had altered by the 1820s, at least for the city's better-off inhabitants. A distinction was emerging between the 'modern' and 'pre-modern' community, and in Edinburgh, as in other European cities, a shift in strategy over controlling the night indicated the pace of change (Schlör 1998: 79–81). Thus, during the 1770s, at the time Fergusson was writing, problems of law enforcement were apparent from the popular repudiation of the curfew regulations. The inept Town Guard had become the object of derision. Mostly discharged soldiers from Highland regiments, their unflattering nickname was the 'Toun Rottens', which translates from the vernacular as 'Town Rats' (Graham 1909: 123–124). Such was elite anxiety about the inadequacy of existing arrangements, in the face of rising crime and the threat to order, that Parliament approved a wide-ranging Police Act for Edinburgh in 1805. The wealthier taxpayers were empowered to elect a Board of Commissioners, which oversaw the operations of a wholly new police establishment. Edinburgh appeared to be adapting to the requirements of modern urban society. Yet, in words that had a familiar echo, an official report of 1807 identified the Board's prime function: 'a watchful Police, by checking the first appearances of vice, and by lighting and watching the streets of a great city, may effectually guard the morals of the people, by removing the opportunity, and consequently the temptation, to do wrong' (Chapman 1807: 2). Vigilance against the threat of moral corrosion was no new phenomenon; it was the mechanism for combating this that proved to be innovative.

Edinburgh: fact, fiction and the night

Crime, danger and darkness are particularly subversive elements of the urban night, which seem all the more insidious because they expose personal vulnerability. They are both intangible and uncomfortably close, and although they often can be explained rationally, they still have the capacity to provoke emotional responses. Thus, the creation of Edinburgh's Police Board did not allay fears about the volatile nature of the deteriorating Old Town. Indeed, New Town development seemed to intensify anxieties, and whatever their efficiency, the police had an uphill task in countering impressionistic opinions about the extent of delinquency. A significant illustration of reactions to nocturnal crime was the Tron riot, which occurred in the midst of celebrations to bring in the New Year, on 1 January 1812. New Year, rather than Christmas, is the traditional Scottish mid-winter festival, and in early nineteenth-century Edinburgh the crowds habitually gathered round the clock tower of the Tron Church, to watch for the stroke of midnight. A good-natured, if sometimes raucous, occasion, it was disturbed by the depredations of the 'Keellie Gang'. This group of adolescents, some only 12 years old, was intent on violent robbery, and eventually assaulted and murdered a night watchman (Ralston 1980: 42–43). Although the ringleaders were quickly apprehended, and three were hanged, the subsequent prolific pamphlet debate identified the riot as evidence of a deep-rooted malaise in Edinburgh. Social boundaries had been relaxed to allow for the public celebration of a special night, but these had been violated. Conviviality had been abruptly transformed into terror, and the security of every other night was called into question. One writer, 'Civis', claimed dramatically, 'we are all in danger', and urged the formation of citizens' street patrols between 9.30 p.m. and five o'clock in the morning ('Civis' 1812: 10). The spectre of the Paris revolutionary mob fuelled the image of Edinburgh in crisis, especially as the prolonged war with France was still ongoing.

As historian Andrew Ralston has shown, the riot had the important outcome of immediately tightening policing arrangements for the city, with emphasis on stricter public surveillance. It also alerted the 'moral' guardians of the community, notably churchmen, to pay more attention to their urban mission. Education, for the reformation of the young, became a vital part of the missionary agenda (Ralston 1980: 45). Yet for all the lessons of 1812, the route to enlightenment was not straightforward, and Edinburgh's dark side was not eradicated. This was disturbingly brought out as yet another moral panic gripped the city towards the end of 1828, when the scandal of the West Port murders unravelled. Although they had a traumatic effect at the time, the murders have not received the same attention from urban analysts as London's Whitechapel murders of 1888, when the elusive figure of 'Jack the Ripper' brutally killed at least five East End prostitutes (cf., for instance, Ackroyd 2000: 272–277; Schlör 1998: 134–136; Walkowitz 1998: 191–228). The Whitechapel legend was perpetuated by the failure of the police to solve the murders, inspiring a deluge of sensationalist speculation as to the identity of the killer. Conversely, the West Port murders resulted in a conviction, although mystery still surrounds the identity of possible accessories to the crimes. What was shared between Whitechapel and the West Port was their corrosive identity as the terrain of the urban underclass. The particularly gross acts of homicide served to highlight the desperate and demoralized life-styles of the inhabitants. Crucially, the night was inextricably connected with the nature of the crimes and the condition of the communities.

The background to the West Port murders was grave-robbing, the illegal trade in human corpses that had gathered particular momentum in Edinburgh and Glasgow during the early nineteenth century, due to demand from anatomists in city medical schools (Richardson 1989: 131–143). However, the murderers were never involved in grave-robbing. William Burke and William Hare came from the burgeoning Irish immigrant community of Edinburgh, and it was in the West Port that Hare and his wife kept a lodging house. Identifying the demand from medical schools, Burke and Hare set about the business of supplying corpses by the expedient of killing, by suffocation, at least sixteen people. The Hares' lodging house in Tanner's Close proved to be an ideal location for despatching several of the victims, who were usually plied with whisky to ease their demise. Owen Dudley Edwards has written a wry and penetrating account of the life and times of Burke and Hare, commenting: 'The murders present a picture of all sorts of people wandering in and out of Edinburgh, in many cases with nobody to know whether they could be dead or alive and with anyone who might care, far away' (Edwards 1993: 75). The search for short-term sleeping accommodation directed the incomers to cheap establishments, like the Hares' lodging house. Burke and Hare preyed upon their vulnerability and effectively became entrepreneurs of serial killing, receiving the substantial sum of £10 in winter and £8 in summer for every corpse supplied to anatomist Dr Robert Knox.

The murders, which occurred during 1827 and 1828, were eventually exposed and Hare's evidence, given under Crown immunity, was sufficient to condemn his partner. A crowd of 25,000 was estimated to have gathered at Burke's public hanging in January 1829. Walter Scott conveyed the nightmare sense of shock that engulfed the city, in reply to a letter from fellow novelist, Maria Edgeworth:

> ... the horrors which you have so well described ... resemble nothing so much as a wild dream. Certainly I thought, like you, that the public alarm was but an exaggeration of vulgar rumour; but the tragedy is too true, and I look in vain for a remedy of the evils, in which it is easy to see this black and unnatural business has found its origin.
>
> (Quoted in Edwards 1993: 83)

It is ironic that the grim reality of the West Port was viewed with disbelief by Scott, the writer of highly imaginative and colourful fiction. He was also incredulous that the 'Athens of the North', the intellectual heart of the Scottish Enlightenment, could nurture such ruthless and unsavoury criminals. The view was widely shared throughout the city. In the introduction to a contemporary account of the murders, one commentator suggested how much they emphasized the superficiality of progress:

... we fear that, with all its pretended illumination, the present age must be characterized by some deeper and fouler blots than have attached to any that preceded it; and that if it has brighter spots, it also has darker shades and more appalling obscurations. ... Thus, the march of crime has far outstripped 'the march of intellect', and attained a monstrous and colossal development.

(Ireland 1829: 1)

It was widely believed that, in his quest for professional recognition, the eminent and respectable Dr Knox had been the manipulative influence behind the killings. The barbed references to progress should be seen in this context; even agencies of enlightenment could fall prey to corruption. Again, this was no new theme in the urban experience, but it had particular relevance for nineteenth-century Edinburgh, because of the city's much-vaunted reputation for learning.

The West Port murders entered the collective folk-memory of Edinburgh citizens, becoming an enduring metaphor for the city's dark side. A more immediate effect was that the scale of deprivation in the urban heartland came under close public scrutiny, and the missionary impulse intensified in an effort to reclaim and regenerate the worst affected districts. From the 1840s the Free Church of Scotland was especially active, although initial plans for evangelical outreach proved to be overambitious. Too many of the voluntary visitors found it impossible to cope with the pressures (Brown 1982: 361). That a doctor, George Bell, thought it prudent to visit the warren-like wynds at night 'under the guidance of a criminal officer familiar with the district' was testimony to the continuing danger (Bell 1849: 6). By this time it was clear that the police had sufficiently strengthened their role as a linking factor between what Schlör calls 'the accessible city' and its 'hidden districts' (Schlör 1998: 125). Vigilance was beginning to have a practical effect, although commentators like Bell repeatedly stressed the failure of technological progress to penetrate the slums. For instance, dirt and darkness were attributed to the absence of piped water and gaslight, the latter an innovation introduced to the city's principal streets as far back as 1818. One late nineteenth-century enthusiast for gaslight made the telling statement: 'the "Burke and Hare" panic could only have been possible in an age of dark and ill-kept streets and closes' ('A. M.' 1892: 60). By 1867 Edinburgh's civic leaders appreciated the urgent need for action, and inaugurated a programme of wholesale slum clearance to open out and illuminate the Old Town.

Not surprisingly, given his intimate Edinburgh connections, light and the shadow were themes which preoccupied the writer Robert Louis Stevenson. His family background was also relevant, as he came from a celebrated engineering dynasty, which specialized in the construction of lighthouses (Stevenson 1912; Bathurst 1999). Stevenson's sensitivity to the technicalities underpinned this wry account of the impact of gaslight when it first illuminated the city:

The work of Prometheus had advanced another stride. Mankind and its supper-parties were no longer at the mercy of a few miles of sea-fog;

sundown no longer emptied the promenades; and the day was lengthened out to every man's fancy. The city folk had stars of their own; biddable, domesticated stars.

(Stevenson 1906: 441)

In a darker mood, in 1886, Stevenson produced his classic fictional exploration of the divided personality, *The Strange Case of Dr Jekyll and Mr Hyde* (Stevenson 1987). A story of psychological complexity, it nevertheless reflects elements of the Scottish supernatural tradition, with strong hints of Satan as the shadowy force prompting Henry Jekyll's evermore nefarious activities. A more contemporary point of reference, the theme of a doctor with murderous tendencies, has echoes of the anatomist Dr Knox. Ironically, the location of the story is London, and one recent, much-lauded 'biographer' of the metropolis has claimed that the story 'could be conducted only through "the swirling wreaths" of London fog where character and identity may suddenly and dramatically be obscured' (Ackroyd 2000: 153). Conversely, others have identified that there is much of Edinburgh in the topographical setting, notably the residential polarities of the Old and New Towns, which came to embody so much about the contrasts between nineteenth-century squalor and gentility (Gibson 1993: 134–135).

Illumination, in various forms, recurs throughout another Stevenson story, 'The Body Snatcher', based partly on the events surrounding the West Port murders. Stevenson portrays Knox as 'Mr K–', and accurately depicts him as charismatic, 'this meteorically famous man'. In contrast, Burke and Hare appear anonymously as 'unclean and desperate interlopers', who arrive in 'the black hours before the winter dawn' with their sinister deliveries for the dissecting tables (Stevenson 1999: 8). The irony, of course, is that the murderers are serving the professional needs of the anatomist in his relentless pursuit of scientific knowledge. Yet for all the dissimilarities in origins, education and social status, the protagonists in 'The Body Snatcher' share a strong predatory quality. One of Mr K–'s most loyal students sternly urges a doubtful colleague to act as a lion rather than a lamb, and not succumb to moral scruples. Significantly, Thomas Guthrie, a prominent Edinburgh Free Church minister and educationalist, used the same imagery in an evocative warning about nocturnal danger in a sermon of 1859:

> Before the shades of night bring out the ravenous wolf, and the wily fox, and the roaring lion, have all your lambs at home. Make it a bright, cheerful home. Mingle firmness with kindness. And from late hours, from dangerous companions, from nightly scenes of pleasure and amusement, more carefully keep your children, than you bolt door or window against the intrusion of those who can but plunder you of property infinitely less valuable than your domestic purity, of jewels infinitely less precious than your children's souls.
>
> (Guthrie 1859: 19)

In their different ways, but deriving inspiration from similar cultural and historic influences, Guthrie and Stevenson were graphically conveying some of the most deep-rooted fears about the urban night, above all vulnerability, corruption and the threat of violation.

Glasgow: eradicating the shadow

That enlightenment and the shadow could coexist in the city, and within its inhabitants, was given powerful expression in early nineteenth-century Edinburgh. The city's dualistic nature was enhanced by the distinctive conditions of its spatial development and cultural profile. Paradoxically, this distinctiveness helped to define Edinburgh's identity and highlight characteristics that were shared with other contemporary communities. The example of Edinburgh demonstrated that urbanization could yield ambiguous benefits, and as the century progressed there were anxieties that the shadow might overwhelm cities elsewhere in Scotland. Demographic increase was generating unprecedented problems of social control, especially relating to the incidence of crime, poverty and disease. The pressures on Edinburgh were intense, but in Glasgow, the dominant city of the west of Scotland, they were awesome. A territorially compact community, between 1801 and 1821 Glasgow's population almost doubled. By the later date Glasgow was irreversibly pulling ahead of Edinburgh, with just over 147,000 inhabitants to the eastern city's 138,000 (Maver 2000: 83). It should be stressed that Glasgow was a longer-established community than Edinburgh, a major pre-Reformation ecclesiastical centre, with one of the oldest universities in the British Isles, dating from 1451. Fergusson in 'Auld Reikie' depicted Glasgow as more physically attractive than pre-New Town Edinburgh. Yet Glasgow was in the process of developing Scotland's most extensive manu-facturing base, and the nineteenth-century designation of 'Second City of the British Empire' came to reflect both the magnitude and the outward-looking focus of local enterprise.

The contradictions of commercial success were commented upon by one city resident during the 1790s:

> There is now a great deal more industry on six days of the week, and a great deal more dissipation and licentiousness on the seventh. Great crimes were formerly very uncommon; but now robberies, housebreaking, swin-dling, pickpockets, pilferers, and consequently executions are becoming more common.
>
> (Sinclair 1973: 329)

It was evident that, as in Edinburgh, there was a growing preoccupation with the threat of crime. In response to sustained public pressure, Glasgow's Police Board emerged in 1800, administering a professional constabulary five years before Edinburgh and some three decades before the inauguration of the Metropolitan Police in London (Maver 1995: 251–252). There was nothing new about the principle behind Scotland's policing authorities; they were an extension of civic powers, set firmly in the context of the 'common good', a collective designation for the public good or public interest. Scottish policing commitment also went beyond obligations to keep the peace and punish offenders; it related to environmental well-being, providing for services such as lighting, cleansing, street-paving and water supplies (Carson and Idzikowska 1989: 270–271). The notion of the common good, with its paternalistic overtones, underpinned the nature of control in Scottish cities during the nineteenth century and beyond. It provided the moral incentive for interventionist strategies at a time when there was often taxpayers' reluctance to commit public expenditure. It was also a key reason why policing, in an institutional form, developed in Scotland relatively early. The notion of the police as 'a bureaucracy of official morality', articulated by Robert Storch in his account of northern England during the mid-nineteenth century, was already an integral part of the Scottish discourse (Storch 1975: 61).

Like Edinburgh in 1812, there were specific incidents in Glasgow which helped to influence attitudes towards 'moral' policing. For instance, although the celebration of the king's birthday in early June was traditionally rumbustious, the 1819 holiday culminated in rioting notable for its night-time destructiveness (Whatley 1992: 177–178). The propensity of the crowd to illuminate the city with impromptu bonfires, uprooting lamp-posts and police-boxes among other combustible materials, was an indication of popular disdain for the symbols of order. A year of severe economic depression, 1819 was also characterized by the threat of civil unrest emanating from Glasgow's textile manufacturing districts. In September a spate of demonstrations against poverty and unemployment culminated in yet more riots, where one of the most notable features, according to the press, was the systematic smashing of street-lamps (*Glasgow Herald* 17 September 1819). Night had become a time of contested authority, and curfews and extraordinary controls prevailed in the city for months thereafter. This uneasy atmosphere was broken in April 1820, when attempts to rally working-class support for an armed insurrection proved to be abortive (Maver 2000: 65–68). Exemplary sentences on leading insurgents, including three executions, helped to restore social equilibrium. A revised Police Act was passed almost immediately in 1821. Not surprisingly, it provided for more vigorous surveillance of the expanding industrial districts, in an effort to detect criminal activity at its earliest stages and offset tendencies towards antisocial behaviour (Maver 1995: 254).

In his history of the industrialization of light, Schivelbusch has explored the phenomenon of lantern smashing, claiming that the first time it became 'an adjunct to general revolt' was in Paris during July 1830 (Schivelbusch 1995: 105). Intriguingly, Glasgow provides an earlier example, although the destruction of the lamps in 1819 was scarcely an act of revolutionary defiance on the French scale. Even so, strict penalties were routinely incurred by persons in Glasgow found vandalizing or removing street-lamps; the minimum fine was £2, and failure to pay could result in a two-month jail sentence (Glasgow Police Act 1800: 1463). Given the extent of official disapproval, lantern smashing in 1819 represented a very obvious act of urban subversion, which may have been compounded by the novelty of gaslight. Scottish cities were quick to respond to the convenience of the new power source, and there had been well-publicized experiments in Glasgow as far back as 1805. William Murdoch and James Watt, who did so much to pioneer industrial gas lighting, were expatriate Scots who retained close connections with their homeland (Griffiths 1992: 268). The metropolis of London had its first gas company in 1814, and both Edinburgh and Glasgow established similar enterprises in 1817. Compared with continental Europe, the three British cities were at least a decade ahead in adopting gas on a substantial scale. One of the driving forces behind the Glasgow Gas-Light Company was James Hamilton, an elected Police Board representative. He used his grocer's shop in the Trongate as an advertisement for the brilliancy of gaslight, which one admirer effusively recollected as bringing the city 'from darkness into the highest state of perfection' (Mackenzie 1890: 147). Early in 1819 there was keen debate within the Board as to the desirability of converting the lamps to gas, and the urge to identify the city at the cutting edge of innovation won out over claims that oil was less expensive (*GPB* 15 April 1819).

Until the mid-nineteenth century, domestic use of gas in Britain was not widespread (Barty-King 1984: 117). High costs, inconsistent quality of light and fear of fire meant that there was consumer resistance, and the Glasgow Gas-Light Company made its substantial profits overwhelmingly from business use. Nevertheless, the transforming impact of gaslight on public space was profound, and by 1836 there were 2,097 gas-fuelled street-lamps in Glasgow (Cleland 1840: 71). Undoubtedly there was a strong element of what Schlör calls 'light as a factor in order' in the extensive use of gas as an illuminant (Schlör 1998: 58). This was vividly demonstrated by one example of civic initiative from 1840. In response to complaints about the deteriorating state of the public clocks, town councillors commissioned handsome new timepieces, complete with gas-lit dials. If citizens were required to regulate their activities, it was evident that they should have a highly visible reminder of the precise hour of day and night (*GTC* 23 July 1840). The ten o'clock drum had become an anachronism in the age of technological innovation, although the rationale behind the renovation of Glasgow's clocks suggested that there were still continuities with the pre-industrial period. Moreover, in 1840 Glasgow's municipal regime was dominated by evangelical Presbyterians, who resolutely believed in the efficacy of 'moral' policing, especially as a device for maintaining public order. Industrial unrest in the manufacturing districts remained a continuing threat during a period of renewed economic depression, and so purposeful and disciplined use of time was encouraged as an antidote to disorder.

In 1840 Captain Henry Miller, Superintendent of Police, expressed the official view on regulation in a detailed appraisal of Glasgow's crime rates. He was careful to present police activity in a favourable light, showing that the incidence of crime in relation to London, Liverpool and Dublin was comparatively low (Miller 1840: 7–8). However, he acknowledged the urgent need for remedial strategy in Glasgow, with emphasis not on punishment, but on the familiar theme of building moral character. He referred to the youth of many offenders, and it is worth noting the city's age profile at this time, with more than two-thirds of the inhabitants estimated to be under 30 years old (Baird 1842: 161). From

Miller's testimony, drinking and prostitution, with their nocturnal associations, were key areas of concern. Boisterous and 'disorderly' behaviour was inextricably connected with alcohol consumption, and he claimed that 'three-fourths of the crime in the city originates in habits of drunkenness' (Miller 1840: 8). His first priority for improving the city was stricter police regulation of taverns and public houses, particularly those of the unsavoury 'low-rented class'. He also focused on the plight of what he euphemistically termed 'unfortunate females', stating that there were 1,475 known Glasgow prostitutes who frequented 'houses of bad character'. Miller praised city agencies that were attempting to rescue 'the vagrant girls who prowl about the streets', notably charitable houses of refuge. He was also profoundly impressed by the efforts of temperance societies, which had risen meteorically during the 1830s and were conducting a vigorous, high-profile crusade against the evils of alcohol.

According to Miller, Glasgow's streets at night were being safeguarded not only by the vigilance of the city's police, but by the commitment of religious, philanthropic and self-help agencies. This emphasis on regulatory activity in nineteenth-century Scotland fits uncomfortably with Murray Melbin's argument about night-time 'colonization' and the liberating effect of gaslight on modes of nocturnal behaviour. As he puts it, the new illuminant 'made people believe the day was longer', allowing for the extension of working hours and greater opportunities for leisure (Melbin 1987: 14). Much depends, of course, on who these people were, where they lived and what value system they espoused. Thus, whatever the outspoken free-trade beliefs of Glasgow's ruling elite, a libertarian approach to the night was not part of their mind-set. For them, gaslight was convenient and a boon to commerce, but it was also an efficient instrument for exerting power over the urban environment. It enhanced the watchful role of the forces of order and represented a luminous expression of the common good. Given its symbolic status, it is revealing that Thomas Chalmers, the charismatic leader of the Free Church of Scotland, took a keen technical interest in the progress of gaslight, and had pipes installed in his manse as far back as 1810 ('A. M.' 1892: 42). By the 1840s the Free Church was one of several evangelical denominations at the forefront of campaigns to reinforce 'prohibited time', both in relation to the night and for safeguarding the special nature of the Scottish Sabbath. They had considerable success in 'decolonizing' Sunday through the imposed closure of shops, drinking establishments and places of entertainment. Beyond Sunday, in the opinion of Free Church minister James Begg, the day had a temporal rhythm based on the unities of 'eight hours for work, eight hours for sleep, and eight for devotion, study and recreation' (Belford 1861: 4). Breaching this cycle, notably through prolonged night-time working, was unnatural, debilitating and counterproductive.

Glasgow: night missions and urban explorers

The evangelical mission was deep-rooted in Glasgow, a spiritual reawakening that had gathered momentum in the early nineteenth century, consolidating a strong strand of radical Presbyterianism in the city's post-Reformation history. As Jay Brown has noted, the 'Old Theology' of the seventeenth century was given a new lease of life, and ministers of religion could attract vast crowds with their robust preaching (Brown 1982: 211). A favourite biblical theme was the fall of cities, as a metaphor for the mutability of civilization. Sodom, in the Old Testament, was the cautionary example of a city that had incurred the wrath of God, while the New Testament Book of Revelation offered hope of salvation in the new Jerusalem, the shining city where there was no night: 'And the nations of them which are saved shall walk in the light of it: and the kings of the earth do bring their glory and honour into it. And the gates of it shall not be shut at all by day: for there shall be no night there' (*The Bible*, Revelation 21: 24–25). For some the revelatory vision represented a call to social action; for others it placed too much stress on human perfectibility. For instance, the Scottish-born writer James Thomson produced a conscious 'reverse picture' in his long poem, *The City of Dreadful Night*, published in 1880 (Leonard 1993: 144). From a millennialist family, which took a literal interpretation of the Book of Revelation, Thomson later lost his faith and hence his belief in personal salvation. His bleak and eerie evocation of the city where there was everlasting night inspired a range of urban commentators, who perhaps have not appreciated the precise cultural influences (Morgan 1993: 7–8).

For Glasgow's steadfast believers, salvation was given practical application through commitment to public service, philanthropy and a formidable propaganda machine. Scotland's first daily newspaper, the *North British Daily Mail*, was founded in 1847, and became one of the most vociferous and influential evangelical outlets for the remainder of the century. Its first editor, George Troup, pioneered crusading journalism, in an effort to secure a range of social reforms, notably sanitary improvement and better housing. The pungent and often sensationalist style of evangelical preaching was adapted, in order more vividly to impress the corrosive nature of the urban dark side. The technique of investigative reporting was especially favoured, whereby an outsider would explore conditions, and then relate the invariably disturbing experience to newspaper readers. There was a documentary quality to the writing, with close attention to descriptive detail and interviews with the protagonists, often presented in the vernacular. However, the moral message and the theme of light and darkness were pervasive. Troup's investigation of the slum heart of Glasgow in 1848 revealed a warren of looming and decrepit tenements, in a 'superlatively offensive' sanitary state. As he wryly observed about buildings in the Bridgegate district, they seemed to be permanently shrouded in shadow: 'it is but a grey cathedral light that ever enters there upon even the brightest of days. There are some narrow lanes, where, by an inconvenient twisting of one's head, it is quite possible to catch a glimpse of a patch of blue sky above' (quoted in Troup 1881: 73).

In two sentences Troup deployed a range of images, some explicit, some implied. He made the shadow seem all the denser by suggesting a subterranean quality to the slums. There was a strong hint of Gothic unwholesomeness in the presence of the murky 'cathedral' light. His distortion of spatial norms helped to emphasize a sense of claustrophobia and constriction. Glasgow's extraordinary incidence of overcrowding underpinned Troup's view of the landscape; by 1851 the territory of the city covered only 3 square miles (4.8 square kilometres), yet accommodated some 329,000 inhabitants. As conditions continued to deteriorate, Troup's methods were elaborated and used more frequently. That the genre of urban exploration had become well established elsewhere in Britain, notably through the London-based writing of Charles Dickens, further familiarized the readership with the literary conventions (Ackroyd 2000: 451–452; Keating 1976: 13). However, journalist Hugh Macdonald's evocation of a summer day in Glasgow Green, an area of public parkland in the heart of the city, took a different slant from usual. Here Macdonald observed the slum dwellers descending 'in swarms' from their confined surroundings to the open space of the Green. The sunny weather served to heighten their unequivocally nocturnal character:

> Unfortunate females, with faces of triple brass hiding hearts of unutterable woe – sleeping girls, who might be mistaken for lifeless bundles of rags – down-looking scoundrels, with felony stamped on every feature – owlish-looking knaves, minions of the moon, skulking half-ashamed at their own appearance in the eye of the day. ... The veriest dregs of Glasgow society, indeed, seem congregated here.
>
> (Macdonald 1854: 12)

Given their identification with the night, it followed that in the netherworld of the city's poor, darkness was the time of most visible activity. This, of course, was according to the interpretation of the urban explorers, posing as the conduit of entry into the terrain of the underclass. They were using the night, and its inverted values, to give substance to life-styles that seemed incomprehensible to most of their readership. In 1858 the social reformer and temperance campaigner 'Shadow' (Alexander Brown) made this evident in his celebrated *Midnight Scenes and Social Photographs*. As John McCaffrey has explained, Brown related his writing to the realism of the camera, although his snapshots of nocturnal life relied on far more than visual images (McCaffrey 1976: 6–8). Brown's acute sensory awareness was apparent in this description of the Bridgegate late one Sunday:

> As we approach, the hum which formerly fell upon our ear, now develops itself into a Babel of noises – oaths, recriminations, and abuse. ... In a few minutes we grope our way, in an inclined posture, through the entrance of one of those low narrow closes. A small stream of impure water flows on the right, and with the odour of putrifying animal substances, it smells to suffocation. ... The close now becomes more open, and we breathe more freely. A score of eyes from every point – staircase, window, and pavement – fall upon us, as we look through the hazy grey of the night. The impression at once felt is that of intrusion. No nautical explorer ever fell among savages who looked with greater wonder at his approach.
>
> ('Shadow' 1976: 17–18)

'Closes and wynds' were literally the narrow passageways and winding alleys that connected the tenements to the backlands, but by mid-century they had become the generic title for the worst housing of the old city. Brown's disturbing nocturnal descriptions served as a blunt warning that the city was blighting its future if young people continued to grow up in such conditions.

The reference to 'savages' was a favoured device of urban explorers, who often identified themselves with travellers to undiscovered parts of the world, notably the African 'heart of darkness'. Historians have commented on the imperialist language they used, to emphasize the scale of social and spiritual destitution, and how the intrepid forces of enlightenment could reverse this (Keating 1976: 14–15; Walkowitz 1998: 18–19). Brown's observations of Glasgow's 'wild-looking creatures', some with 'low brows' and 'monkey-looking heads and faces', evoked a primitive and racially charged stereotype ('Shadow' 1976: 113–114). In this context, the notion of night-time 'colonization' takes on a new dimension, reflecting the civilizing assumptions of explorers like Brown, and their hopes of taming the urban dark side. As has been shown, policing became one vital agency of control; so also was missionary activism. Night missions were distinctive because they consciously embraced the people most associated with corrosive darkness, such as prostitutes, drunkards and the homeless. Using yet more colonizing imagery, Schlör suggests that the missionary aim was to 'penetrate the "hunting grounds" of vice', and ultimately reclaim the contested territory (Schlör 1998: 221–222). A notable Glasgow example from the 1860s and 1870s was the Midnight Meeting movement, inspired by London's Moonlight Mission (Muirhead 1974: 232–234). Specializing in the work of 'female rescue', its mode of operation was for missionaries to approach prostitutes and invite them to late-night meetings where they would be urged to forsake the streets in return for 'respectable' employment, usually domestic service (*Glasgow Herald* 6 July 1860).

Whatever the 'elevating' efforts of the missionaries, journalists and their readers continued to be fascinated with the contradictions of Glasgow's dark side. There undoubtedly was a voyeuristic dimension to the repeated focus on 'the criminal and unfortunate classes', but moral concern legitimized public curiosity. Again, the *North British Daily Mail* was to the fore in exposing urban conditions, featuring a series of lengthy articles between 1870 and 1872 collectively titled 'The Dark Side of Glasgow'. By this time the *Mail*'s editor was Charles Cameron, an outspoken temperance radical, who eventually became a Liberal Member of Parliament for the city. The drinking habits of the population were a recurring theme of 'Dark Side' reporters, with particular scrutiny given to the prevalence of 'shebeens', or illicit drinking establishments. The *Mail* provided a highly coloured account of their influence:

> The effect of the shebeens has been to keep the streets in their neighbourhood in a continued turmoil; drouthy and disreputable characters and thieves turn night into day, prowl about till four or five in the morning, every now and then refreshing themselves at the shebeens until they become

drunk and disorderly and are carried off to the Police Office, making night hideous with their yells and imprecations.

(NBDM 27 December 1870)

Reporters gave dramatic accounts of nocturnal raids by the police, and the presence of 'loose' women among the persons arrested was frequently remarked upon.

The intoxicating thrill of alcohol consumption extended beyond the seedy confines of the shebeens, and *Mail* investigators were determined to show how easily popular entertainment could descend into the murky realm of vice when drinking was involved. Much was made of the negative attributes of the 'Free-and-Easies', described as 'a sort of quasi-music hall in a tavern', where the working-class patrons provided their own entertainment (*NBDM*, not dated). The term itself suggests an unrestrained and mellow environment, where vigilance over self and surroundings could be too readily relaxed. Dismissed by the *Mail* reporter as an inducement to 'silly youths and sillier men and women to misspend their evenings', the irreverent tone to some 'Free-and-Easy' entertainment touched a raw nerve. One singer, known simply as Jamie, went so far as to ridicule the evangelical mission in the course of his risqué performance. Depicted as a louche figure with a mysterious past, possibly even a divinity student who had gone astray, the implication was that Jamie had succumbed to Satan's influence and was intent on corrupting his impressionable, drink-befuddled audience. Jamie's use of parody to undermine the *Mail*'s conception of normality was seen as shockingly subversive; ideological as well as physical danger was evidently thriving in Glasgow's nocturnal netherworld. Even in an era of rapidly advancing technological change, symbolized by the rise of electricity as a power source, the threat of the shadow remained an integral part of the moral quest to protect the integrity of Scotland's cities, and reorientate cultural preferences in the direction of safe respectability.

Conclusion

The nocturnal qualities of Edinburgh and Glasgow in the nineteenth century were not unique to Scotland. Schlör has written extensively about the efforts of urban authorities elsewhere in Europe to ensure that nightlife was more easily 'controlled, domesticated, civilized, reduced to a manageable scale' (Schlör 1998: 251). What this essay has shown, however, is that in Scotland these control mechanisms were introduced relatively early in the century, and that they derived impetus from the long-standing notion of moral vigilance, which eventually metamorphosed into the practical instrument of policing. The old rhetorical legacy underpinned contemporary enthusiasm for progress and order, and became especially important for furthering the evangelical mission, where the city, and the well-being of its inhabitants, were deemed to be vital for national regeneration. The Scottish experience has also revealed that the more technology was developed, the more control was exercised over communities; indeed, technology became a crucial aid to vigilance, especially the power of gaslight.

Moreover, despite the gradual secularization of society, controls intensified during the early twentieth century. In Scotland the impact of the First World War was significant. For all that round-the-clock working became an integral part of the munitions drive, an unprecedented degree of state regulation was imposed, especially on the widespread use of 'prohibited time' in leisure outlets (Maver 2000: 194–195). A disciplined and abstemious workforce was seen as a patriotic necessity, and many of the wartime restrictions remained in place for decades after the 1918 Armistice.

As far as night was concerned, the triumph of individualism and freedom from restraint was not consolidated in nineteenth-century Scotland. Liberalism may eventually have been the prevailing political orthodoxy, but the missionary endeavour to conquer night and its uncertainties was more imperialist than democratic. The theme has relevance for the twenty-first century. The social trends forecaster, Leon Kreitzman, has recently enthusiastically endorsed Melbin's concept of night-time 'colonization', and criticized the 'strong Puritanical undercurrent' which he suggests characterizes opponents of the encroaching '24 Hour Society' (Kreitzman 1999: 5, 153–154). Theologians, philosophers and environmentalists are identified by Kreitzman as the most vocal in their disapproval; conservative and elitist, they constitute the shock-troops of anti-consumerism. Yet Puritanism and consumerism are far from incompatible, just as the link between colonization and liberation is far from reinforcing. In Scotland, which served as a model of Puritan society during the nineteenth century, the evidence of conspicuous consumption is still visibly apparent in the splendid New Town of Edinburgh, now a site of world heritage importance. On the other hand, Scots have moved with post-industrial times by embracing the consumerization of the night. Since the 1970s, economic necessity has dictated that nocturnal constraints should be relaxed in the drive to build up the thriving leisure industries of Edinburgh and Glasgow. Quantitatively they are the two most visited cities in Britain after London; qualitatively they have become the most popular for tourists, with Edinburgh retaining its appeal over Glasgow (*Guardian* 16 June 2001). The cities' strong sense of history, and flair for promoting this, are major selling points. At night visitors are even taken on conducted tours of the locations historically associated with the urban dark side, in an attempt to recreate, from a safe distance, the frisson, fear and danger of the past.

Acknowledgements

Warm thanks first to Brigitte and Lodewijk for stimulating my ideas on Scotland's dark side; second to Biff Carmichael and Enda Ryan of Glasgow's Mitchell Library for locating *The Dark Side of Glasgow* for me; third to John McCaffrey of Glasgow University for his helpful observations on the urban explorers.

Notes

1   The Scots vernacular was widely used in nineteenth-century popular literature. The English equivalents of Scots words used in this essay are as follows: awa' – away; mirk

– dark; o' – of; nicht – night; puir – poor; heid – head; beild – refuge; ha' – hall; malisons – curses; maun – must.

2   Gars a' – sends all; gae dandring – go strolling; mony – many; gie a' – give all.

Bibliography

'A. M.' (1892) *Light Without a Wick: A Century of Gas-Lighting, 1792–1892*. Glasgow: Robert Maclehose.

Ackroyd, Peter (2000) *London: The Biography*. London: Chatto & Windus.

Arnot, Hugo (1998 [1779]) *The History of Edinburgh*. Edinburgh: West Port Books.

Baird, Charles (1842) 'On the general sanitary condition of the working classes and poor in the city of Glasgow', *Reports on the Sanitary Condition of the Labouring Population of Scotland*. London: HMSO, 159–203 (British Parliamentary Papers).

Barty-King, Hugh (1984) *New Flame: How Gas Changed the Commercial and Industrial Life of Britain between 1813 and 1984*. Tavistock: Graphmitre.

Bathurst, Bella (1999) *The Lighthouse Stevensons: The Extraordinary Story of the Building of the Scottish Lighthouses by the Ancestors of Robert Louis Stevenson*. London: HarperCollins.

Belford, James (1861) *A Voice from the Counter; or, A Plea for Early Closing, with a Preface by the Rev. James Begg, DD*. Edinburgh: John Menzies.

Bell, George (1849) *Day and Night in the Wynds of Edinburgh*. Edinburgh: Johnstone & Hunter.

The Bible (Authorized King James Version) (1998 edition). Oxford: Oxford University Press.

Brown, Stewart J. (1982) *Thomas Chalmers and the Godly Commonwealth in Scotland*. Oxford: Oxford University Press.

Carson, Kit and Hilary Idzikowska (1989) 'The social production of Scottish policing, 1795–1900', in Douglas Hay and Francis Snyder (eds) *Policing and Prosecution in Britain, 1750 to 1850*. Oxford: Oxford University Press, 267–297.

Chambers, Robert (1846 [1824]) *Traditions of Edinburgh*. Edinburgh: William & Robert Chambers.

Chapman, Alexander (publisher) (1807) *Report of the Committees Appointed by the Merchant Company, Incorporations, and several other Public Bodies in and about the City of Edinburgh, to Consider the Effects of the Act Lately Passed for Regulating the Police of the Said City*. Edinburgh: Chapman.

'Civis' (1812) *Address to the Inhabitants of Edinburgh on the Necessity of Immediately following up the Measure Recommended by the Magistrates, for the Purposes of Forming an Interim Additional System of Police*. Edinburgh: J. Johnstone.

Cleland, James (1840) *Description of the City of Glasgow*. Glasgow: John Smith.

Dalyell, John Graham (1835) *The Darker Superstitions of Scotland*. Glasgow: Richard Griffin.

Edwards, Owen Dudley (1993 [1980]) *Burke and Hare*. Edinburgh: Mercat.

Fergusson, Robert (2000) *Selected Poems*, ed. James Robertson. Edinburgh: Birlinn.

Gibson, John Sibbald (1993 [1977]) *Deacon Brodie: Father to Jekyll and Hyde*. Edinburgh: Saltire Society.

Glasgow Police Act (1800) George III, cap. 88, Glasgow City Archives D-TC 14.3.1.

GPB [Glasgow Police Board Minutes]. Glasgow City Archives E1.1.17.

Graham, Henry Grey (1909 [1899]) *The Social Life of Scotland in the Eighteenth Century*. London: Adam & Charles Black.

Griffiths, John (1992) *The Third Man: the Life and Times of William Murdoch, 1754–1839, the Inventor of Gas Lighting*. London: André Deutsch.

GTC [Glasgow Town Council Minutes]. Glasgow City Archives C1.1.62.

Guthrie, Thomas (1859) *The City: Its Sins and Sorrows.* Glasgow: Scottish Temperance League.

Ireland, Thomas (publisher) (1829) *West Port Murders; or, An Authentic Account of the Atrocious Murders Committed by Burke and his Associates.* Edinburgh: Ireland.

Keating, Peter (ed.) (1976) 'Introduction', *Into Unknown England, 1866–1913: Selections from the Social Explorers.* Glasgow: Fontana/Collins.

Kennedy, Thomas D. (1995) 'William Leechman, pulpit eloquence and the Glasgow Enlightenment', in Andrew Hook and Richard B. Sher (eds) *The Glasgow Enlightenment.* East Linton: Tuckwell, 56–72.

Kreitzman, Leon (1999) *The 24 Hour Society.* London: Profile.

Leonard, Tom (1993) *Places of the Mind: The Life and Times of James Thomson ('B.V.').* London: Jonathan Cape.

Lockhart, John Gibson (1977 [1819]) *Peter's Letters to His Kinsfolk,* ed. William Ruddick. Edinburgh: Scottish Academic Press.

McCaffrey, John (1976) 'Introduction', in 'Shadow', *Glasgow 1858: Shadow's Midnight Scenes and Social Photographs.* Glasgow: University of Glasgow Press.

Macdonald, Hugh (1854) *Rambles Round Glasgow: Descriptive, Historical and Traditional.* Glasgow: James Hedderwick.

Mackenzie, Peter (1890 [1862]) *Old Reminiscences of Glasgow and the West of Scotland,* Vol. 2. Glasgow: James P. Forrester.

Marwick, James D. (1865) *Sketch of the History of the High Constables of Edinburgh.* Edinburgh (privately printed).

Maver, Irene (1995) 'The guardianship of the community: civic authority prior to 1833', in T. M. Devine and Gordon Jackson (eds) *Glasgow, Volume I: Beginnings to 1830.* Manchester: Manchester University Press, 239–277.

Maver, Irene (2000) *Glasgow.* Edinburgh: Edinburgh University Press.

Melbin, Murray (1987) *Night as Frontier: Colonizing the World After Dark.* New York: The Free Press.

Miller, Henry (1840) *Papers Relative to the State of Crime in the City of Glasgow, with Observations of a Remedial Nature.* Glasgow: W. Lang.

Morgan, Edwin (1993) 'Introduction', in James Thomson *The City of Dreadful Night.* Edinburgh: Canongate.

Muirhead, Ian A. (1974) 'Churchmen and the problem of prostitution in nineteenth-century Scotland', *Records of the Scottish Church History Society* 18: 223–243.

NBDM, 'The Dark Side of Glasgow'; a series of cuttings from the *North British Daily Mail* in the Mitchell Library, Glasgow, originally published between 1870 and 1872.

Noble, Andrew (1985) 'Urbane silence: Scottish writing and the nineteenth-century city', in George Gordon (ed.) *Perspectives of the Scottish City,* Aberdeen: Aberdeen University Press, 64–90.

Ralston, Andrew G. (1980) 'The Tron riot of 1812', *History Today* 30(May): 41–45.

Richardson, Ruth (1989 [1988]) *Death, Dissection and the Destitute.* London: Penguin.

Schivelbusch, Wolfgang (1995 [1983]) *Disenchanted Night: The Industrialization of Light in the Nineteenth Century.* Berkeley, CA: University of California Press.

Schlör, Joachim (1998 [1991]) *Nights in the Big City: Paris, Berlin, London, 1840–1930.* London: Reaktion.

'Shadow' (Alexander Brown) (1976 [1858]) *Glasgow, 1858: Shadow's Midnight Scenes and Social Photographs.* Glasgow: University of Glasgow Press.

Sinclair, George (1808 [1685]) *Satan's Invisible World Discovered.* Edinburgh: T. Macleish.

Sinclair, Sir John (ed.) (1973 [1793]) *The Statistical Account of Scotland, 1791–1799: Volume VII, Lanarkshire and Renfrewshire*. Wakefield: EP Publishing.

Stevenson, Robert Louis (1900 [1878]) *Edinburgh: Picturesque Notes*. London: Seeley.

Stevenson, Robert Louis (1906 [1878]) 'A plea for gas lamps', *The Works of Robert Louis Stevenson*, Vol. 11, ed. Edmund Gosse. London: Cassell, 440–443.

Stevenson, Robert Louis (1912) *Records of a Family of Engineers*. London: Chatto & Windus.

Stevenson, Robert Louis (1987 [1886]) *The Strange Case of Dr Jekyll and Mr Hyde*. Oxford: Oxford University Press.

Stevenson, Robert Louis (1999 [1884]) *The Body Snatcher and Other Stories*. London: Orion.

Storch, Robert D. (1975) 'The plague of the blue locusts: police reform and popular resistance in northern England, 1840–57', *International Review of Social History* 20: 61–90.

Troup, George Emslie (1881) *Life of George Troup, Journalist*. Edinburgh: MacNiven & Wallace.

Walkowitz, Judith R. (1998 [1992]) *City of Dreadful Delight: Narratives of Sexual Danger in Late-Victorian London*. London: Virago.

Whatley, Christopher A. (1992) 'Royal day, people's day: the monarch's birthday in Scotland, c. 1660–1860', in Roger Mason and Norman Macdougall (eds) *People and Power in Scotland*. Edinburgh: John Donald, 170–188.

Youngson, A. J. (1988 [1966]) *The Making of Classical Edinburgh, 1750–1840*. Edinburgh: Edinburgh University Press.

8 Night-time and deviant behaviour

The changing night scene of Japanese youth

Ayukawa Jun

In present-day Japan, hospitals and the police are not the only institutions offering round-the-clock service. From office-supplies provider Kinko's, Don Quixote discount convenience stores, and grocery stores to ATM banking, more and more companies are operating around the clock. One can now obtain groceries, babysitters, hairdressers, recording studios and even fishing tackle well past midnight (*Keizaikai* 33/19 1998: 142–147).

This shift in opening hours has emerged to meet the demands of the public, and business owners say it also widens and maintains their customer base. Consumer convenience is the bottom line for these establishments. Bars, cafés and karaoke lounges stay open late at night to cater to businessmen and students who choose to party hard and miss the last train home. But that is not the only reason some businesses are extending their hours. Japan's jobholders are spending more hours in their offices and sleeping less according to the National Time Use Survey 2000 Report conducted by the Japanese Broadcasting Corporation NHK (NHK hōsō bunka kenkyū jo 2001; cf. Steger in this volume).

Additionally, with more companies introducing flexible working hours, life-styles are changing. These changes in the nightlife of the general population have also drastically affected the night-time behaviour of Japan's youth. Nowadays, young people in Japan stay up much later than previously. When at home, they engage in activities such as listening to CDs, watching TV or accessing the Internet with their personal computers and mobile phones. In September 2001, Nova English School began taking advantage of this trend by offering late-night English lessons online from 10:30 p.m. to 7:30 a.m. Outside of the home, young people walk around the streets or congregate at convenience stores and karaoke boxes, and young women especially also engage in telephone dating services which sometimes lead them to disappear from home for a period of time.

These devices and the others I shall presently discuss can perhaps be considered as passports to a new world, which allow for new forms of behaviour, new ways of thinking and new perspectives on youth and youth cultures. Factors that underlie these changes are: individualism, the slow undermining of cultural norms and society's changing attitudes towards its youth. What was once taken for granted has now become problematic. What was once thought to be ridiculous or extreme has now become the norm. The border between conventional behaviour and deviant behaviour has become blurred in many ways.

My aim in this chapter is first to describe the changes that are taking place among Japan's youth in terms of the night. In my view, these changes are manifold and materialise in many different contexts. The first part of the chapter is an enumeration of these different manifestations, i.e. nightspots, mobile phones, mobile youth, mobile clubs and stores. Next, I will show how the changes in society and youth behaviour have affected the way young people interact with each other in relationships, and how they have affected the definition of delinquent behaviour. And finally, at the end of my chapter, I hope it will become clear if, and how, these seemingly disparate developments I mention in the opening paragraph are interrelated and what effect they have on youth behaviour.

The changing night scene: nightspots

Over the last thirty years, Japanese people have gradually come to sleep less, and are going to bed much later. According to the NHK time-use surveys, 88 per cent of the people went to sleep before midnight in 1970, 85 per cent in 1975, 85 per cent in 1980, 82 per cent in 1985 and 78 per cent in 1990. On Saturdays, the percentages were 85 in 1970, 80 in 1975, 80 in 1980, 78 in 1985 and 73 in 1990 (NHK hōsō bunka kenkyū jo 1991). In 1995 and 2000, this institute conducted research on high school students (teenagers between the ages of 15 and 18). On weekdays, in 1995, 55 per cent of them went to bed at midnight or later; in 2000 the percentage amounted to 61. They were working, watching TV or engaged in some other activity. On Saturdays at midnight, 62 per cent of high school students in 1995 and 66 per cent in 2000 were still awake and engaged in activities such as watching TV or videos, listening to music on their CDs, MDs or audio cassettes, reading magazines or comics, doing a hobby or homework, studying a non-school subject or playing outside the home. The percentage of young men between the ages of 16 and 19 who were still up at 11:45 p.m. on weekdays was 66 in 2000. On Saturdays at midnight it was 53 per cent. The number of young women between the ages of 16 and 19 who were still up at 11:45 p.m. on weekdays was 56 per cent in 2000. On Saturdays it was 72 per cent (NHK hōsō bunka kenkyū jo, 1996; 2001).[1] These statistics show that high school students are staying awake later than they were five years ago.[2] They also show that more young women than men are staying up later at night and are engaged in late-night activities. Just what kind of activities are the youth engaged in so late at night?

In her article 'Osaka South, American Village, Scenery Till the First Train in the Morning', journalist Ozaki Sachi describes scenes of girls waiting to be picked up by boys (Ozaki 2000: 18). These girls have gathered in groups of twos, threes, fours and fives. The groups do not necessarily know each other. They have gathered in a park close to a popular and well-known gathering place for young people in Osaka. The girls are sitting or squatting on the

ground, waiting for men to drive by in nice recreational vehicles, fancily deco-
rated mini-vans or luxury cars. It is well after midnight and the last train or
subway has already departed. These girls are waiting to be picked up by men
with whom they would like to spend some time. Some of the girls are wearing
their junior or senior high school uniforms. Some of them readily get into the
men's cars. The men approach them by talking through the car window. In
many cases, the back side-windows and the rear windows of the men's cars are
covered with a black tint to prevent an onlooker from looking inside the vehicle.
Ozaki returned to the same nightspot a week later on a Saturday night with an
actor to interview the girls. She arrived around 2 a.m. and interviewed two girls
aged 15 and 17. The girls said that they were just walking around this well-
known nightspot and had been hit on by twenty-six men wishing to spend some
time with them.

Not only in big cities but also in mid-size and small cities do young people
gather at popular local spots. In Takasaki, a medium-sized city with a population of 245,000, young people between the ages of 16 and 18 gather at the
Japan Railway Takasaki Station. They do not come just from Takasaki but from
neighbouring cities as well. They gather on Saturday evenings from around 7
p.m. onward, sit on the ground and chat. They come in groups of about twenty
(*Asahi Shinbun* 28 October 1997). In Maebashi city, which is 115 kilometres from
Tokyo, young people gather at the Japan Railway Maebashi Station. They are
called *yoasobi-zoku*, which means 'the tribe that plays at night'. These young
people arrive by car and, according to an article in the national daily, *Asahi
Shinbun*, on 16 October 1997, their principal reason for coming there is to pick
up people of the opposite sex. Some of these youths are hot-rodders (*Asahi
Shinbun* 16 October 1997).

Hot-rodders usually gather after midnight to speed up and down the high-
ways and roadways racing as loudly as possible and performing all kinds of
driving tricks. There have been hot-rodders in Japan since the 1950s. The
present-day name for them is *bōsō-zoku*, from *bōsō*, meaning to drive roughly, and
zoku, meaning tribe. In the 1950s, they were known as *kaminari-zoku*; *kaminari*
means thunder. This name later changed to *mahchi-zoku*, *mahchi* meaning speed,
and then to the current *bōsō-zoku*. In the 1950s and 1960s, there was great cohesion within each individual *kaminari-zoku* group. They would display signs of
group identity such as flags and wear very colourful uniforms with detailed
patchwork. Identification with a group was very important and, at large gatherings, members stayed within their groups. It was easy to identify who was who
and who was affiliated with what group. There was very little intermingling
except at hot-rodding challenges. The hot-rodders generally gathered in the
small hours of the morning between midnight and 5 a.m. However, as run-ins
with the police became more and more frequent and severe, the size of the *bōsō-
zoku* decreased and the unity of the individual groups weakened. Yet, according
to an article by Nakayama Ryōichi, a Kimono Festival was held on 22–24 July
2000 and the *bōsō-zoku* gathered there at around 10 p.m. with their vehicles.
They confronted the local police and began throwing bottles and cans. Around

200 *bōsō-zoku* mingled with a crowd of about 2,000 festival-goers, some of whom got caught up in the excitement of the moment and joined in, throwing stones, chairs or whatever they could onto the railroad tracks and in all other directions (Nakayama 2000: 28). *Bōsō-zoku* are generally known for rough driving but occasionally participate in more violent pursuits.

Presently, when *bōsō-zoku* gather, it is very difficult to know who is who. In many cases group cohesion is just no longer important. There is usually a very small core group of members and the rest are just groupies. Those who love the speed and challenge of hot-rodding, those who are just out looking for excitement, and those who just happen to encounter the group while hanging out characterise the groupies. They form a pseudo-group that exists just for the moment. Once their hot-rodding challenges are over for the evening, they go their separate ways. Their relationships with each other are very weak and temporary. There is no comradeship. They come together just for the thrill of the moment.

The mobile phone

I will now briefly sketch out the prevalence of the mobile phone and the activities that often surround it. In 1992, the number of mobile phones, including those that were installed in automobiles, was less than 1 million. By 1995, it had increased to approximately 10 million and, by July 2000, to over 61.6 million (Nakamura 2001: 47). Initially, businesspeople used them exclusively as the necessary contract with the phone company could only be made by businesses. However, eventually they grew popular among non-businesspeople, the first individuals eager to have them being high school students. More precisely, they first purchased pagers (called pocket bells in Japan) because the price of a mobile phone was prohibitive. Therefore, in the mid-1990s, it was not unusual to see long queues at public telephone booths in the corridors of high schools during break or lunchtime. The price of mobile phones gradually went down and the contract and payment system changed to allow individuals to obtain them. But they were still very expensive to purchase. However, high school girls – very sensitive to fashion and convenience – desperately desired mobile phones.

As high school girls in Japan are the trend-setters and the barometer by which an item is deemed to be commercially viable or not, mobile phone companies took note of this phenomenon and began to make the mobile phone more readily available. It became instantly popular among high school girls, and, in turn, the whole population of Japan followed suit. According to a study conducted by the Bureau for the Administration on Youth and others, the average monthly mobile phone bill is more than 7,000 yen (approximately 60 euro) per teenager (Yoshii 2001: 88). According to the Bureau, 51 per cent of high school students receive help from their parents in paying their mobile phone charges whereas 33 per cent pay for the charges themselves. The Bureau also stated that more than 70 per cent of high school students had a portable phone in 1999. This percentage appears to be smaller than what I observed.

Through my own survey, I ascertained that almost every high school student has one or more mobile phones. Some of them have at least two, one to talk with friends and to send and receive e-mails, and one to communicate anonymously with strangers. The mobile phone has changed the way high school students from all areas of the country communicate with each other.

How has the mobile phone transformed young people's communication habits? The Youth Affairs Administration, Management and Coordination Agency conducted research in the year 2000 in the Miyagi, Chiba, Tokyo, Ishikawa, Nara and Kumamoto Prefectures. According to Sasaki Teruyoshi, a member of the research project, the research subjects were 3,152 high school students who had stated that they have a mobile phone and 1,815 of their parents (Sasaki 2001: 30). Of the students who own a mobile phone, 94 per cent stated that it had become easier to correspond with friends, 56.3 per cent had become more intimate with their friends, 48.9 per cent had increased the length of their phone calls and 48.4 per cent had increased their number of friends. It should also be noted that 40.5 per cent of the students stated that they go out more and stay out longer than before and 65.8 per cent of the students stated that it had become easier to call a person of the opposite sex. They also stated that the number of their friends of the opposite sex had increased and that they had became more intimate with them.

Without mobile phones there is a form of screening of a student's calls by parents or other family members who may answer the phone first and then pass it on to the student. On the other hand, with the use of mobile phones more than 20 per cent of the parents stated that it had become impossible for them to know with whom their children talk on the phone. And, although 52.5 per cent of the students stated that their family is relieved to know where they are, it should be noted that the number of students who lie about their whereabouts has increased. Approximately 20 per cent of high school girls stated that they often lie about their whereabouts (Sasaki 2001: 33). This indicates that, on the one hand, parents are relieved, but, on the other, that relief is based on their children's false report as to where they are.

Social contact also increased as 54.4 per cent of the students stated that they received calls more often with mobile phones, and 37.6 per cent of them stated that after receiving a call they go out more frequently than they had gone out before. Also, more than 25 per cent of the students stated that they tend to return home much later than before. This trend is most evident among female students on commercial and other job-oriented courses of study (Sasaki 2001: 34).

Sasaki concludes that it has become more difficult for parents to know what their children are doing. For high school students, it has become possible to correspond without their parents' surveillance. One parent reported that she discovered her child was out all night after a late-night phone call to the child; she thought her child was sleeping in bed. Sasaki also pointed out that although it has become easier for children and parents to communicate with each other, there has been no increase in the influence of parents on their children's behaviour (Sasaki 2001: 36). In the past, parents set curfews for their children, but even if curfews were not explicitly set, there was a general consensus that high school students were expected to return home before 10 p.m. unless they were attending a particular function and had told their parents ahead of time that they would be getting home late. However, with the widespread use of mobile phones, parents have become less strict in enforcing curfews. Children have convinced their parents that they can call and check up on them at any time, so the parents have relented and allowed their children to stay out late or overnight at a friend's house. As the phone number of an incoming call is displayed on the screen of a mobile phone, the children do not take calls from their parents when they are in compromising situations. They move to a quiet place and return their parents' calls to give the impression that they are doing something different. Herein lies the dilemma. Parents are aware that trust is crucial in the relationship with their children, for without it, friction may occur and the child will resist the dictates of the parents. On the other hand, if the parents trust the child, they will hesitate to call and check up even when they suspect something is amiss. This allows the child to get away with activities that the parents do not necessarily approve of. The end result is that today's children are very clever at getting their parents to believe what they want them to believe.

The Tokyo Metropolitan Police conducted research on 785 youths who had been counselled or arrested by the police and on 2,115 junior and senior high school students as to whether or not they had a mobile phone. They discovered that approximately 70 per cent of the junior and senior high school students had mobile phones. Additionally, 23 per cent of the junior and senior high school students and 42 per cent of the counselled or arrested youths stated that they started going out more after getting mobile phones. The change in young women's behaviour is more pronounced than that of young men. If we set the number of arrested young men in 1950 at an index of 100, then the index of arrests in 1999 is less than 100. If we do the same for young women, the index of arrests in 1999 is approximately 350. Forty years ago, the percentage of girls among arrested youth under 20 was very low. However, in 1960 it grew to 5 per cent, in 1970 to 10 per cent, in 1980 to 20 per cent and in 1999 to 25 per cent. Violent crime among women has also increased in recent years.

Mobile youth

Recently *puchi-iede* (a little disappearance from home) has become popular among young girls. *Puchi* is the Japanese version of the French *petit* (small), *iede* meaning disappearance from home. The term refers to staying away from home for a short period of time. In the past, girls who left home had made up their minds and would declare that they were never coming back. However, nowadays, girls have no clear reason for staying away. They just disappear from home for several days or weeks. Unlike in the past, many parents do not report the disappearance of their daughters to the police. Indeed, many parents do not seem too upset at their daughter's disappearance. As the young woman is aware of this, she feels free to stay out for a while, say, at her friends' apartment, her male companion's apartment or with someone she has met at a club or through telephone clubs (Kon 2000: 266).

Nishiki Mitsue wrote an article recounting her days as a counsellor for troubled youth and those potentially headed for trouble. She worked in front of the Osaka Central Railway Station for more than twenty years. Compared with the present situation, youths in the past were intent on running away. They ran away with the purpose of freeing themselves of their parents. However, beginning in the late 1980s, children who left their homes had no particular reason for leaving. They just wanted some freedom to play around for a while. Once they got bored, they returned home (Nishiki 2000: 35). Nishiki said that in the past, when she reported to parents that their child was found, the reunion was very emotional. Generally, everybody cried. Sometimes the emotion of the reunion was so great that even Nishiki and other counsellors also shed tears. Nowadays, however, both children and parents have changed. She believes that the number of parents who do not stop their children from wandering around at night and staying away from home without their explicit permission has increased. She also feels that the number of children who 'disappear from home for no apparent reason' has also increased (Nishiki 2000: 35).

A probation officer of the Tokyo Family Court, Fujita Yasuhiro, reported on a case that demonstrates the relationship of *puchi-iede*, *enjo kōsai*, speed (methamphetamines) and the mobile phone (Fujita 2000: 24–27): Ryoko, a sophomore in high school, is diligent and obedient according to her parents. She never says a bad word to or about them, and her relationship with her mother is so intimate that they seem more like close friends than mother and daughter. Ryoko's friend Akemi is very active, and the two are in the same group. Ryoko got into the habit of staying over at Akemi's home. She told her parents that she was staying over at Akemi's in order to study. Ryoko and Akemi sat up late at night talking. Akemi smoked and inhaled methamphetamine (which is called *s*) in order to stay awake at night, and Ryoko joined her in using methamphetamine. Akemi engaged in *enjo kōsai* (literally, compensated dating), i.e. prostitution, in order to get money to buy methamphetamine. She recommended that Ryoko should also begin *enjo kōsai* and persuaded her into trying it by telling her that she could earn money just by going to a karaoke lounge or having dinner with men without having any sexual intercourse. However, after a man took Ryoko to a hotel and forced her to have sexual intercourse with him, she began to prostitute herself often. Even when one of Ryoko's parents telephoned Akemi's home while Ryoko was out with a customer at a hotel, Ryoko's parents believed and felt relieved when told that Ryoko was studying at Akemi's home. Ryoko was arrested for the possession of methamphetamines and sent to a juvenile classification home, which is a detention centre for juvenile delinquents and juvenile criminals. In the beginning, Ryoko's parents could not face the reality of the situation. They exclaimed: 'we kept in touch with each other through the mobile phone, and there were no secrets between us'.

On a late August night in 2002, at 2:30 a.m. I interviewed a group of three junior high school girls strolling around a park in the middle of Nagoya. Ikumi, who is 14 years old, said that she had done *puchi-iede* last summer. She had spent most nights last summer away from home with her friends. She had usually stayed at one of her friends' homes. Also, she had spent several nights at an observation platform that few people approach at night in a park that is not far from her home. She sometimes sniffed glue, which is called 'thinner' in Japan. Occasionally she went back home to take a bath, change clothes, eat something and sleep for a while. Since she was given a mobile phone when she was in the sixth grade, her mother could call her easily. At first she answered her mother's calls frequently, but less so the longer the *puchi-iede* lasted. She told us that the reason she did *puchi-iede* was because she had not liked being with her mother the previous year. According to her explanation, there is a stage in life when a girl does not like to be with her mother and for her it had been the previous year. Now, it does not bother her to be with her mother.

Even though it is called 'disappearing from home', young women do it easily. They do not have any feelings of anxiety concerning their situation, and they do not have serious thoughts about their future. Girls such as Ryoko and Ikemi look for momentary pleasure or seek money in order to go out and take part in delinquent behaviour. They also develop rhetoric to neutralise deviant consciousness and maintain that their behaviour 'is such a trivial matter that it is all right. If we are going to do wrong, then we should do it before becoming an adult.' This attitude has caused delinquency to escalate. On the other hand, parents do not think the present activity of disappearing from home is serious. Parents say that, although they do not know the whereabouts of their son or daughter, they are not worried because they can always get in touch with each other. Even when the family court sends an order to a youth and his or her parents to attend the adjudication, some parents call the family court and actually say 'My child has gone for a few days, but he or she will return sooner or later' (Fujita 2000: 26).

Mobile clubs

Telephone clubs, known as *tere-kura* in Japan, started in the 1980s and became very popular in the 1990s. The operation of a telephone club is quite simple. Men who want to become clients of a telephone club go to the establishment and then wait for calls from women who want to befriend them. This form of dating is known as *enjo kōsai*, or 'compensated dating' as mentioned above, a euphemism for prostitution. Women use this form of dating to get money from men. *Enjo* (help) comes from the man in the form of money given to the woman, and *kōsai* (companionship) comes from the female in the form of dinner dates or sexual favours. The association with each other is temporary. It can last just for the time it takes to have dinner or sex, overnight, or for a period of several weeks or months until the woman gathers the amount of *enjo* she desires.[3]

This form of dating has been made easier in that the man no longer has to go to the telephone club. Messages can now be delivered to him via his mobile phone and through e-mails. High school and junior high school girls command the highest fees in this dating practice. It has become another ticket to freedom for them. It also demonstrates how empowered youths have become in their relationships with adults, juxtaposed to how weak adults have become within these relationships.

At the beginning of September 2002, there was a message listed on the bulletin board of an Internet 'encounter site', which most users access through their mobile phones. Two 18-year-old high school girls wanted to find a man who would pay 40,000 yen (approximately 340 euro) for sexual intercourse with no kissing or oral sex. When I met them at midnight in the suburbs of Nagoya, they turned out to be 17-year-olds. During an interview that lasted approximately one hour at a family-style, 24-hour restaurant, the lights on their mobile phones flashed frequently indicating that several messages had reached them and several people had called them. They read and wrote e-mails in front of me.

Both girls' families permitted them to stay at the other's house. By talking to their parents as if they were staying at each other's house, they could do what they wanted at night. They told me that they had posted the ad because they needed money in order to pay their huge mobile phone bills and in order to accumulate the deposit that is needed to rent their own apartment.

Access to the Internet, telephone clubs (which now allow access through Internet sites), hot-rodding, karaoke clubs (which will be discussed next) and disappearing from home are just the tip of the iceberg in the opportunities that are open to young people to enjoy night-time pleasures. The downside is that the relationships formed and people encountered within these newly found freedoms are temporary and dissatisfying, leaving young people with a feeling of emptiness. They thus seek new and better thrills to assuage the emptiness temporarily.

Karaoke box

A karaoke box is a place that contains many rooms with sing-along equipment in them. Customers rent one of the rooms for a certain period of time. Karaoke has become a very popular amusement among Japanese people. There are also karaoke sets that can be bought, set up at home, and enjoyed by the entire family.

Not only adults but also junior and senior high school students go to karaoke boxes to sing and drink, both in the daytime and at night. They are usually celebrating something such as the successful completion of a school project, someone's birthday, or their success in examinations. Students also go there to relieve stress or just to have fun. Often at the weekend, high school students stay overnight at the karaoke box. In the past, it cost a lot to have a night out on the town, but renting a room in a karaoke box is now very affordable for high school students.

A study conducted by the Leisure Development Centre indicates that 63 per cent of young men aged 10 to 19 and 83 per cent of young women aged 10 to 19 visited a karaoke box at least once in 1997. The percentage of young women aged 10 to 19 who have been to a karaoke box is greater than the combined totals of those over 20 (Yoka kaihatsu sentā 2000). According to one of my students who works at a karaoke box, the majority of the customers there are junior and senior high schools students. They bring alcohol and cigarettes into the karaoke box. The staff at the karaoke box ignore their drinking and smoking for the sake of business. If they try to stop high school students from drinking and smoking, altercations may occur resulting in fights. This in turn will bring in the police who will charge both parties. The students will receive a warning and a juvenile record. The karaoke management will be fined and/or charged with other penalties for illegal activities. As a result, the reputation of the karaoke box will be tarnished, which, in turn, will precipitate a decrease in customers among the high school crowd.

As it was very easy for minors to purchase alcohol at stores and to drink at karaoke clubs, pubs and other clubs, the law governing this was changed in November 2000 increasing the punishment for such infractions. However, the law has had little effect on curbing behaviour and is not strongly enforced. Interviews with a few managers and owners of karaoke clubs in the spring of 2001 showed that they still serve alcohol to high school students if they are not wearing high school uniforms.

Suzuki Kenji, chief doctor in the Department of Psychiatry at the National Kurihama Hospital, which is famous for its treatment of alcoholism in Japan, conducted research on high school students' drinking behaviour in 1995 at two public high schools in the Tokyo and Kanagawa Prefectures. In his analysis he divided the students into three categories. Category 1 was the group of students who do not drink or drink only a few times a year. Category 2 was the group of students who drink more than several times a year. Category 3 was the group of students who drink more than once a week, or the heavy drinkers (Suzuki 1996: 22).

Among the high school boys, the percentage in category 1 was 39.5 per cent; that in category 2 was 35.7 per cent; and that in category 3 was 24.8 per cent. Among high school girls, category 1 contained 43.2 per cent, category 2 contained 42.7 per cent and category 3 contained 14.1 per cent. In category 3, the number of students who had part-time jobs was 74 per cent; the number who went to karaoke boxes often was 23.3 per cent; the number who sometimes went to karaoke boxes was 73.6 per cent; and the number who had never been to a karaoke box was 3.1 per cent. On the other hand, in category 1, the number who had part-time jobs was 37.4 per cent; 6.1 per cent went to a karaoke box very often; 64.3 per cent sometimes went to a karaoke box; and 29.6 per cent had never been to a karaoke box. In category 3, the frequency of having part-time jobs and going to karaoke boxes is significant.

Among high school girls in category 3, 85.4 per cent had a part-time job; 47.9 per cent went to karaoke boxes very often; 50 per cent sometimes went to a karaoke box; and 2.1 per cent had never been to a karaoke box. In category 1, 39.9 per cent had a part-time job; 3.4 per cent went to a karaoke box very often; 87.7 per cent went to a karaoke club sometimes; and 8.9 per cent had never been to a karaoke box (Suzuki 1996: 24). Suzuki thus established a relationship between the frequency of going to a karaoke box and the frequency of drinking alcohol among high school students, both boys and girls.

Convenience stores

The definition of a convenience store according to the MITI (Ministry of Trade and Industry) is an establishment which sells mainly food, has a floor-space not exceeding 250 square metres but more than 30 square metres, and operates more than fourteen hours a day. There were 23,837 convenience stores in 1991, and 39,627 in 1999. Among the latter, 25,919 or 60 per cent of them were open twenty-four hours a day. Stores classified as 'other supermarkets' by the MITI, which are in reality very similar to convenience stores, totalled 120,721 in 1997, a great increase from the 72,027 registered in 1991 (Tushō sangyō daizin kanbō chōsa tōkei bu 1997; 1999; 2000).

Convenience stores have become a way of life in Japan. Sometimes several competing stores are all situated on the same corner. At night, convenience stores become gathering places for young people. Some just sit on the floor, some eat snack food and some smoke. Generally, they are just hanging out. According to research done by the Federal Organisation of Convenience Stores, 5 per cent of customers are aged 15 and under, 47 per cent are between 16 and 25, 23 per cent between 36 and 45 and 6 per cent are aged 55 and over. Cashiers are required to punch in a code indicating the sex and estimated age of customers at checkout time. A student of mine who works at a convenience store says that most customers after midnight appear to be between the ages of 16 and 25.

Generally, students in their last year of junior high or in the second year of senior high school take a three- to four-day educational school trip. All students are expected to take part in the trip. Many junior high schools take their students to important historical places such as Kyoto and Nara, the former capitals of Japan in ancient times. Even in such historical surroundings the major activity in which students participate in their free time is to visit convenience stores to compare the items in that store with those they have back home, according to a junior high school teacher.

Young people are not only customers but also employees of convenience stores. The number of employees in convenience stores increased from 189,611 in 1991 to 406,490 in 1997. The number of employees at twenty-four-hour convenience stores was 300,504 in 1997 and had increased to 425,737 in 1999.

It is also very easy for minors to purchase alcohol at convenience stores. There are laws that prohibit young people under the age of 20 from drinking alcohol and smoking cigarettes. However, these laws are not strictly enforced in Japan. Although the laws prohibit people under 20 from smoking and drinking there are no provisions for punishment. Usually those who sell cigarettes or alcoholic beverages to minors or who force them to partake of these vices are prosecuted. Generally, around ten people per year are fined for this infraction. Additionally, there are vending machines everywhere that sell cigarettes and alcohol to anyone able to operate them and many minors purchase these products in this way. Although recent agreements have been established prohibiting the operation of vending machines from 11 p.m. to 5 a.m., many retail shops do not follow these agreements. One can also see high school students in school uniform smoking cigarettes in front of convenience stores.

The law governing the sale of alcohol to minors was changed in November 2000, increasing the punishment. However, as there is no custom of checking IDs at checkout counters in Japan, this law has never been seriously enforced, rendering it ineffective. I feel that this type of behaviour is symbolic of young people's increasingly adult-like behaviour. The gap between the behaviour of youth and that of adults is narrowing. The Research Institute of Public Health in the Ministry of Health, Welfare and Labour researched the smoking habits of high school students. Among high school boys, 24.7 per cent of first-year students (15–16 years old), 31.0 per cent of second-year students (16–17 years old) and 36.9 per cent of third-year students (17–18 years old) had smoked at least once in the previous thirty days, while 10.8 per cent of first-year students, 18.3 per cent of second-year students and 25.4 per cent of third-year students had smoked cigarettes daily during the previous thirty days. Among high school girls, 9.2 per cent of first-year students, 13.3 per cent of second-year students and 15.6 per cent of third-year students had smoked cigarettes at least once in the previous thirty days, while 2.4 per cent of first-year students, 4.5 per cent of second-year students and 7.1 per cent of third-year students had smoked cigarettes daily in previous thirty days (Osaki *et al.* 1996: 18–20). The number of youngsters who smoke has been increasing in Japan for several reasons, including the influence of advertisements and the incentive of smoking imported cigarettes from the United States (Ayukawa 2001: 224–227).

A staff writer on the *Asahi Newspaper* once described the scene at a convenience store in Kyoto. A young woman, 18 years old, visited this convenience store often. At 11:30 p.m., she could be seen chatting with a girl in senior high school and a girl who was a second-year student in a junior high school. She became acquainted with them at the convenience store and had in fact acquired thirty friends who were customers at this convenience store. At around 12:30 a.m., she and the two girls she had just met started to wander around the city. The girl had her small motorcycle and the other two girls had their bicycles. When they departed from the convenience store, they left behind their empty plastic drink bottles on the pavement in front of the store. After a while they returned to the store. The girl said that she usually goes home at 5 a.m. The reporter thus noted that convenience stores have become a place for the young to gather and socialise (*Asahi Shinbun* 30 September 2001). As we can now ascertain, the changes that are taking place in Japanese society, especially at night, are complex and diverse. Now, in the second part of this chapter, I will reflect on how these separate developments are interrelated and how they affect the everyday behaviour of Japanese youth in a more profound manner.

Changing attitudes

Junior and senior high school students must wear school uniform in Japan. However, many students oppose this rule saying that it deprives them of their freedom to choose to wear what they want and that it also symbolises the intrusion of school on their private lives. Then, with the revision of school rules fifteen years ago, only junior and senior high school girls could wear the girls' school uniform. Thus, the uniform became a symbol of their youth and privilege. Accordingly, high school girls began to customise their uniforms by shortening the skirts and wearing baggy leggings that cover their ankles and calves. High school girls also put on make-up in the trains after school and wear pierced earrings, both strictly prohibited in the school rules of just five years ago. My students tell me it is very difficult to distinguish high school students from college students when the high school students change into their private wear.

Hida Daijirō, a professor of sociology of education, conducted research at the same ten high schools in the same prefecture in 1979 and 1999. He questioned the students on what kinds of things the high school expends its energy on in counselling students. The percentage of students who think that the high school expends a lot of its energy on the enforcement of school rules was reduced from 55 per cent in 1979 to 39 per cent in 1999. This indicates that the deregulation of school rules is being promoted (Hida 2001: 21).

Many female students now wear their uniforms at game centres or when walking around in amusement areas late at night. In the past, police and adult watch-groups on the lookout for juvenile delinquency would instantly target them. Presently, very few people would dare to say anything to these young people. This indicates that the meaning ascribed to delinquency is transforming. However, there are still some areas where the police will pick up youths who are out late at night. The City of Hiroshima is one of them. In 1998, the Hiroshima police stopped and warned 1,992 young people about being out after midnight in amusement areas. However, as the definition of what constitutes delinquency becomes blurred, these warnings by police are becoming meaningless for the youths and are not at all altering their behaviour (compare the Hamilton case elaborated in Nottingham's contribution to this volume).

Do these changes also affect the youth's psyche? I will explore this question with reference to three issues: (1) individualism, (2) the erosion of cultural norms and (3) the reshaping of society's views of its youth.

Individualism

One of the main reasons leading to the previously described changes in youth behaviour is the current social trend towards individualism. People are no longer dependent on traditional groups or organisations, and, likewise, groups and organisations can no longer offer as many benefits or support facilities. The guarantees that were once in place are slowly eroding away leaving youths with the feeling that they can only depend on themselves.

According to the pattern variables of Talcott Parsons (1951), Japanese society has been defined as a group-oriented society. However, the power of the various groups to wield control or influence over their members has declined steadily in recent years. The ties within the family unit have likewise weakened. A short time ago, children were not only raised by their parents, but also by extended family members. Grandparents, aunts and uncles had considerable power over children and their behaviour. However, this strong influence now seems all but extinct. Many parents, devoted to their jobs and careers, no longer know what their children are doing. The quality time they used to spend with their children is now non-existent.

The notion that children have rights has taken hold in Japan. This has resulted in a loss of the high schools' and junior high schools' power to exert influence and control over children. If schools now try to apply school rules in an effort to stamp out minor offences or pre-delinquent problematic behaviour, they confront cries that the rules are an invasion of the child's privacy or right to free expression.

Previously, when young people graduated from school they applied for employment with a company that they liked and devoted their entire working lives to that company. In turn, especially in the case of a man, the company guaranteed lifetime employment. However, with the advent of the economic depression in 1992 (still a reality at the time of writing in 2002), the pressures of globalisation and the advancement of information technology, companies have been forced to restructure in order to stay competitive. This has led to the laying off of personnel and the complete erosion of the guarantee of lifetime employment. The permanency of the company in an individual's life has now fallen into the realm of a temporary relationship. Those companies that have been forced to change their ways are not just fringe companies in the economic network. Every company, large and small, has had to face the new reality; even a few of the largest banks in Japan have gone bankrupt. One major national department store and a few major supermarket chains faced financial ruin and are now out of business. Most national research institutes have been privatised. The national universities and the national postal service, which come under the umbrella of the Ministry of Education and the Ministry of Posts and Telecommunications – that is, national government agencies – will soon be privatised. The public telephone network, which has dominated the business and private lives of everyone in Japan, has been divided into regional companies. Young people, who have witnessed the laying off of middle-aged company workers and the restructuring of companies left and right, have been made very aware that the dreams that they were raised on are no longer a reality. The stability and reliability of companies and other organisations has eroded leaving young people to realise that the only thing that they can depend on is themselves.

Additionally, the notion of privacy has taken root in Japan. This notion of privacy was introduced into Japan by Western society after the end of the Second World War. However, the Japanese are still confused about what comes within the private sphere. A child's belief that it is their right to bar their parents from entering their room is seen as the child's right to privacy. Some adolescents even lock the door to their rooms when they are away. According to research conducted by the Council of Education in the Fukuoka Prefecture in 1996, pupils at elementary, junior and senior high schools spend the bulk of their free time at the weekend in their own rooms reading comics, playing computer games, listening to CDs, watching rental video movies or watching TV. They know how to entertain themselves and escape from the older generation in their own rooms. Very young children still sleep with their mother or parents in Japan. But by the age of 10, 80 per cent leave their parents' room to sleep in their own room or a room shared with siblings (Shinoda 1990: 49). Current standards dictate to parents that they must provide each of their children with their own private room. The belief is that a private room will assist parents in raising children who are unique, independent and self-reliant. However, once children get their own rooms, they sometimes claim the right to privacy and declare their private rooms off-limits to their parents.

Karl Taro Greenfeld, a Japanese–American who was born in Kobe in 1964, documented the life-style of a girl who returns home on the first train in the morning. The girl says of her father that 'he hadn't been in her [Keiko's] room since she had begun puberty, pointedly staying away – he didn't want to know about whatever it was young girls thought, felt or did' (Greenfeld 1994: 131). Even if parents wash and dry the child's clothes, in some households they are not permitted to enter the adolescent's room to place the clean clothes in the dresser. The child's rights have become stronger as the power of the parents has weakened. This has led to the creation of borders that were non-existent just fifteen years ago. With the advent of a child being given their own room, the behaviour of the child inside that room has increasingly become a secret from the parents. Parents are under the notion that when their child enters their private room, the child must be studying. Although this may be the case 10 per cent of the time, the reality is that most children are in their rooms playing video games, accessing the Internet, including the viewing of adult sex sites, or reading comics.

In society, family dynamics dictate that the children are dependent on their parents. Children are not expected to pay for their room and board, their clothes, their secondary or higher education or even, sometimes, the bills for their mobile phones. It is accepted that these expenses are the responsibility of the parents. Children nowadays feel it is their right to have their parents shoulder the burden of these expenses. They say it is only common sense. When it comes to commodities that children desire that fall outside of these categories, the children get part-time jobs, earn the money and purchase the commodities they want. They feel no obligation to share the pocket money they earn from part-time jobs with the family. It is their own private money to do with as they please and they decide how it will be spent. Focus is thus only on their individual needs, not the needs of the family.

A quarter of a century ago, many high school students and some junior high school students used to get up very early in the morning to deliver papers to earn money to pay for their high school tuition or for pocket money. The German word *Arbeit* has been incorporated into the Japanese language to mean part-time work. Yet, if these students wanted a part-time job, they had to get permission from the school. The school only permitted it when the job was considered proper for a student and when necessary to support the family. Working as a retail shop seller was not permitted. However, many students secretly entered into part-time jobs. With the revision of school regulations, schools now tacitly permit part-time jobs. Nowadays, many high school students have part-time jobs at fast-food outlets, convenience stores, family restaurants and retail shops. In order to keep overheads low, employers prefer to hire part-time help. When their jobs are finished for the day (usually around 10 p.m.), students are often invited to go drinking at a pub or singing at a karaoke box. Therefore, the job is the initiation of many high school students into nightlife.

Currently, parents expect children to study and do not place responsibility on them to contribute to the family income. Parents will pay for tuition, and in the event that they cannot, the social system will pay for it. Children are not expected to work in order to support the home. Young people take that for granted now and are no longer prepared to get up very early in the morning to deliver papers. At the same time, the decreasing number of children in the population as a whole makes it easier to enter university, and high school students are not required to study as hard as before. When students get a part-time job, they see it only as a very temporary thing, a means to get the money to purchase what they desire. Once their goal is met, they say goodbye to the job. They change jobs frequently because of the low pay and simplicity of the work.

In the 1950s and 1960s, many graduates from junior high schools in rural areas were transported to urban areas by what was called the '*shūdan shūshoku ressha*', or 'the trains that brought large groups of junior high school graduates to urban area companies for employment'. They would work for companies such as clothing, steel or machinery manufacturers. Many of these companies have now gone out of business or have scaled back their employment rosters. Only very highly skilled or manual labourers are needed nowadays. The manual labourers' jobs tend to be very strenuous and dirty. Japanese youths refuse to take these jobs, so the bulk of the jobs tend to be filled by foreigners, mainly second- and third-generation Japanese–Brazilians. They are diligent, hardworking people reminiscent of Japanese youth thirty years ago. These foreigners do not mind the hard work, the long hours or the dirtiness of their jobs. In contrast, Japanese youths would have, and have, given up these jobs after only a short period of time. They lack the stamina, patience and endurance for this type of work. In addition, because they have been raised in affluence, they are easily bored. They treat jobs just like their video games – good for a moment's pleasure and then easily cast aside.

Professor Mimizuka Hiroaki talks about '*kōsotsu mugyōsha sō*'. A *kōsotsu mugyōsha* is a person who does not go to university, college or any other school, and does not have a full-time job. Most work part-time, which means they are deprived of social insurance and medical benefits. Their jobs are very simple, such as cashiers at convenience stores, and they do not work at the same place for long. The percentage of *kōsotsu mugyōsha* among high school graduates was 4.7 per cent in 1992. Since then, it increased to 10 per cent in 2000. It is higher in large cities: for example, the percentage of *kōsotsu mugyōsha* among public high school graduates in Tokyo is 20 per cent (Mimizuka 2001: 5).

Not only has the number of high school graduates who do not seek full-time jobs increased, but also the number of youths who drop out of high school has recently exceeded 100,000 in one year. These individuals prefer to enjoy themselves in pursuing the pleasures of night-time entertainment without a care in the world for the future. Instant gratification is the name of the game.

Changing norms

In Japan, anyone over the age of 60 knows that young people were taught that masturbation was deviant behaviour. A great deal of shame was associated with masturbation. In particular, girls were viewed as not having any sexual desires. These views have recently undergone dramatic changes. Among young people, masturbation has taken on the fashionable term '*hitori-ecchi*' in Japanese and has gained acceptance by authorities in the field of sexual development as a natural thing to do. Young people are now encouraged to masturbate and often do so in the privacy of their own rooms. They no longer feel a sense of shame in masturbating. Young girls are now even proud to announce that they have the desire to masturbate and that they do masturbate. As young people have gained this newly found freedom to masturbate behind the closed doors of their own room without shame, they have also gained newly found freedoms in more advanced sexual behaviour outside of the home, away from the scrutiny of their parents. As explained previously, through the use of mobile phones, young people can now meet up with people that their parents would most likely disapprove of or forbid them from seeing if they were aware of such meetings. Changing cultural ideas, such as the notion of the right to privacy, afford young people this freedom. They meet up for friendship, companionship, sex or all of these. Rendezvous take place at love hotels (places where people go for sex for a two- to three-hour period or longer anytime of the day or night) or in their rooms at home when their parents are away.

According to research conducted by a study group responsible for sex education in elementary, junior and senior high schools in Tokyo, 12 per cent of the senior girls (students aged 17 to 18) in high school had had sexual intercourse in 1984, but this figure reached 37.8 per cent in 1999. Among boys in the same age group, 22 per cent had had sexual intercourse in 1984 while 39 per cent had done so in 1999 (*Mainichi Shinbun* 21 June 1999). This research shows that the sexual behaviour of girls has undergone a more drastic change than that of boys. According to statistics from the Ministry of Health, Welfare and Labour, the number of girls under the age of 20 who have had abortions has risen steadily for the last six years, from 26,117 in 1995 to 44,477 in 1999.

The advent of information technology has promoted a sense of freedom in young people in that they can enjoy more freedom of expression, independence and active social mobility at night. They can travel to places that their parents never dreamed of. One such place is an adult entertainment homepage on the Internet. Children, even in elementary school, can access these homepages with ease. Parents are anxious about this easy access to such pages but can do little to prevent it. There is no border distinguishing children from adults. In the world of anonymity, this symbolises that the borders in many areas of society have become ambiguous.

The government is now promoting deregulation in many areas of society. One such area is the length of time a business can remain open. In the past, most large-scale retail shops, department stores and supermarkets had to close by 6:30 p.m. With the advent of twenty-four-hour convenience stores, these retail shops and department stores can now remain open until 8 p.m. while supermarkets can remain open until 9 p.m. The notion that we are meant to work or study in the daytime and stay home at night is slowly disappearing. The border between day and night is thus also blurred.

For young Japanese women too, the domestic and social borders are disappearing. In the past, high school girls were expected not to wear make-up or use cosmetics. At the very least, they were expected not to wear heavy make-up or use expensive cosmetics like adults. If they did, they were expected to put them on at home. They now put on cosmetics in trains and subways in full view of other passengers. First they proceed with the application of foundation using powder puffs, then they apply eye shadow and lipstick, and next the heavy-duty equipment to curl the upper and lower eyelashes. What astonishes most middle-aged and older passengers is that these young girls sit directly on the floor of the train. This behaviour is unimaginable for many who feel that the border between what is clean and what is dirty is no longer commonly shared knowledge.

Just fifteen years ago, wearing make-up, piercing ears, wearing pierced earrings and dying hair were the litmus tests for what was and what was not delinquent behaviour. Nowadays, these tests are no longer applicable. Many girls as well as boys dye their hair and the wearing of pierced earrings is common among high school boys. There is no longer a clear border between what is and what is not delinquent behaviour.

Changing societal views of youth

To glean a definition of juvenile delinquency, I will turn to the statutes. A new juvenile statute was established in 1947 after the Second World War. According to this statute, there are three categories under which youths can be adjudicated at Juvenile Court (in Japan, the Juvenile Division of Family Court): (1) juveniles between the ages of 14 and 20 accused of criminal behaviour; (2) juveniles under the age of 14 accused of criminal behaviour; and (3) status offences, i.e. juveniles accused of pre-criminal behaviour. It is in category 3 where we can find a definition of juvenile delinquency. Here, there are four types of behaviour that are considered pre-criminal behaviour: (1) out-of-control youths who will not obey and cannot be controlled by their parents or guardians; (2) young people living apart from their families for no good reason such as in the case of 'disappearing from home'; (3) young people in the company of adults involved in criminal activity along with youths who frequent establishments that entice them into criminal and/or deviant activity; and (4) youths exhibiting behaviour deemed offensive or detrimental to the moral values of their own person and/or that of others.

Adolescents who display any of the behaviours listed in category 3 were previously considered juvenile delinquents. Society and the police were in complete agreement with category 3 and vigilantly policed youths for such crimes. In 1970, approximately 5,000 youths were sent to Juvenile Court for a status offence, but, in 1999, only 839 cases were considered. At first glance, it looks as though this law has been very effective in curtailing juvenile delinquency. However, upon closer inspection, one realises that this is not the case. Delinquent behaviour of this kind is on display everywhere, especially at night. The two tickets to freedom are the promotion of individualism, and the awareness and acceptance of children's rights. Category 3 of the juvenile statute has consequently been severely compromised. Society and the police no longer vigilantly police for these offences because society, at least, no longer views them as offences. In many instances, young people's night-time behaviour is seen as a rite of passage. More importantly, it is viewed as activity belonging to the youth's private sphere. With this redefinition of juvenile delinquency, we now have some idea of what it is *not*, but we are still not quite clear about what it *is*. This crucial redefinition is still in progress.

Conclusion

The results of the recent trends in society and the changes in youth night-time behaviour have led to major changes in relationships in Japan. In the past, there was stability and permanency in relationships. This was assured through a person's association with a group or an organisation. Lifetime employment at a company was one such pillar of stability. However, as companies and other groups and organisations have lost a great deal of their ability to hold segments of society together, relationships in society have become more fluid and temporary. On this level it can be appreciated that many of the above-mentioned developments in nightlife are interrelated. Young Japanese in particular seem to be entering a completely new world, where the old one has been dealt with and forgotten. How this will affect Japanese society as a whole remains to be seen.

Acknowledgements

I would like to express my greatest thanks to Professor Sanford Taborn who helped me challenge the frontier and make sense of the theme for people who do not know the Japanese way of life.

Notes

1   As the method of doing research has changed since 1995, it is impossible to compare the results prior to 1995 with those after 1995.
2   While some statistics show little change in the amount of sleep among young people between ages 15 and 24 (Sōmuchō tōkei kyoku, 1993; 1998), the research done by NHK is more precise and reliable.

3   As this activity became a social problem, regulations at the level of the prefecture were changed and a new law was established. Now, if a man receives sexual favours from a woman under 18 years old in exchange for money, he can be prosecuted. But it is estimated that most people go unpunished.

Bibliography

Books and articles

Ayukawa Jun (2001) 'The United States and Smoking Problems in Japan', in Joel Best (ed.) *How Claims Spread: Cross-National Diffusion of Social Problems*. New York: Aldine de Gruyter, 215–242.

Fujita Yasuhiro (2000) 'Keitai denwa to oyako no kizuna: puchi iede o tsūjite' (Mobile phones and the bond between child and parent: considerations of little disappearing from home), *Gekkan seito shidō* 30(12): 24–27.

Gaishoku sangyō sōgō chōsa kenkyū sentā (Institute for Research on the Food Service Industry) (2000) *Gaishoku sangyō tōkei shiryō shū* (Statistics on the food service industry 2000), Tōkyō.

Greenfeld, Karl Taro (1994) *Speed Tribes: Days and Nights with Japan's Next Generation*. New York: HarperCollins.

Hida Daijirō (2001) 'Kosei jūshi rinen, shin gakuryoku kan to itsudatsu tōsei kinō' (Principle of esteeming individual personality, new way of learning ability, and the function of control on deviance), *Seishōnen mondai* 48(7): 21.

Keisatsu chō (National Police Agency) (2000) *Keisatsu hakusho, Heisei 12 nen ban* (White Paper on Police 2000), Tōkyō.

Kon Isshō (2000) 'Keitai motte kigaru ni iede' (Disappearing from home is getting easy with mobile phone), *Sinchō* 45(April): 265–271.

Mimizuka Hiroaki (2001) 'Kōsotsu mugyōsha no Zenzō: Sono haikei to kadai' (Gradual increase of jobless among high school graduates), *Seishōnen mondai* 48(6): 4–7.

Mizutani Osamu (2000) 'Doraggu ni oboreru kanashiki jūdai' (Miserable teenagers devoted to drugs) *Sinchō* 45(April): 253–258.

Nakamura Isao (2001) 'Keitai denwa no fukyū katei to shakaiteki imi' (The spreading of mobile phone use and its social meaning), *Gendai no espuri* 405: 46–57.

Nakayama Ryōichi (2000) 'Bōtoka suru bōsō-zoku' (Hot-rodders who become mobs), *Gekkan shōnen ikusei* 45(12): 26–31.

NHK hōsō bunka kenkyū jo (NHK Broadcasting Culture Research Institute) (1991, 1996 edn) *Kokumin seikatsu jikan chōsa 1990, 1995* (Nationwide research on peoples' time use 1990, 1995), Tōkyō: Nippon hōsō shuppan kyōkai.

NHK hōsō bunka kenkyū jo (NHK Broadcasting Culture Research Institute) (2001 edn) *Dēta bukku: kokumin seikatsu jikan chōsa 2000* (Data book: nationwide research on peoples' time use 2000). Tōkyō: Nippon hōsō shuppan kyōkai.

Nikkei sangyō shōhi kenkyū jo (The Nikkei Institute for Research on Industry and Consumption) (1998) *Dēta de miru wakamono no genzai* (Present situation of youth seen through data). Tokyo: Nihonkeizai Shinbun-sha.

Nishiki Mitsue (2000) 'Osaka ni okeru shinyahaikai nado no hensen (1): Shōnen hodōshokuin no me o tōshite' (The change of night wandering and others in Osaka (1)– seen through memo by guiding personnel), *Gekkan shōnen ikusei* 45(12): 32–42.

Nishiki Mitsue (2001) 'Osaka ni okeru shinyahaikai nado no hensen (2): Shōnen hodōshokuin no me o tōshite' (The change of night wandering and others in Osaka (2) – seen through memo by guiding personnel), *Gekkan shōnen ikusei* 46(1): 34–41.

Osaki Yoneatsu *et al.* (1996) '1996 nendo miseinen-sha no kitsuen-kōdō ni kansuru zenkoku chōsa' (National survey on smoking behaviour among juveniles in 1996), *Kosei no shihyō* (Indexes on welfare) 46(13): 16–22.

Ozaki Sachi (2000) 'Osaka minami, Amerika mura, shihatsumade no fukei' (Osaka South, American village, scenery till the first train in the morning), *Gekkan shōnen ikusei* 45(12): 17–24.

Parsons, Talcott (1951) *Social System*. New York: The Free Press.

Sasaki Teruyoshi (2001) 'Keitai denwa no shoyū to seishōnen no komyunikēshon kōdō' (Possession of mobile phone and communication behaviour of youth), *Seishōnen mondai* 48(4): 30–36.

Shinoda Yūko (1990) 'Ko-suriipingu: shūshin keitai ni miru Nihon no kazoku zō' (Co-sleeping: the picture of families in Japan seen from sleeping arrangements), *Gendai no esupuri* 271: 40–50.

Sōmuchō seishōnen taisaku honbu (Management and Coordination Agency, Bureau for the Administration of Youth) (2000) *Seishōnen hakusho, Heisei 11 nendo ban* (White Paper on Youth 1999). Tōkyō: Ministry of Finance.

Sōmuchō tōkei kyoku (Management and Coordination Agency, Statistics Bureau) (1993) *Heisei 3 nen Shakai seikatsu kihon chōsa hōkoku* (1991 Survey on time use and leisure activities, Vols 1, 6, 7). Tōkyō: Nippon tōkei kyōkai.

Sōmuchō tōkei kyoku (Management and Coordination Agency, Statistics Bureau) (1998) *Heisei 8 nen shakai seikatsu kihon chōsa hōkoku, zenkoku seikatsu jikan hen* (1996 Survey on time use and leisure activities, Vol. 1, results for Japan, daily time allocation by sex, age and economic activities). Tōkyō: Nippon tōkei kyōkai.

Sōmuchō tōkei kyoku (Management and Coordination Agency, Statistics Bureau) (1998) *Heisei 8 nen shakai seikatsu kihon chōsa hōkoku, chiiki seikatsu jikan hen* (1996 Survey on time use and leisure activities, Vol. 3, time use by prefecture). Tōkyō: Nippon tōkei kyōkai.

Suzuki Kenji (1996) 'Kōkōsei no inshu to fasshon' (Drinking by high school students and fashion), *Seishōnen mondai* 43(12): 20–25.

Suzuki Rieko (1998) 'Chūkōsei ni hirogaru kakuseizai osen' (Diffusion of the usage of methamphetamines among junior and senior high school students), *Chuō kōron* 113(10): 142–158.

Tsushō sangyō daijin kanbō chōsa tōkei bu (The Ministry of International Trade and Industry, Bureau of Statistics) (1997) *Shōgyō tōkei hyō, Shōwa 60, Heisei 3, 6, 9 nen* (Statistics on Commerce 1985, 1991, 1994, 1997). Tokyo: Tūsan tōkei kyōkai.

Tsushō sangyō daijin kanbō chōsa tōkei bu (The Ministry of International Trade and Industry, Bureau of Statistics) (1999) *Shōgyō sokuhō, Heisei 3, 4, 11 nen* (Bulletin on Commerce, 1991, 1992, 1999). Tōkyō: Tsūsan sangyō chōsa kai.

Tsushō sangyō daizin kanbō chōsa tōkei bu (The Ministry of International Trade and Industry, Bureau of Statistics) (2000) *Wagakuni no shōgyō 2000* (Commerce in Japan 2000), Tōkyō.

Wakamono raifu sutairu shiryō shū henshū iinkai (The Editorial Committee for Data on Lifestyle of Youth) (1999 edn) *Wakamono raifu sutairu shiryō shū '99* (Data on lifestyle of youth 1999). Tōkyō: Shokuhin ryūtsu jōhō sentā (The Information Centre on Food Distribution).

Yoka kaihatsu sentā (Leisure Development Centre) (2000) *Rejā hakusho 2000* (White Paper on Leisure 2000), Tōkyō.

Yoshii Hiroaki (2001) 'Wakamono no keitaidenwa kōdō' (Behaviour of youth using mobile phones), *Gendai no esupuri* 405: 85–95.

Yūsei shō (The Ministry of Post and Telecommunications) (1998, 1999, 2000) *Tūshin hakusho, Heisei 10, 11, 12 nendo ban* (White Paper on Posts and Telecommunications 1998, 1999, 2000), Tōkyō.

Newspapers and magazines

Asahi Shinbun (Asahi Newspaper)
Mainichi Shinbun (Mainichi Newspaper)
Keizaikai (Business World)

9 Between day and night

Urban time schedules in Bombay
and other cities

Lodewijk Brunt

Under the pressure of globalisation local cultures are changing drastically, including local ways of dealing with time. Global standard time is expected to transform thoroughly the plurality of local time patterns. Based on specialised technology, humankind seems to be adopting a kind of 'world time', which, according to many experts, is a necessary condition for the foundation of a global network of communication and transportation and an important aspect of the globalisation process as such. In the lobbies of large hotels around the world, guests are able to determine their position on the global time scale by comparing local time with the time in London, New York, Tokyo or Delhi.

Apparently the world is being subjected to one singular yardstick for the measuring of time. But, in fact, we do not know much about the consequences that this will have for local ways of dealing with time. Our relationship to time appears to be linked quite organically and naturally to our daily lives, so much so that we find it hard, if not impossible, to imagine other people dealing with time in ways different than our own.

In this chapter I deal with time in cities, particularly with the relationship between day and night. I try to show the development of urban night-time in general, and especially the development as a consequence of lighting technology. Street lighting has enabled people to lead a nightlife, either working night shifts in factories and studios or having fun in night clubs and other entertainment facilities. Technological potential is moulded by (local) culture.

In some cities the night becomes almost completely 'colonised' by daytime activities extending into it, whereas other cities seem to accentuate the differences between day and night. In this chapter I point out various examples. In urban sociology we do not know much about the background of such arrangements; therefore, I will try to show some of the theoretical complexities involved. I am much inspired by the way time is organised in the Indian metropolis of Bombay from where many of my empirical examples originate. The lighting technology in this city is not only frail – leading to frequent power failures in different parts of the city and sometimes in the city as a whole – but also quite unevenly distributed. More than half of the total population lives in slums or on pavements, deprived of elementary facilities. The resulting situation is a badly balanced coexistence of different worlds and different living conditions. In this respect the city seems to have some kind of similarity to the nineteenth-century cities of Glasgow and Edinburgh, as depicted by Maver in this volume. I have been doing anthropological fieldwork in this city from the middle of the 1990s onwards, having lived in the northern suburb of Dahisar for almost half a year in 1996 and 1997, and returning to the city each succeeding year for shorter periods of about one month. Bombay is one of the largest cities in the world, with somewhere between 15 and 20 million inhabitants – and it is still growing rapidly. The city is an important anchor for the Indian economy as a whole, being the subcontinent's most important centre of commerce, industry, administration and culture. People are drawn to this huge conglomeration from all over India, hoping to find work and strike fortunes.

Time has been a central topic of interest in my study of cities, especially the ways in which ordinary people deal with time in everyday situations and how this is adapted to overall time patterns in the city as exemplified by public transportation schedules and opening and closing hours of shops and institutions. As a consequence of the complicated structure of the local economy in Bombay, for example, it is possible to find extremely different time schedules and also different interpretations of day and night. This has to do not only with the large heterogeneous population, but, in some respects, also with the technological base of the economy. The variations and differences are, however, held together by a polychronic time pattern (Brunt 1999). The flexibility of this pattern enables the mutual adaptation of widely differing experiences of time. Keeping this in mind, it is difficult to see the dawning of a new, uniform, global time pattern in the city.

Lighting

First, we will consider technology and its consequences for urban nightlife. In *The City as a Work of Art* (1986) Donald Olsen states that every city deserving of the name attends to certain basic functional requirements: a sewerage system, a network of roads and street lighting. In the modern sense of the word, however, street lighting is a relatively recent development, even in many Western countries (cf. also Maver in this volume). In this sense Olsen's remark is rather ahistorical, which is quite remarkable for a historian. Johann Pezzl, in his well-known sketches of eighteenth-century Vienna originally published in 1786 (partly reproduced in Robbins Landon 1991 and Rotenberg 1992), meticulously describes what takes place during a normal forty-eight-hour stretch in the city. In his famous *Skizze von Wien*, in which he tried to depict every aspect of life in Josephinian Vienna, he also devotes attention to the life at night. He sees Vienna as being subjected to utter darkness during the night hours. Modern urban lighting is what enables the introduction of shift work in different economic sectors, which leads to non-stop activities. At the same time, this gives rise to specialised forms of nightlife. In some urban neighbourhoods special facilities develop to meet the needs of those who make use of the night. On the one hand, there are coffee houses and restaurants for the shift workers, on the other, a world of entertainment emerges for the privileged sector of humanity, people who can afford to 'paint the night'. In Charles Dickens' *Sketches by Boz*, he depicts London nightlife in the 1830s. In his report on nightlife in the streets, Dickens draws attention to the people who have been to the theatre and are looking for a nice place to sit and relax after the show: 'and chops, kidneys, rabbits, oysters, stout, cigars, and "goes" innumerable are served up amidst a noise and confusion of smoking, running, knife-clattering, and waiter-chattering, perfectly indescribable' (Dickens 1957: 56). Henry Mayhew (1862), writing some years later, illustrates the relatively limited and more or less segregated character of this kind of nightlife. After the theatres and other establishments of fun and entertainment are closed, he writes, merely the homeless and destitute wander the urban night; they gather at benches in the parks, below bridges or near the refuse of the markets. Only at dawn do they again stir, when the rest of the city wakes up as well.

But gradually the endless specialisation of labour, so characteristic of cities during the day, begins to manifest itself in the night as well. The night is being colonised and increasingly utilised by vast categories of people. Much can be deduced from the diversity of services offered. In Budapest, for instance, many coffee houses are open day and night throughout the year. Some base their reputation on their special services offered at night. Around 1900, as the city grew into one of the most outstanding cultural centres of Europe, local specialties were available from 2 a.m. onwards. These places were full of people, not dining after the show, but eating the special 'hangover soup' before breakfast (Lukacs 1988: 150). Something similar can be found in the Amsterdam Nes, one of the outstanding amusement spots of the nineteenth-century city. Next to the night restaurant Bis-Nihil one could meet friends in Aal Biefstuk's, where day and night

> baked eel, sour eggs, marinated herrings, cutlets, and – with reference to the name of the place [Eel Steak] – steaks were being served, in heavy competition with *Oesterput* [Oysterpit], where this arrangement was topped not only by the display of oysters but also by the presence of a number of beautiful daughters helping out with the business.
>
> (Makken 1991: 59)

Schedules

No big city seems to be able to withdraw from this process of colonising the night, although there appear to be considerable differences between cities in the extent to which the process has advanced. Rotenberg's concept of the 'public time schedule' might be of some help in clarifying what is going on (Rotenberg 1992). Such a schedule results from many different forces, among which the government, companies, trade unions, schools and similar institutions, but also the specific urban culture and the history of the city, are involved. In general, the time schedules of individual urban inhabitants are subordinated to this overall arrangement. The public schedule of Vienna, for instance, has been thoroughly influenced by the Austrian central government, in which the specific history of

Vienna as an important administrative centre played a pivotal role. Since Pezzl's time, the separation of work and recreation has increased greatly, whereas work time has been transformed into one continuous daytime period in the framework of a five-day workweek. When added to the strict closing times of the shops, one arrives at the typical dualistic public schedule of Vienna with its very strict distinction between the domains of work and free time.

Such a tightly regulated public schedule can also be found in the Scottish city of Glasgow where I conducted research in 1998, although this city does not have an administrative background such as Vienna has, but, rather, an almost classical industrial one. Until quite recently most urban public facilities in Glasgow were closed somewhere between 10:30 and 11 p.m. – except for private clubs, taxis and certain night buses that were originally meant for shift workers in the shipping industry. In Glasgow, the owners of the big wharfs along the River Clyde were very influential in determining the public time schedule, especially in the second half of the nineteenth century and the first half of the twentieth century. Their interests often dictated the nature of other time schedules, for instance those of public transportation, public houses or public schools. Even in the years after the Second World War, when Britain was slowly being transformed into an economy with a five-day workweek, the shipping managers could freely decide on the resulting changes in time schedules. Representatives of trade unions were likely to complain about the discrepancy between working hours and the schedules of the public transportation on which they were dependent for reaching their workplaces on time, but the management were always confident of their capacity to adapt the schedules according to their own interests. The result was a 'co-ordinated time schedule', a complex of different schemes, more or less adapted to each other as a consequence of higher authorities who were able to force individual institutions to take into account the interests of the whole community.

The strict Glasgow scheduling presents a sharp contrast to urban life in cities such as Hong Kong, Singapore or Bombay, characterised mainly by an over-powering commercial orientation and small-scale industries, which function like 'incessant communities' (Melbin 1987: 7). Life seems to go on day and night and can hardly be categorised into clear-cut sectors of work and 'free time', i.e. time for recreation or consumption. Here you have 'correlated schedules'; they have no unifying underlying principle from which the individual time schedules can be inferred. In Hong Kong, for instance, Josephine Smart (1989: 57, 58) distinguished at least six 'shifts' for street hawking and markets: in the morning, shifts from 6 until 10 and from 9 until 12; in the afternoon, from 12 until 6 and especially from 3 until 6; in the evening and night, from 7 until 10 or later and from 10 until 2 or later. Apart from the hawkers found at every market selling foodstuffs, drinks and hot meals, concentrations of tailors and textile merchants can be found during the 'dawn markets'. At night, markets are mainly visited for dentists, herbal medicine specialists, palmists, fortune-tellers, writers, singers and artists.

Some cities such as Amsterdam could be said to find themselves on a continuum, moving rapidly from a relatively tightly scheduled city at the one pole towards the twenty-four-hour economy at the other. In the Netherlands a secular government has allowed the liberalisation of opening and closing hours for shops during weekdays as well as on Sundays. This flexible timing, which is an important addition to the growth of flexible working hours, has become quite popular and appears to satisfy the needs of a considerable portion of the city's relatively large population of single households (less than a quarter of the total population lives in 'traditional' households consisting of two parents and their children). It is perhaps to be expected that the Amsterdam public time schedule will move further away from a 'co-ordinated' one towards a 'correlated' one. Thus, although the extension of time, based on the elaboration of lighting technology, seems to be increasing on a worldwide scale, this does not necessarily always lead to a further colonisation of the night. As already mentioned, cities sometimes show considerable differences in their public time schedules. Moreover, these schedules are changing constantly (compare the situations depicted by Ayukawa and Nottingham, both in this volume).

To return to 'flexible' Amsterdam, the move towards a twenty-four-hour economy has been celebrated as an important step in the direction of the global economy. Yet, during the first decades of the twentieth century the city's public schedule seemed to be considerably more flexible than it is now. Recalling his youth in Amsterdam, the writer Maurits Dekker mentions the fact that the city became extremely 'dull' after the Second World War. 'The smaller Amsterdam of 1910', he writes, 'was less of a village than the bigger Amsterdam of 1950' (Dekker n.d.: 168). He continues:

> Even in the most out-lying streets of the suburbs some shops were open late at night, while there were still some old men waiting at the hairdresser's at 11 p.m. Hawkers pushed their carts with smoked fish in the shining of the gaslight and sellers of chestnuts walked about in the darkness with an oil lamp and a burning iron stove on their carts.
>
> (Dekker n.d.: 170)

From Dekker and his contemporaries one learns that in the old parts of the inner city there were numerous bakery cellars with non-stop activity during the night. This is where people who had been out and about could get fresh buns. In the Jewish district, Jodenbreestraat or Waterlooplein, there was ample opportunity to buy fresh fish eggs at 4 a.m. or to drink hot chocolate with the Jewish merchants on their way to the market. But you would find a fair number of evening and night markets as well, full of life. The best known is the Nieuwmarkt on Saturday nights. Dekker writes a long list of the things you would be able to get there, such as: fish and cigars, butter cake, cheese, sweets and herring, but also spiritual nourishment from the 'idealists' gathered around the Waag trying to get their message across. Dekker (n.d. 150, 151) writes: 'there were debates about heaven and hell, about politics and vegetarianism'. Members of the Salvation Army, freethinkers, abolitionists, anarchists and anti-militarists all tried to attract attention and sell their magazines. Therefore, it seems clear that the development of street lighting had no unifying or unilateral impact on city life in general. In some periods, nightlife appeared to blossom, whereas in later periods it became quite subdued – in the very same city.

Night and day

As a result of the great increase in free time after the Second World War, the 'colonisation of the night', as Melbin has called it, expanded to new dimensions – especially in Western cities. Nowadays, the night is no longer the exclusive domain of night-workers and nocturnal passion and romance seekers, but is used by a much broader segment of the population. In Amsterdam, nightlife appears to be moving again in the direction of the way it was during Dekker's youth. Urban lighting is constantly being improved and extended (Bowers 1998) and nightly facilities are becoming more common, not only in the area of entertainment, but also in urban public transportation, shopping and other services. Life is fastening its grip on both night 'time' and night 'space'. The distinction between night and day is diminishing most rapidly at the crossroads of transport systems, such as train stations, airports and taxi stands.

One of the features of Bombay nights I like best is the almost festive atmosphere one encounters when arriving at a railway station after dark. During my stay in Dahisar I often returned quite late from interviews, meetings or visits, but whatever the time there were always considerable numbers of people about in and around the small station. Hawkers were selling their goods and especially the sellers of perishable products like fruits or snacks were eager to attract the travellers' attention by shouts and demonstrations. All the time there was a continuous arrival and departure of buzzing auto rickshaws going on, the drivers manoeuvring their vehicles noisily through the narrow lanes which were packed with buyers and sellers, pedestrians on their way home or arriving at the station. After midnight many people were sleeping, but life went on, even in suburbs like Dahisar. In Jhabvala's beautiful short story 'An Experience of India' (Jhabvala 2000: 128) there are a few lines about the small town where the American woman, from whose perspective the story is told, spends the night. She is exhausted but finds it impossible to sleep in her hotel room because of the noise coming from the street. It was nearly midnight but all the shops were open, people were having a good time, talking and laughing, music was being played. In this particular case it is because the hotel appeared to be situated near a brothel, but generally speaking such a set-up is common for many areas in Bombay. Life often seems to go on day and night and one cannot help but wonder whether Indian people ever sleep.

Many times on my way home from the station in the night I watched cricket games being played near a street lantern where even very small boys participated or watched. I often visited the Muslim bakery halfway between the station and my compound. At one o'clock in the morning the bakers are resting, sitting around the store, smoking and listening to the music from an old radio. With the bread or cookies that I buy still warm, we exchange a few words about work or life in general. Next to the bakery the blacksmith is often still in the middle of some complicated task. Because his furnace is so hot, he often prefers to work at night. During my visit to the city in the early spring of 2002, I noticed that the bakery had disappeared. The blacksmith took over the premises. In the one or two slum areas that I have to pass, life always seems to be as busy as it is during the day: children running around, parties going on, lit-up roadside shops. Even those shopkeepers who have already cleaned and closed their shops are often sitting in the front, having conversations with other shopkeepers or passers-by. Many of them I know; we exchange pleasantries or simple greetings before I enter my compound. No matter how exhausted I am sometimes upon returning home after a long day of seeing people and travelling around in the merciless Bombay heat, I am usually revitalised once I arrive at the railway station and walk home through the night. As the noise of human laughter, shouting and talking dies down and the traffic on the streets vastly diminishes, other sounds become more prominent. From my nights in Dahisar I also vividly remember the excited howling of the packs of wild dogs that have chosen the empty site next to my compound as their home base. All these examples are reminders of the fact that, in many ways, Bombay can be considered a city that never sleeps, a qualification proudly used by many Bombay natives themselves. The thought often strikes me that the city would even have a busy nightlife without any modern street lighting, whereas I find it quite easy to imagine a perfectly still and quiet Amsterdam, Vienna or Glasgow at night.

Nightlife

In many cities nightly entertainment centres add to the excitement of city life for the local population and, of course, for the visitors from elsewhere whose experiences form a substantial part of a city's reputation. Many city guidebooks have special chapters dedicated to such places. For example, the *Instant Guide to New York*, which is in front of me while I write these words, mentions ten or so 'nightspots' in Greenwich Village. They are indicated on a detailed map of the area and their names vary from Bitter End to Sweet Basil or Knickerbocker Saloon. We should not be too surprised if some of these nightspots no longer exist, because they rely greatly on the trendsetters' ever-changing taste.

In contemporary Bombay, around midnight the 'young and beautiful' can be found at places like Bachelor's, conveniently situated on Marine Drive where many people pass by on their way home from the theatre or the cinema. One simply parks somewhere near the place to be served. Some people stay inside their cars, but many get out and meet others who are standing around. On hearing the shouting and the animated discussion, outsiders might think some kind of riot is going on, but in fact the atmosphere is friendly and 'cool'. It is a great place to observe and to be observed and, owing to the fact that one can only arrive there by private car (or taxi), one is sure to be 'in closed company'. Bachelor's is famous for its ice creams in a rich variety of flavours and its huge assortment of fruit drinks. Although the entire establishment is not much more than a small workbench on the sidewalk, during the latter half of the 1990s the place was packed night after night. (It is very typical of Bombay's dynamic economic atmosphere to make something out of nothing.) Other quite similar establishments, such as Bharat Juice near Chowpatty Beach and Haji Ali Juice at the entrance of the Haji Ali Mosque, have also sprung up in other parts of the city.

In recent years, so-called 'ladies' bars' or 'beer bars' have become quite popular as city nightspots, although not to everybody's pleasure, and probably for a completely different kind of public than is to be found at the above-mentioned establishments. Representatives of the Bombay municipality and the local police have declared time and again that these bars have a sleazy character. Their message seems to be that no upright citizen would even think of entering such a place. During my fieldwork in the city, some people told me about the ladies' bars and urged me to go and visit them. Although I gladly went along with some informants, I sometimes suspected that I was providing a welcome cover. What nobler reason could one have to visit notorious spots than the necessity of accompanying a naive stranger? The things that go on in there are supposed to be a slap in the face of Indian culture and – despite the name – decent people would consider them extremely degrading for women.

What actually does go on in a ladies' bar? I must admit that my own experience is quite limited. The interiors of the bars I visited looked somewhat like theatres, with small stages in front. The seats for the audience resemble two-seater school benches, including the table in front. These are a type of private cubicle and from one's own seat it is difficult to observe the other members of the audience or the things they are doing, except of course the person directly opposite, but it is possible to choose your own seating. My impression is that many visitors do, actually, seat themselves. The table in front is not meant for writing but for putting down drinks and to confine the audience to its seats. These bars mainly serve bottles of beer. The exclusively male waiters standing in every corner of the bar provide never-ending full bottles. On stage a number of girls dance. The music is so loud that all communication must occur through gestures. The girls are neatly dressed in nice and colourful saris and nothing sleazy seems to be going on at all. It takes a while before one understands what the purpose of being here could be. Despite the deafening music, something is going on between the dancers and the exclusively male audience. Only the girls are in the spotlight; the audience, the bar and the large number of waiters standing around are nearly in the dark. The men in the audience are supposed to attract the girls' interest through eye contact. As soon as this contact takes place, the girl, by smiling and accentuating her body while dancing, gives the impression of dancing exclusively for the one who has made contact. She highlights this by dancing towards his table in order to pick up her reward in the form of some cash. Of course other men try to 'steal' her away from this symbolic bond by trying to divert her attention and, possibly, offering more cash. As far as my experience goes, no yelling or shouting goes on, which would be senseless anyway because of the volume of the music. About all that takes place is intense gazing and ogling. The audience is not allowed to touch the girls or to leave their seats for any purpose other than to go to the toilet.

The ladies' bars remind me of what I have read about the so-called 'taxi dance halls' which used to be quite popular (and equally despised by upright citizens) in American cities during the 1920s and 1930s. These were halls in which one could buy a ticket for a couple of minutes' worth of dancing with one of the girls employed by the owner. Both the girls and their customers were from recent groups of immigrants; the dance halls offered an opportunity to meet with members of the opposite sex, however brazenly commercial and vicious that may have seemed to outsiders. As in the case of the taxi dance halls, the ladies' bars are very much associated with illicit sexuality and prostitution. If this were true, however, it completely escaped my attention. To the degree that these ladies' bars can be considered a facility for the many young (male) migrants who continue to flock to the city, it would certainly seem likely, though, for prostitution to be an integral part of them. It is also quite interesting that one of the few forms of commercial nightly entertainment in the city is quite specific as far as the customers are concerned. This underscores the exclusive and segregated nature of Bombay nightlife, a point that is made somewhat more explicit later in this chapter.

Bohemian nights

The development of this sort of nightlife in general can be distilled in detail from Seigel's fascinating study of the Parisian *bohème* (Seigel 1987). During the Third Republic, the concept of the *bohème* called forth images of the numerous coffee houses and cabarets in Montmartre, especially the Momus café that was frequented by Henry Murger and his friends, and somewhat later the equally (in)famous Chat Noir or Le Mirliton. People who go there are looking for a mixture of sensuality, metaphysical inspiration and vague political passions. Here one is able to express the kind of feelings that have to be suppressed in an ordinary, civilised existence. This 'romantic' nightlife, where the extremes of society meet, climaxed in the 1920s. The Berlin nights, manifested in and around the many small cabarets and 'Kneipen', have been immortalised by designs and impressions made by artists such as George Gross and the songs performed by Marlene Dietrich (Jelavich 1990). The nights of Paris have been equally immortalised by the French–Hungarian photographer Brassaï (1976), as were the New York City nights by Weegee (1996). Urban nightlife of this historical period was also popularised in numerous songs composed by the likes of Cole Porter and George Gershwin. In Amsterdam, the local *bohème* was established in havens such as De Uilenkelder or Het Honk, as Maurits Dekker described in hindsight: 'In addition to drinking rivers of Stout and eating massive quantities of cheese with mustard and performing plays, in which the actors went on stage with toilet seats around their necks', he recalls, 'people did sometimes dream about strange "political actions"' (Dekker n.d.: 104–105) The visitors were poets, playwrights, academics, students and musicians. And sometimes a wealthy nobleman turned up who was offered ample opportunity to read his poetry, as long as he continued to buy enough champagne to keep his audience happy (Decker n.d.: 114–115).

In the same period, artists were conceiving alternative notions of time. The new 'aesthetics of time', according to film-maker Sergei Eisenstein, was expressed in modern poetry, cubism, jazz and modern design and architecture in general. In Eisenstein's words:

> The modern image of the city, especially the nightly metropolis, forms the physical equivalent of jazz music. The nocturnal sea of electric advertisements is undermining every feeling for perspective or true realism. ... The headlights of passing cars, the lights above the gliding rails and the glittering reflections on the wet surface of the streets – all of this is being reflected in the shiny rainwater on the ground and while we are quickly moving forward between these worlds of electric signals, we don't see them on the same level anymore, but as different wings of a theatre that hangs in the air and through which the nightly flood of traffic lights is flowing.
>
> (Quoted in Boyer 1994: 50)

Following Rotenberg (1992) we could perhaps consider this period of the romantic urban night as a transitory phase between a pre-industrial and industrial economy. The atmosphere from this period is, perhaps somewhat watered down, still to be found in tourist 'hot spots' such as ski resorts, spas and pleasure centres at the seaside. These places for spending free time have been aptly called 'spaces in the margin' (Shields 1991). These are localities of a peripheral nature, at the border of respectable society. Here people are able – for a time – to 'let it all hang out', to indulge in alcohol, drugs and sex and all sorts of behaviour that is considered uncivilised under 'normal' conditions. Shields uses the English seaside resort of Brighton as an example of such places, but it would be easy to add other examples, for instance the American gambling resorts of Reno and Las Vegas, or their Asian counterpart, Macau. Another feature of these spots is their non-stop character; the difference between day and night has ceased to have any relevance here and, consequently, is hardly perceived at all. As far as I can tell, the 'border sector' in Bombay nightlife is still limited and has not developed into the kind of entertainment industry one finds in some Western cities – although the Bombay red-light district is quite extensive.

Evening raga

We must not confuse general, mainly Western developments with local ones in other parts of the world. Olsen's previously cited remark about cities providing street lighting for its inhabitants is not only ahistorical, but rather ethnocentric as well. In Bombay, the development of street lighting took place in the same period as in many parts of imperial Britain, but the context was very different. The romantic nightlife that took place in cities such as Berlin or Paris or New

York in the early decades of the twentieth century hardly existed in Bombay or was strictly confined to particular groups or people. Consequently, in contrast to what we saw earlier for Western cities, the urban night in Indian cities has had an overwhelmingly private, segregated character. As we have seen above in connection with the ladies' bars, this segregated nature still seems to be a central feature today. Wealthy Indian or Parsi families entertained their guests in their own 'salons' and organised elegant evenings of (Indian) dance and music at home, where sometimes a few Europeans were also invited. Examples are to be found in Gita Mehta's novel *Raj*, which takes place in Calcutta rather than Bombay, although these cities are very similar in this particular respect. The main character of the novel is Jaya Singh, wife of the Maharajah of Sirpur, the most prestigious of the Indian kingdoms. In the period between the world wars she has irregular but intense contact with members of the Indian nationalist movement. One evening she is invited to the house of Mrs Roy, her former English teacher. There is some kind of soirée going on and Jaya meets not only her host but also people such as Rabindranath Tagore, Motilal Nehru, Sarojini Naidu and Annie Besant. After having been introduced to the guests by Mrs Naidu, Jaya joins the relaxed gathering in discussing the political situation. At a certain moment Mrs Naidu exclaims that the evening is too beautiful to just discuss politics. She says: 'Come, let's sit in the Music Room and listen to an evening raga.' While Jaya is hanging somewhat back, the musicians are busy tuning their instruments.

> Incense spiralled toward the musician's platform. Jaya watched Mrs Naidu lean back against a bolster cushion, her eyes closed in pleasure as she listened to the Raga Durbari, the evening raga of the king. Beside her, the poet brushed his white beard with his long fingers and smiled at the Angrez woman.
>
> (Mehta 1989: 243, 244)

This privatised kind of nightlife, where socially segregated communities are entertained in isolation from the rest of society, has not yet disappeared altogether from contemporary India.

Jhabvala (2000) gives an overview of the way a Westernised Indian woman is supposed to express her station in life socially. Typically, she has studied in Oxford or Cambridge or some ivy-league American college, just like her father had done. She speaks flawless colloquial English and has a degree in economics or English literature. Her parents have always had a Western life-style, with a preference for Western food and an admiration for Western culture. She herself thinks one should be more Indian in outlook, which motivates her to wear hand-loomed saris and be interested in classical Indian music and dance. Jhabvala (2000: 16) says:

> If she is rich enough she will ... hold delicious parties on her lawn on summer nights. All her friends are there – and she has so many, both Indian

and European, all interesting people – and trays of iced drinks are carried around by servants in uniform and there is intelligent conversation and there is a superbly arranged buffet supper and more intelligent conversation, and then the crown of the evening: a famous Indian maestro performing on the sitar.

In many respects this could have taken place seventy or a hundred years before. Jhabvala continues:

> The guests recline on carpets and cushions on the lawn. The sky sparkles with stars and the languid summer air is fragrant with jasmine. There are many pretty girls reclining against bolsters; their faces are melancholy, for the music is stirring their hearts, and sometimes they sigh with yearning and happiness and look down at their pretty toes (adorned with a tiny silver toe ring) peeping out from under the sari.

Jhabvala aptly concludes: 'Here is Indian life and culture at its highest and best.'

In line with the privatised and segregated nature of Indian colonial society, British officials had their own clubs and societies where, normally speaking, Indian people would not be welcome. In *Raj*, Jaya Singh is travelling to Calcutta with her friend and chaperone Lady Modi – appointed by Jaya's husband to introduce his traditional wife to the 'ways of the [Western] world'. As they drive through the city, Lady Modi explains what they see. Pointing out some dark-skinned women in European clothes she remarks:

> Anglo-Indian girls, darling. Fathered by Englishmen working on upcountry tea estates. Of course, those same Englishmen are more discreet in Calcutta. At night they go to the brothels on Cryer Street, and in the daytime they drink at the Bengal Club or Calcutta Club – two of the many clubs in Calcutta with signs saying 'Dogs and Indians not allowed'.
>
> (Mehta 1989: 231)

Public life was heavily coloured by the political situation of the British colonial authorities being fiercely attacked by the freedom movement. Of course there have always been exceptions to the rule. In the same novel, Jaya and Lady Modi meet a common friend in a restaurant containing

> a high-ceilinged room reproduced in the fourteen-foot-high mirrors hanging on the walls. An orchestra dressed in white tailcoats was playing dance tunes that Jaya recognised from Lady Modi's collection, and a Christmas tree threw coloured lights onto the wooden dance floor. Indians and Englishmen leaned forward with unselfconscious ease to make themselves heard over the music. Jaya could not believe that only three hundred yards away British clubs carried signs saying DOGS AND INDIANS NOT ALLOWED.
>
> (Mehta 1989: 238; capitals in the original)

When we discuss recent times, we must mention that apart from the privatised and segregated nature of urban nightlife, the application of electricity and street lighting is lagging behind other developments, especially population growth. The facilities available, deemed so elementary by Olsen, are unevenly distributed throughout the city's population. Although many Bombayites are proud of the city's 'golden necklace', the well-lighted strip of skyscrapers in the south of the city that forms a semi-circle along the coast of the Arabian Sea (of which Marine Drive is an integral part), only a small percentage of the population is able actually to enjoy this. More than half of the inhabitants of the city live in slums or on the pavements of the street, far removed from the luxurious dwellings along the coastline. Only a minority of these slum-dwellers and homeless have access to electricity, or other public facilities such as fresh drinking water and sewerage. Many slum areas, with their narrow lanes with scant space for two people to pass by each other, are practically always dark, even during the day. For outsiders it is not easy to imagine what these places look like at night. In order to be able simply to observe their environment, people have to steal electricity, make (dangerous) fires or rely on oil lamps or (expensive) generators. Although some posh neighbourhoods can be characterised as oceans of light in which people can bathe themselves, the most densely populated and extended areas could be called worlds of darkness. At night, travelling by train through extensive neighbourhoods of slum dwellings, one does occasionally observe a fire burning between some huts and a sharp eye could perhaps detect a shimmering light shining through the rudimentary roofs or walls of individual structures. However, as mentioned previously, many parts of Bombay's slums already seem to feature eternal darkness. Sharma (2000: 103, 104) describes some of the narrow lanes of Dharavi, Bombay's largest slum area, as frightening. 'If there is a hell', she writes, 'you will find it … where primitive foundries fashion brass buckles for leather belts and bags.' She walks down a lane that is barely 3 feet (0.9m) wide, sided with 'dark, soot-covered rooms, 8 feet by 6 feet, the hell-holes that are integral to the buckle trade. … Through the haze you can see figures, young men who are working using a medieval method to forge buckles out of molten brass.' In general, however, the million or so inhabitants of this slum must live in constant semi-darkness. 'There is hardly any natural light in the lanes separating rows of houses', Sharma says, emphasising a situation that is well known to anyone who has walked around in the area (2000: 131, 132). The reason is obvious: namely 'because people have built lofts that extend upwards and outwards and almost touch the loft on the opposite side' (Sharma 2000: 132).

A similar condition is highlighted in a realistic way in one of Anita Desai's novels, *The Village by the Sea*, where the young Hari decides to give up life in the poor fishing and farming village of Thul and run away to Bombay to start a new life – leaving behind his three sisters, his sick mother and his father, who is an habitual drunkard. Hari finds a job at a roadside eatery where he has to clean the tables, serve the customers and run errands, almost day and night. He sleeps somewhere in a little neighbouring park, but in the rainy season he has to sleep inside the tiny, oppressively hot and stinking eatery. During this time, however, he falls ill and his boss, Jagu, offers to take him home. The house appears to be situated in a slum.

> There were not enough houses or flats in the city for the millions of people who came to work in it and earn a living in it, and since there were not enough, the rents of even the smallest flats were too high for people like Jagu. He counted himself lucky to be able to rent a shack in a 'zopadpatti'. These shacks clung to the side of a hill by the sea. ... On the boulevard side of the hill the houses had been large and tall, pink and green and yellow, with names like Sunshine and Seagull, in which the rich people lived. On the other side of the hill were the shacks of the poor, tumbling downhill into an open drain and a busy road. As Hari followed Jagu along a narrow path, he felt his feet slipping in the soft mud. The whole hill seemed to be turning into mud. The shacks seemed to be coming loose and sliding into the gutter that separated the zopadpatti from the street.
>
> (Desai 1982: 15)

Desai's description may perhaps seem overdone to some readers, but it is not. During each Bombay monsoon many people are made homeless or even die as a consequence of serious landslides in which sometimes hundreds of huts and shacks are swept away. After a dangerous descent Hari and his boss arrive at the latter's dwelling.

> Several pairs of eyes peered at him from under the rags they held over their heads to keep off the rain from the leaking roof. It was very dark inside although there had been a faint glow outside from the street lamps across the gutter.
>
> (Desai 1982: 116)

Apart from the unequal distribution of elementary facilities, Bombay also suffers from frequent power failures. This too makes for urban nights which are far more erratic, insecure and perhaps adventurous than comparable nights in many (wealthy) Western cities. This condition puts Olsen's remark about the elementary nature of urban street lighting in a peculiar perspective. Bombay does provide for street lighting, as do many other cities, but not for all its inhabitants. Excluded are, mainly, particular neighbourhoods in the northern and north-eastern parts – the suburbs where many of the recent middle-class or lower-middle-class immigrants live, areas which are avoided by the rich and the powerful. As already mentioned, during a period of about six months between the end of 1996 and the first half of 1997 I lived in such a suburb. This was Dahisar, on the northernmost administrative border of Bombay municipality proper. In December 2000 I was visiting a good friend and excellent informant, Sunil Nimbalkar, and his wife Neela, who live in Nalla Sopara. This is even beyond Dahisar, and part of what is administratively called 'Greater Bombay'. Nalla Sopara can be found at what is nearly the north-western border of Greater

Bombay at a distance of some 60 kilometres from the lush nightspots along Marine Drive. This is what I wrote in my diary on the day after the visit:

> Nalla Sopara is a horrible place, where even the roads have not been properly levelled. It consists of hastily assembled compounds without the least ornamentation – despite the fact that the area has a famous past, according to Sunil. He himself is living in one of the first compounds that were constructed some eight years ago. From the windows of his apartment at the western side he could see the railway tracks where all the local and interlocal trains go by. At the eastern side he had a free view of the hills that enclose the city of Thana at the northernmost part of the bay from which Bombay derives her name. All this has disappeared behind rows of high-rise flats. His compound is now surrounded by a fast growing part of the city. I would become extremely sad if I were forced to live here, and I know Sunil is desperate to get away from here as well. The whole infrastructure is miserable. Water is provided for just a few minutes a day and there are power failures on a daily basis, sometimes lasting for days on end. Especially in the blazing heat of the Bombay area this leads to nasty conditions. It is impossible to open the windows in view of the mosquitoes, and of course one cannot use electric fans. One must feel like one had been put into a boiling prison. During my very visit a power failure occurred. Although this lasted for not much longer than an hour, I was instantly reminded of the many times I had felt like such a prisoner.

Although insecurity about basic facilities is concentrated in the suburbs where the large majority of Bombay's inhabitants live, sometimes the entire city is reminded of the frailty of its technological basis.

Against this background, what should we make of Olsen's conviction that street lighting is to be considered a prime facility of any city? Should Bombay be considered as not a 'real' city because it is unable to provide for this basic need? At least once during my stay between December 1996 and June 1997 I witnessed a power failure that hit the entire city, lasting from about 9 p.m. until well into the early hours of the following morning. I was just entering Churchgate Station, the starting point for the local trains that run between the southern Fort Area of the city and the northernmost local railway station of Virar, which is even beyond Nalla Sopara. Suddenly the entire city was flooded in complete darkness, except for the headlights of cars and buses and the oil lamps and gas lighting of hawkers' outlets along the streets. All the trains had come to a halt at whatever part of the track they were situated, and consequently no single train could leave Churchgate Station. It was a matter of minutes before the gigantic platforms of the station were absolutely packed with people not knowing what to do except wait for the trains to resume their normal courses again. There was a lot of speculation about the seriousness of the power situation among the passengers and, in general, one could see the well-known signs of what happens when complete strangers are suddenly transformed into co-victims of a particular inconvenience. People started having conversations, borrowed each other's mobile phones to inform the family at home and told each other stories about corresponding circumstances they had found themselves in before. After about one and a half hours the trains started moving again, despite the fact that the city as a whole was still covered in darkness. At each station that we passed on our way north we could observe similar situations, platforms that were packed with people waiting to continue their journey. In between the stations the city was hardly noticeable, except by the lights of vehicles at railway crossings, the occasional campfires along the tracks where people were cooking their meals or faint lights from candles in the windows of far-away apartment complexes. Because one is well aware of the many millions of people somewhere 'out there' there is a feeling that the city, which is normally thriving and humming with energy, has suddenly been transformed into a ghost town. As a consequence of the special circumstances and the resulting feeling of togetherness some people on the train were singing songs accompanied by drumming and the tones of a sarangi. All this gave rise to a truly remarkable atmosphere. When I finally arrived at Dahisar Station, my destination, it was well past midnight. As usual I walked home trusting that I would be able to find my way quite easily in the dark. That's what I actually succeeded in doing, although I felt compelled to walk in the middle of the road as often as possible fearing that otherwise I would perhaps trip over sleeping people or heaps of garbage on the sidewalk. By far the most difficult task I had to perform was to open the lock of the gate to the compound and the three odd locks on my front door in the pitch-dark staircase of the building where I lived. Once inside my small flat, the choking heat could not be driven away by any fans, of course, and I had to feel my way around with my fingertips to locate a box of matches and some candles. Over the course of the night the power was returned and the city was on its feet again. It is obvious that some cities have difficulty providing adequate lighting and other facilities. This does not deny their urban nature, although it does lead to complicated patterns of time and makes for a staggering sort of colonising of the night.

Kinds of cities; kinds of time

In trying to show the development of the urban night it might be of help to compare cities on the basis of how they could be situated along a continuum, although this does not necessarily explain what is going on. In Rotenberg's view the economic background of a city shapes its time schedule. Administrative cities could be characterised as 9-till-5 cities, whereas harbour cities tend to have a twenty-four-hour model. But most cities cannot be so easily categorised as one might perhaps think on the basis of Rotenberg's analysis of the Vienna case. How would Bombay fit into Rotenberg's scheme? Bombay, for example, is a conglomerate of many different cities. It used to be called the 'Manchester' of the East because of its important cotton industry. Only since the final years of the 1980s, after the longest industrial strike in history, has this sector's prominent position in the city's economy been greatly reduced. But Bombay has always been – and still is – a first-class harbour city as well. Apart from being an industrial centre and a harbour, Bombay must also be considered a prime administrative centre, being the seat of both the government of the state of Maharashtra and the extensive Bombay Municipal Corporation. Both administrations employ many tens of thousands of people. The city, moreover, is by far the most important globalised centre of India, where all the central banks, insurance companies, advertising agencies, computer industries and financial institutions are concentrated. And Bombay is also an outstanding cultural and artistic city: in the film industry of Bollywood alone, the number of films being produced easily exceeds that of any other film centre in the world. And also not to be forgotten is that the city also has India's largest service sector. It would seem that Rotenberg's dimensions are much too simplified to encompass Bombay's nature.

The city's economic base is extremely diversified not only in terms of the kinds of activities but also on the basis of the kinds of energy being used. In addition to the industrial sector with its heavy machinery and the post-industrial corporate sector that depend on electricity and computers, one finds a substantial, predominantly informal 'pre-industrial' sector where energy is mainly derived from the power of the human and the animal body. Perhaps several sectors of the city have some kind of a 9-till-5 schedule, especially foreign agencies and international corporations, but the time schedules of other sectors are quite different. Correspondingly, the meaning of work time and free time varies greatly in different sectors and, as a consequence, people likewise have varying notions about day and night. The world of artisans and small home-based industries is governed not by the clock but by the tasks that have to be accomplished. Time is different from money; time is flexible. Consequently, in Bombay very different time worlds coexist in one single space. As Ramesh Kumar Biswas remarks, just beneath the surface of Bombay urban life one can observe a world containing different rhythms and each of these rhythms is linked to varying historical periods: British colonial time, the time of the Moghuls, a traditional era and our own modern time. In Bombay, according to Biswas, time is manifested in a series of realities, myths and ghosts.

> Look beyond the surface and you will discover a city here that runs on different rhythms and, though young, incorporates several eras in it: colonial, traditional and modern. … A city where the ticking of the wristwatch is overlaid with the beat of archaic drums, different 'tablas'. Any cheap Bombay calendar bought on the street would illustrate, with its intricate overlapping of Vedic, Gregorian, Buddhist and Islamic cycles, the complexity of simultaneous existences that a Bombay resident lives through every day.
>
> (Biswas 2000: 54)

The author distinguishes ten different kinds of time. Among them the time of languages – for instance, in Sanskrit (and contemporary Hindi as well) the words for yesterday and tomorrow are identical, as are the words for the day before yesterday and the day after tomorrow – the epic time, the time of the sun, the cosmic time and the time of the Internet. One can only understand what is really going on in the city if one is able to distinguish between these forms of time, says Biswas. Perhaps he is right. The juxtaposition of different forms of time does not imply that these are adapted to each other or that they are in any way harmoniously integrated. In other words, the different schedules Biswas is speaking about are correlated, not necessarily co-ordinated.

One would be able to find co-ordinated schedules in Dutch society. Despite becoming more flexible in recent years, most opening and closing times are regulated and have been mutually adapted: generally speaking there are no sharp conflicting interests between schools, factories and shops concerning their times of opening and closing. In the country as a whole there is even a co-ordinated holiday period for all of these institutions in order to permit the even spread of holidays among each region. In the Dutch consensus democracy, a considerable number of concerned parties have been involved with such efforts at co-ordination: not only political parties but trade unions, industrialists, consumer organisations, school boards, parents' associations and others. As the basis for this, one can detect a clear and simple worldview: in the daytime people are working or attending school, at night people ought to sleep and during the evenings people watch TV or go out to be entertained and have fun. During the weekend, stretching from late Friday afternoon until Monday morning, people do as they like; they are free and they can take a rest, whether motivated by religious beliefs or not. Compared with this orderly existence, life in Bombay often seems to be chaotic and unpredictable, not least by the unreliability of the public facilities. Therefore, entirely new theoretical concepts seem necessary in order to grasp Bombay's complex, many-layered condition.

Conclusion: between day and night in Bombay

Living in my flat in Dahisar I had to get up at about 6:30 a.m. at the latest to get water. The water pressure never started at exactly the same time and I had to avoid the risk of missing the daily ration. Sometimes the water pressure lasted for half an hour or even longer, offering me plenty of time to fill every bucket and container in the flat, but sometimes time was in short supply and I had to do the job in ten minutes or a quarter of an hour. If possible I tried to bathe in the previous day's water in order to be able to use every available container for the new day. After this nervous episode, I made telephone calls, unless I had scheduled early appointments in which case I had to leave at about 8 a.m. Many people have accomplished their morning prayers before 7 a.m. and are having breakfast while preparing for the workday ahead. Phone calls are an important part of these preparations. In my diary I read that I sometimes woke up at 6 a.m. because somebody in the neighbourhood thought it important to try out his fireworks at that time. In some auspicious periods the number of weddings was so large that the musical bands heading the wedding parties were marching the streets from 5 a.m. onwards. At other times I heard the early bells of the temple opposite the compound, but many times I had to get up because my phone was ringing or because my neighbour was banging my front door to warn me that this morning 'the water had come early'. Often I was woken up by ordinary street noises: the nervous honking of auto rickshaws and cars which, like bats, seem to orient themselves through Bombay traffic by sound instead of sight; the yelling of the little kids from the slums next to the compound when their mothers ordered them home for bathing or a meal; the excited calls and shouts of the adolescent boys from my compound starting their first cricket games of the day before they had to leave for school or work. The first lines of Anita Desai's novel *Clear Light of Day* also sound very familiar to me:

> The koels [a kind of cuckoo] began to call before daylight. Their voices rang out from the dark trees like an arrangement of bells, calling and echoing each other's calls, mocking and enticing each other into ever higher and shriller calls. More and more joined as the sun rose.
>
> (Desai 2001: 1)

As I said before, work went on till late at night, even after midnight, both on the streets and in shops, offices and studios. In my diary I wrote about New Year's Eve of 1996. I had just returned from the city centre where I had attended some festivities organised by the Sassoon Library. On the roof of the building, right in the middle of Bombay's Fort Area, there had been a generous offering of delicious snacks followed by a game of musical chairs. I arrived by train in Dahisar around 11 p.m. and to my immense joy I was in time to see the party organised by our neighbouring compound. There were pleasant games, not only for boys and men, but also for young children, girls and women. Everybody was having a good time, as far as I could tell. From all over the neighbourhood people had come to watch what was going on within the compound walls. At the same time, at a distance of some 200 metres, one of the neighbourhood roads was being repaired. Behind the background of the happy sounds ascending from the compound and the gathered audience at the gate was the heavy noise of pneumatic hammers and tractors manoeuvring to and fro. At midnight I was home and I opened the doors to my small balcony. I could see people standing on the roofs of far-away skyscrapers shooting fireworks into the sky to celebrate the New Year. At much less of a distance the repair work on the road went on without any break or hesitation, as if there was nothing else around. 'One city; widely different times', I thought.

Bibliography

Biswas, Ramesh Kumar (2000) 'One Space, Many Worlds', in Ramesh Kumar Biswas (ed.) *Metropolis Now! Urban Cultures in Global Cities*. Vienna and New York: Springer, 51–60.

Bowers, Brian (1998) *Lengthening the Day*. Oxford, New York and Tokyo: Oxford University Press.

Boyer, M. Christine (1994) *The City of Collective Memory*. Cambridge, MA, and London: MIT Press.

Brassaï (1976) *The Secret Paris of the 30's*. New York: Pantheon.

Brunt, Lodewijk (1999) 'Op tijd in Bombay' (On time in Bombay), *Sociologische Gids* 46(6): 457–475.

Dekker, Maurits (n.d.) *Amsterdam bij gaslicht* (Amsterdam by gaslight). Utrecht and Amsterdam: Het Spectrum.

Desai, Anita (1982) *The Village by the Sea*. London: Heinemann.

Desai, Anita (2001) *Clear Light of Day*. London: Vintage.

Dickens, Charles (1957) *Sketches by Boz*. Oxford: Oxford University Press.

Jelavich, Peter (1990) 'Modernity, Civic Identity, and Metropolitan Entertainment: Vaudeville, Cabaret, and Revue in Berlin, 1900–1933', in Charles W. Haxthausen and Heidrun Suhr (eds) *Berlin: Culture and Metropolis*. Minneapolis and Oxford: University of Minnesota Press, 95–111.

Jhabvala, Ruth Prawer (2000) *Out of India*. Washington, DC: Counterpoint.

Lukacs, John (1988) *Budapest: A Historical Portrait of a City and its Culture*. London: Weidenfeld & Nicolson.

Makken, Bert (1991) 'De Nes in het fin de siécle' (The Nes during the fin de siécle), in Ronald de Nijs (ed.) *In de Nes daar moet je wezen* (The Nes is the place to be). Amsterdam: Stadsuitgeverij, 47–62.

Mayhew, Henry (1862) 'The Great World of London', in Henry Mayhew and John Binney (eds) *Criminal Prisons of London and Scenes of Prison Life*. London: Cass.

Mehta, Gita (1989) *Raj*. New York: Fawcett Columbine Books.

Melbin, Murray (1987) *Night as Frontier: Colonizing the World after Dark*. New York and London: The Free Press.

Olsen, Donald J. (1986) *The City as a Work of Art*. New Haven, CT, and London: Yale University Press.

Robbins Landon, H. C. (1991) *Mozart and Vienna*. London: Thames & Hudson.

Rotenberg, Robert (1992) *Time and Order in Metropolitan Vienna*. Washington, DC, and London: Smithsonian Institution Press.

Seigel, Jerrold (1987) *Bohemian Paris. Culture, Politics, and the Boundaries of Bourgeois Life 1830–1930*. New York: Penguin Books.

Sharma, Kalpana (2000) *Rediscovering Dharavi*. New Delhi: Penguin Books.

Shields, Rob (1991) *Places on the Margin: Alternative Geographies of Modernity*. London and New York: Routledge.

Smart, Josephine (1989) *The Political Economy of Street Hawkers in Hong Kong*. Hong Kong: The University of Hong Kong, Centre of Asian Studies.

Weegee (Arthur Fellig) (1996) *Weegee's New York. 335 Photographs 1935–1960*. London and Munich: Schirmer Art Books.

10 'What Time Do You Call This?'

Change and continuity in the politics of the city night

Chris Nottingham

Listeners to BBC Radio were recently informed about a new kind of social tension in South Korea. A correspondent argued that while young Koreans are still prepared to acknowledge that the day is meant for work they are increasingly of a mind that the night should belong to them and to pleasure. The pleasures in question are apparently less than Bacchanalian consisting mainly of the playing of computer games, and the move from day mode to night mode seems to involve no more than a couple of clicks on the mouse. Nonetheless the information was clearly presented with a hint of *schadenfreude*. One of the darker suspicions in the West underlying discussions of the relative decline of Europe and North America has been a fear that we have ceased to be capable of transferring a work ethic to our rising generation while in the East this can still be taken for granted. In making their claim for the night as a time of pleasure, the young Koreans were echoing a claim long celebrated in popular Western music: that the night was made for fun, for love, for escape from the attention of parents, teachers, employers; for anything other than useful study or quiet rest in preparation for the rigours of the next working day.

In most societies at most times, time and the moral order are seen as being intimately related. The relationship is usually at its most acute in respect of the division between night and day. A proper understanding of and compliance with the rules that attribute particular forms of behaviour to one zone or the other is widely seen as an essential element of moral decency. In our time, in the West, the inability of the 'underclass' to regulate their lives according to accepted time disciplines is regularly cited as a defining characteristic. Those who habitually choose to flout the conventions of night and day, even though the activities they choose to perform at an inappropriate time may in themselves be blameless, become objects of suspicion. 'What time do you call this?' is a familiar moral reprimand uttered by those who see it as their duty to recall laggards to a sense of the appropriateness of particular activities for particular moments; a rhetorical question which we can imagine on the lips of a parent scolding a child who has left the light on too long, a foreman confronting a worker arriving late in the morning, a spouse upbraiding a partner for arriving home too late in the night, or, at least at one time, a policeman reminding a nocturnal drunk that the hour had come to go home.

It is now twenty-five years since Daniel Bell set his concerns about the hedonistic individualism of youth culture in the West in a theoretical context. Bell argued: 'the economy, the polity and the culture – are ruled by contrary axial principles: for the economy, efficiency; for the polity, equality; and for the culture, self-realization (or self-gratification)'. 'The resulting disfunctions', he claimed, 'have formed the tensions and social conflicts of western society in the past 150 years' (Bell 1976: xi). Whether the BBC correspondent was correct in suggesting that young Koreans are beginning to succumb to self-gratification is a question beyond my competence, but his mode of analysis clearly has a track record. In the conflict over appropriate behaviours for the night we can identify an argument about social order that has a history.

Fears of disorders of the night are probably eternal, but it was clear to Bell that the rise of industrial societies gave them a new precision. A capitalist economy with a scientific division of labour required everyone to turn up for work at a set time (Thompson 1967). The popular ideologues of political economy, such as Samuel Smiles and Harriet Martineau, hammered home the lesson that the successful individual was one who internalised time discipline. Their heroes knew that 'early to bed, early to rise' was the only route to health, wealth and happiness. The failing individual could be identified by a profligate 'spending' of time and, in particular, an inability to resist the pleasures of the night.

Yet the capitalist ideologues were building on cultural foundations already in place. It is difficult to discover a time when the night has not been an issue in the contest between 'authorities', anxious to enforce a code of respectable behaviour, and variously defined 'others', no less anxious to avoid the humiliation and boredom of compliance. One of the most readily recognisable stereotypical conflicts of Western literature is between the noisy reveller and the awoken sleeper: the former belligerently uncomprehending of how anyone could fail to share his boisterous pleasure, the latter, always at a disadvantage, making a case for decorum and order. At a certain time of night it is difficult to make the case for the routine demands of the morrow when set against the immediate pleasures of the moment. This is a fact that even the reveller's most aggrieved opponent finds difficult to ignore entirely. The contest is usually an uneven one not least because the reveller represents life and pleasure, a fact that even his most aggrieved opponent is forced to acknowledge. His very annoyance is often intensified by a sense of exclusion. The decrepit country magistrate in Shakespeare's *Henry IV Part 1*, first annoyed and then carried away by the virility of Falstaff's band of revellers, bleats to his companion of student days when he too 'heard the chimes at midnight'. This equivocation has always been, and remains, a complicating factor in attempts to regulate the night.

And, indeed, the matter may well go deeper still. Bryan Palmer has presented an account of the 'dark shelters of the peasant night' which shows that our night anxieties can be traced back at least as far as the mythologies of medieval Europe (Palmer 2000: 23–48). The peasant night, Palmer argues, could provide an escape from the ordered hierarchies of the day. Night could represent both in reality, and perhaps even more in imagination, an opportunity to break the bounds of individual identity, the obligations of domestic relationships and, on the wilder shores, involve debaucheries and blasphemies, which symbolically usurped secular and spiritual hierarchies. For those in authority and others of a conservative disposition the night represented a time when the delicate threads which prevented a Gaderene descent into anarchic sensuality were at their most fragile. The physical darkness of the night was firmly associated with moral darkness and disorder.

In an attempt to identify a developing politics of the city night I shall first look briefly at some problems of definition before considering the early perceptions of, and responses to, the dangers of the night in the new industrial city. I shall then examine how the problem was redefined towards the end of the nineteenth century as the city night became associated with a greater range of pleasures offered to a wider social spectrum. I shall then concentrate on present perceptions and, in particular, on recent innovations designed to produce safer nights, both to ask what they tell us about current perceptions of the night and to consider whether they are likely to achieve their stated objectives. Next I shall look at those groups who have been proposed as potential regulators before moving to consider modern visions of the constants of night-inspired political speculation: those groups the Victorians called the 'creatures of the night', the homeless beggars and the prostitutes who remain on the streets of the city night after the revellers have departed. My examples are mainly drawn from the city of Glasgow. This is largely a matter of convenience. I am more interested in what Glasgow might tell us about city nights in the West in general than in its own particularity. Readers with a closer interest will find in Maver's contribution to this volume an intriguing account of the development of the city's individual nocturnal character.

Towards a politics of the night

Politics is a word that is easier to use than to define. For present purposes, I suggest politics is most usefully understood as that process whereby societies seek workable solutions over matters that cause conflict between groups or individuals within them, or put another way, how order is created out of social diversity. Those who hold official positions in the state, whether as politicians, bureaucrats or agents, have a privileged, but not monopolistic, position within this process. Even that ultimate and defining power of state officials, their claim to the exclusive legitimate use of physical force, must, in reality, be exercised with prudence. They are few, their responsibilities are vast, and their powers are invariably greater in theory than in reality, so in practice their ability to operate often rests on a capacity to mobilise existing prejudices and reinforce or formalise understandings or arrangements already in place within the broader society. This is a practical principle that acquires a normative dimension in liberal societies. The process works most effectively where decisions can be achieved by agreement, but in complex societies this is rare and the achievement of working compromises will usually rest on a brokering of interests between those who are too powerful to be ignored and the use of power, whether ideological or coercive, to exclude, deter or subdue the others.

How, then, does this help us in investigating the politics of the night? The night we can see does not sit easily with politics. Joachim Schlör argues:

> There are a series of relationships and frames of reference in which the essence, the peculiarity of the nocturnal city emerges in rough approximation: night and violence, night and sexuality, night and pleasure, night and solitude.
>
> (Schlör 1998: 11)

All four of these associations suggest nothing but difficulty for those who operate in the political sphere. They suggest states of mind in which individuals are at their most private and least inclined to bend to political reason. Moreover, the very darkness of night holds the promise of anonymity for those who wish to harm their enemies, pursue illicit obsessions, indulge the grosser pleasures, or simply escape the social gaze. It is not coincidental that the folk-devils that have most afflicted the imagination of the defenders of order and the law-abiding citizens, from witches through to the 'lads' and 'ladettes' of our time, have been firmly associated with the night.

The difficulties of dealing with such breaches of discipline are further increased by the fact that it is widely accepted, even by the respectable, that different standards of behaviour apply at night. Even at an academic conference one would be judged a dull dog if one were not capable of unbending over a drink and revealing a less serious side of one's nature. Who could deny that an eminent citizen who returned home the better for drink, on his hands and knees, would stand a better chance of retaining his good reputation if he did so at two in the morning rather than two in the afternoon? Sexuality is another matter which convention confines to the hours of darkness. Only the brave, desperate or stupid would advance a speculative sexual proposition in the full light of day. This may be a matter of socially constructed convention or it may represent an accommodation with some deeper structural symbolic impulse, or it might be a bit of both, but it remains a fact. Night can produce a sort of madness, a wilful evasion of everyday self-discipline, all the better if accompanied by later amnesia. Thus, William McIlvanney's account of an ideal Glasgow Saturday night: 'Ye shoulda been with us last night boy. Fantabulous. One of the best nights known to man. Ah don't remember a thing' (McIlvanney 1981: 208). Two hundred years earlier in Edinburgh, James Boswell awoke with a hangover and an all too vivid memory of a night of debauchery:

> It is curious how differently bad conduct appears to a man when he himself is guilty of it from what it does in the abstract. What would I have thought had I been told of a counsellor-at-law and the father of a family doing what I did last night!
>
> (Ryskamp and Pottle 1963: 86)

The night, then, not only produces tangible problems for those in authority and renders their charges less susceptible to political appeals, but it can also remind them of a certain moral equivocation within themselves. The virtues that lie at the heart of citizenship, sobriety, calmness, openness to persuasion, an ability to forsake the immediate pleasure for the longer-term gain, are not at their strongest after dark. Night-time gatherings are more disorderly, raucous and resistant to any but the most basic appeals. Were it possible, politicians would be well advised to ignore the night altogether.

The nineteenth-century city night

Historical sociologists tell us that the developing cities of the Industrial Revolution were characterised by the development of horizontal solidarity and vertical division (Dandekar 1990). In pre-industrial societies, class – perhaps here more accurately called rank – reinforced social hierarchy. Personal relationships stretched across status hierarchies. Authority had a human face. In the city, however, class difference became an anonymous matter. The debates of mid-nineteenth-century Britain were much informed by conservative anxieties set off by precisely this problem. Thomas Carlyle, in *Past and Present* (1965), produced the most pessimistic account of a society, which rested on nothing more than the 'cash nexus'. How could the new mill owners, who, true to the dictates of their 'dismal science' of political economy, regarded their charges as units of production, 'hands' to be used by day but abandoned at night, employed or discarded according to the dictates of the market, possibly achieve the authority of traditional rulers? Samuel Taylor Coleridge, in *The Constitution of Church and State* (1972), pointed out that the new cities were also beyond the influence of spiritual leaders. In a single journey the new city dwellers escaped the influence of both squire and parson.

The direct experience of cities, and no less the imaginative machinery through which they came to be understood, created powerful anxieties. The world that was lost was undoubtedly idealised and fears of the new were over-dramatised, but it was difficult to see how the basic dysfunctions of the modern industrial city, the vast numbers concentrated in squalid, unsupervised slums, constantly supplemented by successive waves of newcomers, would sort themselves out. Respectable inhabitants of the nineteenth-century 'cities of strangers' (Ignatieff 1983) were haunted by new spectres of disorder and, like all spectres, these achieved their greatest potency in the dark. Charles Dickens was adept at evoking this sense of respectability threatened by nocturnal transients obeying only their own mysterious dictates.

These concerns set off a whole range of measures based on a perceived need to establish some control of the disorder of city life. These included new institutions, the creation and application of a new social knowledge, the assumption of new administrative powers, and the creation of new types of functionaries. In Glasgow, the insecurities of the new city life developed a clamour for 'police' (De Swaan 1991). 'Police' was defined broadly in

Glasgow. It included such public health measures as compulsory cleansing and the inspection of lodging houses as well as those directly related to the maintenance of public order (Checkland 1982). By the outbreak of the First World War, the City of Glasgow's Police Department was responsible for baths and wash-houses, cleansing, the fire brigade, the lighting of streets, public works, sewage and public health administration, which included food inspection, control of the port, and responsibility for infectious diseases (Corporation of the City of Glasgow 1914). Though fears were great, most nineteenth-century cities could be characterised by energetic, if intermittent, social and political activity, driven by a variety of forces such as evangelical Christianity, utilitarian reason, fear of disorder and self-interest (Brown 1982). All, however, pursued the goals of security and order. By the end of the century there were numerous charitable organisations providing, among other things, education and training, material assistance for the destitute, and nursing services for the poor. Most in Glasgow were eventually co-ordinated within the Charity Organisation Society, the aim of which was specifically to ensure that rather than merely receiving handouts, failing individuals should also encounter 'a friend' (Charity Organisation Society 1924). There was a Lock Hospital with its attendant organisations, dedicated to the cure and reform of prostitutes. Temperance organisations were exceptionally active (King 1979). Most of these organisations were run by middle-class people, often the same people who were involved in municipal affairs (Robertson 1998), but there has recently been a re-evaluation of the efforts of working people themselves. Clearly they too used voluntary organisations, trade unions, friendly societies, religious fraternities and the like as a means of reducing the risks of life in liberal society and escaping the disconnectedness of urban life.

It is difficult to take too seriously those accounts, which seek to reduce this complexity to simple principles. Michel Foucault (1991: 205) suggested Bentham's Panopticon as a model of the order that had developed. While it is clear that Bentham himself felt he had provided the blueprint for an ordered society (Himmelfarb 1965: 32–81), government practice never approached his ambition. Bentham himself had wildly creative ideas about the uses of darkness: in his model penitentiary, criminals were kept in the dark and were only allowed gradual access to light as they were judged to be in the process of reform (Bowring 1838–48: 29). In Chadwick's model workhouses, inmates were denied any night-time sociability, being banished to their dormitories from early evening to morning. Chadwick took the concept of 'police' to its logical conclusion by proposing a night-time curfew for his model workers (Donajgrodzki 1977: 78). Yet while such cases provide a useful illustration of the operation of organising radical minds untrammelled by political complexity, the panoptic ideal offers little insight into the actual processes of social control in nineteenth-century industrial societies. The process of state development was too complex, too subject to the ebbs and flows of live politics, too far beyond the control of any single force, to be so summarised.

The problems of pleasure

Fear of disorder, however, is but one element of the imaginative life of the industrial city night. The anonymous observer who boldly went into the Glasgow night in the mid-nineteenth century ostensibly to record its horrors produced an account which, alongside a very proper account of social misery, was run through with an unmistakable excitement ('Shadow' 1976). In his record of phenomena such as the 'moral tempest of Saturday night' and the 'dangerous dens of the worst of thieves and prostitutes' we can catch a glimpse of that unresolved mixture of repulsion and fascination that became a feature of many later excursions into the 'abyss'. As well as disorder and moral degradation, the relative anonymity of the city night promised excitements beyond the wildest dreams of 'rural idiocy'. Towards the end of the nineteenth century, the hedonistic possibilities came to be celebrated more openly. Numbers of young middle-class people were going out at night. One account of London nights spoke of a country 'getting gay' and 'inclined to frolic'; entertainment was ceasing to be entirely domestic and 'men and women lived the life of the town, the restaurant and the theatre and the music hall prospered together' (Gaunt 1988: 163). Thomas Escott argued that it was a question of public pleasures being more widely available and spoke of 'the revolt of the sons and daughters of the middle class against their exclusion from modes of enjoyment that to their contemporaries slightly above them in the social scale had long been allowed' (Escott 1897: 203–4). 'Never indeed', wrote the radical journalist Holbrook Jackson, 'was there a time when the young were so young and the old so old' (Jackson 1988: 11). For a comparative consideration of the contribution of Bohemia see the contribution by Brunt in this volume.

Throughout the nineteenth century, social critics were forced to recognise that it was not only the rule of 'squire and parson' which the new urbanism had dissolved. The family itself, hitherto the most effective institution in imposing a sense of time discipline on the young, was also under threat. The sociologist Ferdinand Tönnies despaired of the urban household as 'sterile, narrow, empty and debased to the conception of a mere living space which can be obtained elsewhere in equal form for money' (quoted in Banks 1973: 111). As early as the 1840s, Friedrich Engels had pointed out that children in industrial cities, sometimes as young as 14 or 15, had begun to pay their parents a fixed sum for board and lodging and keep the rest for themselves: 'In a word, the children emancipate themselves, and regard the parental dwelling as a lodging-house, which they often exchange for another as it suits them' (Engels 1987: 167). Charles Booth, in his pioneering study of social conditions in London, also noted a weakening of family ties that he felt had occurred in the last two decades of the century (Booth 1903: 43). Emile Durkheim associated the weakening of the authority of the family with cultural dynamism:

> Great cities are the uncontested homes of progress: it is in them that ideas, fashions, customs and new needs are elaborated ... temperaments are so

mobile that everything that comes from the past is somewhat suspect ... minds naturally are there orientated to the future.

(Quoted in Banks 1973: 112)

With the expansion of lower-middle-class employment in the later decades of the century, even greater numbers of young people enjoyed a period between escaping the authority of the parental home and assuming the responsibility of their own families. For many, this became an opportunity to flirt with the future. Edwin Muir, a self-made man of letters, recorded a social life in Glasgow at the turn of the century structured around progressive organisations, suggesting that there was a network that might constitute a 'soft city' (Raban 1976). The gatherings Muir attended were for the most part earnest, but they involved an independent social life in the evening (Muir 1980). The anonymity and discontinuity of city life allowed young radicals to reconstruct themselves as socialists, vegetarians or feminists. Moreover, in the new public spaces of the cities – in the museums, institutes, galleries and theatres – young men and women could meet on their own terms.

The generational revolt of the last two decades of the nineteenth century seriously complicated debates about urban order. Those who joined progressive societies heralded the development of a body of opinion that would specifically challenge prevailing notions of how the 'dangerous classes' should be treated. The lower orders and, in particular, 'the creatures of the night' became objects of fascination. Beggars and prostitutes were presented as victims rather than predators, most notably in Walt Whitman's *Leaves of Grass* (Whitman 1993). Some literary men had a personal fascination with low life. For Ernest Dowson, Arthur Symons recalled, no night out was complete which did not end in one of the shelters frequented by all-night cabmen (Symons 1896). For the socialist visionary Edward Carpenter, the prostitute stood as a mute indictment of respectability; reviled, but nonetheless the foundation stone of the very society which rejected her. In *Civilisation, Its Cause and Cure* he presented the criminal in similar terms: 'But is he there in the dock, the patch-coated brawler or burglar, really harmful to society? Is he more harmful than the mild old gentleman in the wig who pronounces sentence upon him?' (Carpenter 1900: 100). In Joris-Karl Huysmans's novel *A Rebours* (Huysmans 1891), which served as a Europe-wide manifesto for those who wished to proclaim their indifference to bourgeois order, the hero achieves the ultimate expression of the new mental state by transferring all his activities to the hours of darkness.

To Max Nordau these things were nothing less than the signs of irreversible degeneracy; a Europe-wide surge of wild young men and 'ecstatic women' in the grip of Dionysus, inspired, he thought, by Friedrich Nietzsche (that 'means of raising a mental pestilence'), afflicted by a collective 'ego-mania', committed only to self-gratification, which was leading the whole continent of Europe down the path of degeneration (Nordau 1968: 14). Nordau exaggerated but he had identified a new dimension, a section of the middle classes beginning to find excitement in what had aroused only fear in their parents. Controlling the night would now be a more politically sensitive matter.

Nights in the present-day city

A nocturnal walk around the pleasure centres of any of the major cities of Western Europe in the present day would surely convince Max Nordau that all his worst fears had been fulfilled. In most cities earlier attempts to regulate hours devoted to drinking and public pleasure have been reduced to a point where it is difficult to detect much effect. The night belongs to youth, to its high decibel signalling and its pleasures. Life in the entertainment centres really does seem to begin 'after midnight' and life involves the visible casting-off of restraints. A recent report for the Economic and Social Research Council concluded that 'aggressive hedonism is now the norm and unruly, violent behaviour is a central feature of this new economy' (*Guardian* 27 November 2000). Recreational drugs are an important aspect of the culture. A recent estimate suggested that half a million ecstasy tablets are consumed each weekend in Britain; but this has not reduced the importance of alcohol. In Manchester between 1997 and 2000 the number of licensed premises (i.e. pubs, clubs and restaurants) rose by 242 per cent. Glasgow has seen a less dramatic rise although the number of licences granted to 'places of entertainment' (largely clubs) rose from 169 to 828 between 1980 and 1999 (Her Majesty's Chief Inspector of Constabulary for Scotland 2000). Certainly drink is becoming an ever-more significant part of the British economy with pubs and clubs turning over £22 billion per annum and employing 500,000 people. This trade is currently responsible for a fifth of all new jobs (*Guardian* 27 November 2000).

The widespread moral concern over this culture is exacerbated by the recognition that drink-fuelled aggressive behaviour on city streets at night is no longer confined to a particular class or gender. 'The drunks of Tony Blair's nightmares are as likely to be young female professionals as tattooed, underclass no-marks' (*Guardian* 11 July 2000). The most emphatic demonstration of the spread of the new culture was when Blair's 16-year-old son was taken home by the police after being found drunk and unconscious in Leicester Square after celebrating the conclusion of his school examinations. The boy's headmaster commented: 'Children are growing up much earlier than they used to.' Most public reaction reflected this sad resignation.

Yet most of the population of Britain have little or no direct experience of the new hedonism. Even those who do desert their suburbs in the evenings are rarely in the places or out at the times when it is most visible. Television, however, ensures that they can experience it vicariously. A number of producers have recognised that following a group of 'clubbers' with a hand-held camera makes for cheap and compelling programmes. The formula involves, typically, spectacular drinking, public nudity, fights, vomiting, and sexual encounters with easily acquired and quickly discarded strangers. *Ibiza Nights* was an early attempt at the genre and Ibiza has become the adjective for the life-style. Newspaper journalists have not been slow to follow:

> By 4 a.m. they are unconscious and one of the girls they came with is exchanging her thong for a lightstick while her mate is getting her tits out for

this bloke who says he's got a jeep. The next day they will sleep for three hours, get up, have a cup of coffee, rinse out their mouths with the Listerine they bought at the airport and repeat the whole routine.

(Guardian 11 July 2000)

Efforts by local authorities, such as Westminster's attempt to regulate Soho by the designation of 'stress areas' and the deployment of 'enforcement officers', are seen, no doubt correctly, as pathetically inadequate in the face of huge popular and commercial pressures (*Guardian* 12 August 2000).

Is it possible to take consolation from the fact that such stories fit pretty well into a long tradition of moral disorder as entertainment? Since the beginnings of popular media the British have enjoyed being 'shocked' by tales of what their fellow citizens are getting up to in the 'secrecy' of the night. What is the significance of the crush of youthful pleasure seekers in the city night? Does it represent a novel challenge to an ordered society or is it, as Zygmunt Bauman suggests, merely that modern Western societies have abandoned older forms of internal social control, concentrating on 'border controls' and leaving those inside to the seductions of consumption (Bauman 1998)? Can we console ourselves with that traditional liberal construct of the 'moral panic', or perhaps Nordau was correct and we have been living in a progressive degenerate hell for so long that we no longer notice?

Control in the present-day city

While Western cities seem to have abandoned many controls over the night, and police numbers are small in the face of the thousands who flood into the centres, it would be a mistake to believe that the forces of order had nothing at their disposal. Regulations may be different but they are still in place. Attention, however, tends to be focused on the new devices. One such, which has raised some hopes and more fears, is the network of CCTV cameras that has recently spread through cities. The average Briton is now seen on CCTV at least 500 times a week (*Guardian* 2 February 1999).

The Scottish Office produced its first evaluation of the impact of official CCTV cameras in 1995 on the basis of twelve cameras in the small town of Airdrie, and found a measurable beneficial effect on crime (Scottish Office 1995). However, a 1999 report on the impact of the thirty-two cameras in central Glasgow concluded: 'the CCTV cameras could not be said to have had a significant impact overall in reducing recorded crimes and offences'. Nor had the cameras had any effect on the clear-up rate of crimes. It was suggested that the contrast between Glasgow and Airdrie arose because the former is bigger and has a more transient population. Another hypothesis was that awareness is the key to deterrence and only 33 per cent of those questioned were aware of the cameras. The report acknowledged that CCTV operations were compromised by the prejudices of the observers: their suspicions seemed to be aroused 'by young men wearing "puffa" jackets, football shirts, baseball caps, pony tails and

woolly hats' (Scottish Office 1999a). The finding that cameras lose their deterrent effect when the individuals involved are drunk raised doubts about the
ability of CCTV to tame the city night.

In spite of these qualifications, popular views are supportive. Around 70 per
cent of people sampled in Glasgow were in favour and believed they would
prove effective (Scottish Office 1999a). The fact that they have proved helpful in
tracing the culprits in high-profile cases, such as the murder of James Bulger
(*Guardian* 16 December 1999) and the Brixton nail bomber (*Guardian* 30 April
1999), has inevitably tended to legitimate their deployment. They have even, on
occasion, proved useful in upholding civil liberties. A number of recent cases
have seen the conviction of police officers for the use of excessive force on the
basis of camera evidence (*Guardian* 7 October 1999). They are also becoming
part of the pattern of expectations: when the memorial to Stephen Lawrence,
the black teenager murdered by a racially motivated gang, was defaced,
complaints were made that there was no camera in the dummy box guarding the
site (*Guardian* 26 February 1999).

However, most of those who have written about the subject are hostile to the
idea. There have been rumblings on the Right – CCTV has prompted the
Conservative *Daily Telegraph* to launch a 'freedom web site' where readers can
report breaches of their civil liberties (*Daily Telegraph* 12 July 2001) – but most
criticism has come from the Left. Some criticisms are about the way systems
operate: 'In a busy street there are hundreds of issues to focus on. Deciding who
the trouble makers are, and deciding if anything should be done about the incidents becomes a matter of crude stereotypes' (Norris and Armstrong 1999). It
has also been pointed out that the regulation of CCTV operations under the
Data Protection Act, which specifies, for example, that surveillance must be
'adequate, relevant and not excessive' and recorded images must not be kept
'longer than is necessary', is inadequate. Most studies concede that CCTV is
useful for making arrests when strangers are assaulted or robbed, but Norris and
Armstrong suggest that in cases of fights between those already acquainted,
CCTV might discourage intervention by their 'mates' or other citizens, which
the authors regard as the proper way to handle such things. They also suggest
that cameras remove the anonymity that is one of the delights of city nightlife:
'people have affairs, people hide their sexuality. Are these really matters for state
concern?' (Norris and Armstrong 1999: 90)

In other accounts, however, CCTV can appear as nothing less than a threat
to urban diversity and individual freedom, a surrender to 'middle-class' and business pressure in the interest of 'property values in the gentrified enclaves of inner
cities and profits in the malls' (Fyfe and Bannister 1998: 254). For Nick Cohen,
'the new electronics ... seem to thrust forward into a future with no place for the
freedom of the individual' (Cohen 2000). Fyfe and Bannister present a sombre
view of present-day Glasgow:

> Gated residential communities, the private policing of office and shopping
> spaces, local curfews to reduce the risk of public disorder at night in city-

centre streets, and, within the last five years, the proliferation of public space CCTV surveillance systems are all increasingly common strategic responses to anxieties about crime and concern at declining consumer and business confidence.

(Fyfe and Bannister 1998: 256)

Recent sociological literature from Britain and the United States demonstrates conclusively that CCTV has hit a collective raw nerve. For those influenced by Foucault it offers irresistible confirmation of the master's vision. Here is the ever-expanding 'gaze', the remorseless advance of 'social control', the elevation of panopticism into 'a network of socio-spatial control and discipline across the streets of Britain' (Fyfe and Bannister 1998: 267). Among sociologists driven by the nostalgic communitarian ideal, reaction is no less hostile. For Richard Sennett, CCTV is another nail in the coffin of that urban heterogeneity which teaches citizens to tolerate healthy disorder (Sennett 1996: 108). For Iris Young, the new 'fortress cities' are eliminating the public space where 'people encounter other people, meanings, expressions and issues which they may not understand and with which they do not identify' (quoted in Fyfe and Bannister 1998: 263). CCTV becomes, in this developing orthodoxy, a factor in the 'imposition of a middle class tyranny', the 'purification of space' and a means of driving 'troublesome others' off the street and out of sight (Fyfe and Bannister 1998: 263). There are commentators whose criticism is qualified – for David Lyon, the new surveillance 'spells control *and* care, proscription *and* protection' (Lyon 1994: 219; emphasis in the original) – but they are in the minority.

This is not the place to develop a response on the scale demanded by the new orthodoxy but a number of questions can be raised. In the first place we might ask whether the present situation is as novel as has been suggested. Cities have indeed provided the conflict and diversity that has often proved critical in destroying political authoritarianism and making its reimposition difficult. Yet there were always forces seeking, often in the interests of the preservation of property and the protection of commercial interests, to drive those who created diversity off the streets. The question then is not one of motive but of effectiveness: is there something in the present situation which makes it possible for one set of interests to eliminate the others permanently? In this sense CCTV is surely carrying more baggage than is justifiable. It is reasonable to suggest that CCTV cameras represent inadequate 'technological fixes to chronic urban problems' (Fyfe and Bannister 1998: 256) but no less a mistake to assume new technology will overwhelm all other political and social considerations. In a near totalitarian society with a terroristic penal code and a cowed population, an additional means of surveillance might indeed make a significant difference, but any changes it may work in a city such as present-day Glasgow would surely be marginal and complex. Nights do indeed lack the general vibrancy and diversity that was present twenty or thirty years ago, but it is more realistic to see the security cameras as consequence rather than cause.

Some of the current pessimism can be traced back to Jane Jacobs' lament for the demise of American cities. Her prescription for a healthy city is 'an eclectic mix of land-uses in city centres generating street activity twenty four hours a day' providing 'eyes upon the street' belonging to the 'natural proprietors of the street' (Jacobs 1961: 45). Leaving aside the question as to whether this too might not have authoritarian overtones – for states are not the only threats to liberty – we can ask whether CCTV might not actually help persuade people to venture onto the city streets after dark. Shouldn't we view those 'middle-class' residents as a vanguard of regeneration rather than dismiss them (us?) as symptoms of the disease? Isn't it possible that CCTV cameras, even granted their limited effect, might encourage the opening of the small businesses that are the base of a diverse urban nightlife?

Finally we might ask whether the view of the city at night as a 'stagnant fortress' has any relationship with reality. Anyone walking through central Glasgow in the late evening, as I regularly do, is faced with a more complex reality. There are indeed far fewer people about, even at weekends, than there were thirty or forty years ago. But at the top of pedestrianised Buchanan Street it is often possible to see a number of skateboarders, precisely the sort of impecunious youths which commercial pressures are supposedly anxious to eliminate from city centres, indulging their passion under the gaze of a CCTV camera. Outside Central Station there is invariably a congregation of 'undesirable others' conducting their businesses of begging and drug dealing with little attempt at concealment. Occasionally the police are there as well but they seem to be concerned only with containment. I am sure skateboarders, dealers and beggars all experience public and private harassment but I doubt if it is of a qualitatively different sort from that which has always taken place. One element of confusion on this issue may arise over the question of punishment. Present-day developed societies are exceptionally effective at punishing those who wish to preserve their respectability, and their credit rating, but relatively powerless over the others. For those who have no wish for respectability and its attendant bene-fits, or have no hope of regaining it, one more conviction is unlikely to exercise much deterrent effect, and hence, maybe, the cameras are not much feared.

In the case of CCTV it seems possible that the general public, less alienated from commercial society, less susceptible to visions of past glories and future dystopias, and, hence, more impressed by evidence of marginal gains, and, perhaps, more inclined to trust in the emergence of a tolerable future even when it is, as ever, impossible to see how it can be constructed, has a more realistic view than the social scientists.

Glasgow has also been the centre of national attention over another policing initiative designed to calm fears of the night. This initiative focuses on a very different location: not the relatively tiny, brightly lit, intermittently busy areas of the city, but the vast, gloomy, sodium-lit, largely deserted, dormitory estates, which form by far the greater part of the city night. In 1997 the Strathclyde Police introduced a child curfew in the Hamilton district, which is on the fringes of the city. In the rundown housing estates there were complaints that young people were congregating in gangs in the night, damaging property and preventing older people from leaving their homes. The police were given powers to pick up unaccompanied young people after 9 p.m. and take them home. The scheme was originally directed at children of 12 but later extended to the 12–15 age group. The pattern of reactions has been similar to those over CCTV. Some have been troubled by the implications for civil liberties and others have questioned whether the parents the children were returned to were capable of exercising appropriate authority (Springham 1998). Public pronouncements confirm it is a very sensitive issue. Even the word curfew is taboo: Strathclyde Police insist that their main concern is with the safety of young people at risk and always refer to the Hamilton scheme as the 'Child Safety Initiative'. Reports speak of 'the protection of vulnerable young Scots' (Scottish Office 1999b). Positive aspects are stressed, such as the provision of 'state of the art' youth cafés (*BBC2 Newsnight* 7 December 2000). In the first year of operation police made 229 interventions, 31 on children less than 8 years old, and 200 children were returned to their homes. A 40 per cent reduction in reported crime was recorded in the intervention area, although it was recognised that other safety initiatives taking place at the same time could have contributed. Opinions in the older section of the intervention group (12–15) were evenly divided and one survey of 100 residents found 44 per cent in favour. Tony Blair, perhaps stung by the failure of local authorities to take up powers under an earlier national scheme to introduce curfews and prosecute parents who exercise insufficient discipline over their children, made the extension of the Hamilton Initiative the centrepiece of the creation of 'a new moral purpose in Britain' (*Observer* 5 September 1999).

The positions taken up in the new debate are largely predictable on the basis of the functions and ideologies of those asked to comment. Many young people, particularly those 14 and 15 years old, resent the fact that they cannot go out on their own after 9 p.m. Left-wing groups see the measure as an attempt to simplify complex social problems. Civil liberties groups stress the dangers of stigmatising all young people with measures designed to curb an unruly minority. Local authorities express reluctance to invest in a scheme that promises ongoing difficulties and doubtful returns. A community worker, familiar with the Hamilton Initiative, warned that such curfews simply encourage residents to transfer problems to the police and discourage the citizens' interventions, which he felt were the only effective way of re-establishing control. There are examples of successful curfews but these rest on the effective co-operation of parents and are in areas where the original problems were not acute (*BBC2 Newsnight* 1 July 2001). Finite numbers of police available and the absence of major investment in leisure facilities inevitably cast doubts on the future effectiveness of the initiative. The government might claim that it at least reinforces the message that parents should be held responsible for the conduct of their children but its actions do not match its grand moral designs. It is difficult to escape the impression that its prime motive is to demonstrate to the suburbs that it is 'doing something'.

Judges of normality

Behind the Hamilton Initiative is a widespread sense that traditional controls have broken down. Police are no longer visible on the streets and are constrained in the efforts to discipline delinquents. Older people frequently remark that they no longer feel comfortable about intervening to prevent antisocial behaviour. Nobody seems willing to risk abuse by asking the young what time they think it is. There is a related assumption that other authority figures have also ceased to use the opportunities their functions present them with. Foucault raised the question in an interesting way: 'Judges of normality are present everywhere. We are in the society of the teacher judge, the doctor judge, the educator judge, the social worker judge; it is on them that the universal reign of the narrative is based' (quoted in Dandekar 1990). The Foucault school, for which opposition to 'social control' is an article of faith, is clearly very much at odds with British popular opinion, which would seem to prefer a situation in which these 'judges' were even more active. Foucaultian suspicions also seem very much at odds with the experience of the potential 'judges' themselves. Teachers seem too burdened by new controls and aggressive pupils to contemplate broadening the control they exercise. Besides, while the public in general may favour a more active disciplinary role for teachers, parents often take a very different stance when their own children are involved. Doctors, too, are frequently heard to protest that, far from showing deference or openness to influence, their patients tend to be assertive, if not aggressive.

The Accident and Emergency Departments of the Glasgow hospitals, where the flotsam of the city night routinely presents itself, should provide a useful site to look for examples of the exercise of social control. I was able to talk to eight qualified nurses with current or recent experience of the night shift in Glasgow's A&E units. With a quite striking uniformity, and no prompting, they all divided night-time clients into those they described as 'genuine' and others. The others seemed to be defined by the fact that that their problems were self-inflicted, through drink or drugs either directly, or as a result of accidents or fights resulting from intoxication. Thus the first criterion for acting as 'nurse judges', an element of moral disapproval of certain types of behaviour, was always present. However, all spoke of codes that prevented them from expressing their disapproval. While some did admit that they deliberately delayed treating those they judged to be simply drunk (waiting times in A&E Departments in Scottish city hospitals can be up to three or four hours if the case is not an emergency) and others spoke of withdrawing the minor signs of reassurance, all felt constrained in their conduct. Far from nurses being able to act as judges they are more likely to end up as victims. It is a sad fact that assaults on nurses in A&E units are currently running at record levels and in some departments there is now a police presence on Friday and Saturday nights. There are also indications that some 'judges of normality' are so uncertain of their powers that they employ some ingenuity in transferring responsibilities. Not untypical is the A&E doctor who complained that the police were using such units as 'places of safety' for awkward clients (*British Medical Journal* 1997, 315: 886). One female nurse recalled how two policemen brought in a violent prisoner, took the handcuffs off him and left him in her charge. Certainly A&E Departments do exercise general functions associated with the maintenance of order – for instance, they routinely record child injuries in order that others can detect cases of possible abuse (*British Medical Journal* 1997, 315: 855–856) – but in general such duties are not popular and the outlook of their staff was dominated by the difficulties of doing the job as formally defined and avoiding the displeasure of their clients which can often result in formal complaints being made. The 'gaze' may be present but there would be some doubt as to deciding who was its director and who its object. Nurses certainly disapprove of some of the behaviour they encounter but feel incapable of doing anything about it.

'Creatures of the night'

The 'creatures of the night', the prostitutes, beggars and homeless, have always claimed the attention of those expressing fears about the disorder of the city night. For some they have been a cause for pity, for others moral disapproval, but for all they have been a subject of serious curiosity. There are several reasons why this should have been the case, but underlying them all is the compelling illusion that such people, by evading control mechanisms, can serve as witness to the ultimate potential of the city night. The order of the industrial city, in theory and practice, rested on the notion that nobody should be autonomous. For most this was a matter of being subject to the disciplines of employment. In the course of the nineteenth century strenuous efforts were made to ensure that those who were not employed were nevertheless controlled through the disciplined use of charity and the regulation of the places in which they congregated at night. Those who evaded, or existed on the margins of, such control were naturally a cause for concern.

Prostitution is still seen as much of a problem in present-day Glasgow as it was in the mid-nineteenth century. The language in which it is discussed has changed but there are few public voices that do not define the ideal end of policy as its elimination. Clearly there is far less inclination to place blame on the prostitutes themselves. The fact that almost all legal activity in Glasgow is dedicated to punishing the prostitute is widely seen as unacceptable. This may be a reflection of the feminisation of the control of prostitution. Of the thirty-three directors of the Lock Hospital in the 1880s none were women. Now it would seem that virtually all of those who work with prostitutes are women. Those involved in prostitution believe that hostels should have exclusively female staff. Publications are dominated by a feminist perspective; and official publications of BASE 75, which runs, among other services, a drop-in centre for medical advice and needle exchanges, specifically reject a 'masculinist way of knowing' (Stewart 2000: 8).

BASE 75 has 1,140 prostitutes registered ('Shadow' in 1858 estimated the number of prostitutes in Glasgow to be 1,600) and makes a conscious attempt to provide a service 'which the women want'. The effectiveness of its work demands that it establishes a clear division between its work and the criminal justice system and while it sees its aim as helping women to escape from prostitution, it does provide services and support to those who choose not to:

> On first contact women are introduced to a staff member who speaks with the woman to determine her reasons for becoming involved in prostitution and to explain alternative options. ... However if a woman has clearly decided [to begin or continue prostituting] she is registered with the drop-in centre and given information about the range of specific services available.
>
> (Stewart 2000)

The only exception is with under-age girls who are automatically put in contact with the social services.

In many respects the life of the Glasgow prostitute in 2001 can seem remarkably similar to that of 150 years before. Debt, disease, drink and drug abuse, assault, and the occasional murder are the constants. It is still an outcast profession firmly linked to other underworlds. Of Glasgow prostitutes, 92 per cent have injected drugs at some time and around two-thirds are heroin addicts. Levels of HIV infection are very low, largely perhaps because 97 per cent report using condoms 'all of the time', but a large majority have hepatitis C. Glasgow has 100,000 injectors and ex-injectors who are so infected (Stewart 2000: 7). 'Drug injectors in Glasgow spend an estimated £160 million a year on drugs most of which comes from the sale of stolen goods and drug dealing' (GGDAT 1999: 7).

Heroin is often presented as a new dimension but Victorian Glasgow already had the taste. In 1858, 'Shadow' commented on 'the pernicious and deadly habit of using opium as a narcotic': 'the druggists shop is wont to be frequented by artisans going to their work' ('Shadow' 1976: 118). He also recorded that girls became seduced into prostitution in the very institutions which were supposed to redeem them: 'A procuress had even managed to effect an interview with a comparatively innocent girl in hospital, for the purposes of assisting her trade in this horrible vice' ('Shadow' 1976: 127). This can be compared with 'Shirley's' description of a hostel for the homeless in 1999: 'They can be horrible places, the violence and the bullying. You see young girls, "fresh" wee new lassies being targeted to work, to earn money for the older women and the men' (Stewart 2000: 33). It is for these reasons that the Scottish Executive is committed to developing homeless accommodation with more controls and compulsory detoxification (*Herald* 2 June 2000).

Prostitutes in Scotland cannot be sent to prison for their occupation but fines are imposed and many get into a cycle of unpaid fines that ends with incarceration. Of a sample interviewed, 88 per cent had had experience of the criminal justice system. The experience of prison is real for many, and a fear for all. Many record abuse from strangers, verbal abuse from other women being most common. A Dickensian note enters the women's descriptions of where they have spent nights: 'Up closes', 'On heaters in alleys', 'In doorways', 'Old buildings',

'Walk about all night', 'Lanes', 'Under motorway bridges', 'Garden sheds' and 'Anywhere' (Stewart 2000: 26).

If there has been some shift of opinion in favour of the prostitute, public discussion is still cast in a moral framework. Disapproval, though, is generally directed more towards the client; thus the spokesman for the Catholic Church in Scotland was reported as saying: 'I have been saying for years that men who use prostitutes should be prosecuted.' The Church of Scotland representative was similarly inclined: 'It is an injustice that ... the men who use them get off scot-free' (*Herald* 23 March 1999).

The present situation is difficult enough to regulate though not impossible. In investigating the murder of a Glasgow prostitute in 1998, it was reported that police had interviewed 2,500 male clients, friends and family relatives. An additional 870 clients of other Glasgow prostitutes had been traced, some as far away as Hong Kong (*Herald* 23 November 1998). If clients were to be regularly prosecuted it seems unlikely that such investigations would be possible. Street prostitution is an almost exclusively night-time phenomenon and many such prostitutes now work in an area of the city that is well lit and covered by CCTV cameras, normally enjoying tacit police approval. The more the criminal justice system intervenes, whether with prostitutes or their clients, the more likely is the business to be conducted in darker corners. This, however, is not the sort of argument that the moral campaigners listen to, or have ever listened to, in Glasgow.

The greatest change is in the nature of the agencies that deal with prostitutes and beggars. The days of philanthropy are gone and the agencies responsible are now largely funded by the state. Politicians prefer the agencies to retain a measure of autonomy but they are subject to frequent regulation and monitoring, facilitated by their reliance on state funding. BASE 75 was recently rescued with £1.8 million from the Scottish Executive (*Herald* 23 August 2000). The Talbot Association, which runs hostels for the homeless, spent around £3 million per annum on its hostels in 1998, of which only £16,000 came in the form of private donations. The active members of its committees tend to be retired social work administrators and the like which facilitates relationships with official agencies (Talbot Association 1999).

The treatment of the overlapping problems of homelessness and begging has, in Scotland, as elsewhere, become more a matter of public debate as it has become a more visible feature of city life. As in the case of prostitution, the debate reflects both differences and similarities to what has gone on before. There is far greater understanding of the factors which cause people to live on the streets: 'those who beg have generally experienced a disrupted family background, substance abuse, exclusion from the labour market and institutionalisation ... or usually a combination of these factors' (*Guardian* 15 September 1999). There is a growing, if not universal, recognition that begging is not an easy route to a reasonable life. Yet while there is a great deal of money and activity directed at the problem, every effort is made to demonstrate that policies are based on hard-nosed realism. Louise Casey, the London government's homelessness 'Tsar', provoked much opposition when she advised citizens that kindness to beggars was actually counterproductive. A previous Conservative prime minister argued we should 'condemn a little more and understand a little less', and the current New Labour administration is committed to a policy of 'tough care' that will force the homeless into the labour and housing markets and to accept responsibility for themselves. Policies on prostitution are essentially similar (Scottish Executive 2000). It would be over-fanciful to see an exact parallel with Victorian attitudes. Practices are far more respectful of the individual rights of the 'creatures of the night' even though the debate on principle may seem familiar.

Conclusion

> A sacredness of love and death,
>   dwells in thy noise and smoky breath.
> (Alexander Smith 1857, Whyte 1983: 1)

During the nineteenth century it was recognised that the modern industrial city created a need for a new kind of politics. The complexity and dynamism of city life broke down traditional authority structures and seemed to defy all attempts to discover any lasting alternatives. The maintenance of tolerable order not only required a plethora of official and civil organisations and activities, but a willingness on the part of its rulers to involve themselves in a continuous process of invention and innovation. Even then the cities could never be subjected to the degree of control that their more nervous guardians might require. Cities inevitably involve a large measure of disorder and always contain the seeds of deeper disturbances. In this sense the city has probably shaped modern politics more than politics has ever been able to shape the city.

Cities have their own dynamics and, as such, stand as an obstacle for those with grand political designs. Some such leaders, Pol Pot for example, have taken this to its logical conclusion and physically destroyed what they could not control. Others, such as Adolf Hitler, attempted a process of incorporation, not only seeking to eliminate the spontaneity of the city, and particularly city nights, by organised terror, but by inventing a set of alternative meanings and rituals. For the most part, though, even politicians and political ideologues who have disliked cities – from nationalists who have disliked their cosmopolitanism to conservatives who have hated their moral pluralism – have decided they have to live with them.

Early approaches to the problem of the modern city night tended to be authoritarian. This was really a variation on the theme of curfew: to make sure that the vast majority of citizens were in their homes, or at least off the street, at night. However, the functioning of the modern city always demanded a certain level of night-time activity. Markets are the obvious example; and if markets were permitted so the public houses and restaurants around the market had to be allowed to open as well. There were also pressures for public entertainment. If these were resisted, the result would be unregulated activities, so they came to be permitted under licence. As Schlör has shown for the city of Paris, once different focal points of night activity were in existence, pathways would be established between them (Schlör 1998: 37). Pleasure seekers, when their entertainment concluded, would seek out the bars in the market areas. The pathways that linked the points could be used by others, such as prostitutes, to provide additional services. The authoritarian attempt to control the night was thus gradually breached, albeit in the face of the displeasure of other citizens with different ideas of night-time activity.

Inhabitants of large cities are continually being reminded of the fragility of the arrangements that make their lives tolerable, but nowhere is this awareness more sharply felt than in the night. Characters appear who do not seem to share their habits and outlook; even fellow citizens who might seem acceptable in their daytime personas take on a different aspect at night. Cities generate a degree of moral ambiguity with even respectable citizens capable of demanding both more order and less control as it suits their immediate interests. Material necessity may have been the primary motive for driving people into cities, but the journey also represented an opportunity to escape the impositions of ascribed status and those organic relationships with superiors, so prized by traditional conservatives, postmodernist historians and others who were never likely to experience them. Most city dwellers at some point in their lives gain something from the anonymity and relative disorder of the urban night. It should therefore not surprise us that the order of the modern city is something that has to be continually reasserted and reinvented. There is a Hobbesian interdependency to city life, the ability of all to inflict damage on all, which imposes an inevitable complexity on the process.

New innovations in the policing of the city night can only be evaluated in this broader political and historical context. For instance, the deployment of CCTV cameras has been opposed on the ground that it will detect activities that individuals would prefer to keep secret, such as adulterous meetings. However, the costs of interpreting data in such a crusade would surely be prohibitive. Moreover, CCTV represents only a relative breach of anonymity in that the cameras are not in private places; the illicit pleasures of the city were always linked to the risk of discovery. In any case the mores of urban living are dynamic: changes are constantly taking place in what individuals are prepared to reveal in public. City dwellers have always shocked rural visitors by what they are prepared to do in front of others. The more serious objection is that CCTV will tend to produce a more totalitarian society. Here it is useful to remember that in Britain, innovations in security, from the introduction of efficient police services in the nineteenth century to the current running argument about citizens having to carry identity cards, have always been rejected by libertarians of the Left and Right on the assumption that the price of liberty is eternal state inefficiency. Current controls on the use of CCTV cameras are undeniably inadequate but we need not assume they must continue to be so. In any case, the prevailing assumptions about the relationships of governments and populations do not alter because state agents have more information at their disposal.

We should not assume that the progress from the early nineteenth-century city can be represented by continuous lines of development from curfew to bacchanalia or control to anarchy. We should, I believe, be no less sceptical of the currently dominant theme of the sociological literature that pictures the modern city as having entered, or being on the road to, a zone of total regulation. The visible signs of bacchanalia are, of course, still supported by a deal of regulatory activity, some of it of a traditional nature, some representing innovation. In modern Glasgow many of the most immediate problems of order at night are dealt with by the private security firms and privately employed doormen or 'bouncers' who now regulate entry into all city centre pubs and clubs. The instructions under which they operate reflect the nature of the premises they are guarding. At the more basic end of the market, doormen are under instruction 'to admit all women but exclude neds' ('ned' being a term to denote a young male person of a high degree of undesirability) while at the other end entry can depend upon age (i.e. neither being too young nor too old), sobriety and style of dress. Prevailing views, at least the views of those who gain admittance, tend to be in favour, even of the 'frisking' for weapons and bottles that sometimes takes place, on the grounds that it contributes to safety and enables people to relax in the company of those like themselves. Thus these and other controls should not be seen as serving one interest at the expense of others. It would indeed be foolish to overlook the influence of commercial interests but it is equally mistaken to suppose that those interests never coincide with the public's own wishes. Present arrangements also satisfy a number of the variegated, and sometimes conflicting, needs of modern states, anxious to limit the costs and potential embarrassments of traditional policing and regulation. States, partly because they are faced with more articulate populations, more sensitive to their individual rights, now find it more difficult to undertake the extensive responsibilities they acquired from the mid-nineteenth century onwards. However, they have discovered that they can achieve acceptable results by using licensing and fines to persuade private businesses to undertake such duties.

Neither should we assume that changes in the city night itself always move in one direction. Certainly the entertainment centres, at least those that cater to young adults, stay open much later than they used to and some other facilities have followed suit. A few Internet cafés, one appropriately named Insomnia, and some branches of the large supermarket chains have recently started to stay open all night. But there are many services that have gone in the other direction. In Britain the running of the railways on commercial principles has led to the elimination of almost all night trains. Even the stations that used to provide all-night public spaces with some basic facilities are now closed before midnight. Doctors no longer make night calls except in the most exceptional of circumstances. The wholesale markets, which were indirectly responsible for much of the nightlife of cities, have now moved to peripheral industrial estates and are entirely self-contained. It is also remarkable in Glasgow how much of the other night entertainment, which took place before midnight and involved a broad section of the population, has disappeared. For instance, in the early 1960s,

Glasgow had many cinemas, theatres, pubs, cafés and, as a consequence, night streets which were busy. Only four theatres now remain and these only operate part-time. There are only four cinemas (albeit multi-screen ones) in the centre of town. Home entertainment has no doubt accounted for most of the decline, but there is also the phenomenon of out-of-centre entertainment complexes which are difficult to access except by car. Most of the cafés are shut before 8 p.m. Even the more interesting shop windows are now behind shutters and many of them are shut away in locked shopping centres. Now much of the city centre is relatively empty from about 7 p.m. onwards.

What has really disappeared from Glasgow, most particularly during the last thirty years, are the pleasures of the streets themselves, of 'noise and smoky breath', of joining a mixed throng, of walking in the company of strangers, some moving purposefully, others just drifting. Even the draconian pub closing time, which prevailed in Glasgow until the mid-1970s, at least ensured that at 10 p.m. city streets became crowded with people attempting to prolong the pleasures of the night. Now later opening times mean people tend to drift out in dribs and drabs and often decant themselves directly into taxis. Certain city streets do become very busy at different times of the night but the crowds are largely stratified by age. For the most part the night street is less a place in which to dawdle and watch others, more a zone to pass through quickly. Many people were, then as now, in transit to a particular place of entertainment, but it was the progress through the crowded city street that conveyed much of the sense of 'being out'. Many factors are involved; Glasgow like many other cities has suffered a huge loss of population and the planning fashions of the 1960s removed many of those who might otherwise have remained to the peripheral 'schemes'. Cowcaddens, close to one of the main entertainment areas, which contained 40,000 people in the 1950s, now has no more than a thousand. By an irony, much of the direct responsibility for the city being a less entertaining and more threatening place lies not with the youthful revellers or other folk-devils of the suburban imagination or even the police for failing to get a grip, but with those very masses in suburbia huddled before their television screens who, when they do go out, go to a dedicated entertainment complex and travel by car. It is their absence which makes the city night a more stratified, specialised, intermittently threatening, not to mention boring, place.

Bibliography

Banks, Joseph (1973) 'The Contagion of Numbers', in Harold Dyos and Michael Wolff (eds) *The Victorian City. Images and Realities*, Vol. 2. London: Routledge and Kegan Paul.
Bauman, Zygmunt (1998) *Globalization. The Human Consequences*. Cambridge: Polity Press.
Bell, Daniel (1976) *The Cultural Contradictions of Capitalism*. New York: Basic Books.
Booth, Charles (1903) *Notes on Social Influences and Conclusion (Life and Labour of the People in London*, Final Vol.). London: Macmillan.
Bowring, John (ed.) (1838–48) *A View of the Hard Labour Bill (The Complete Works of Jeremy Bentham*, IV). Edinburgh: William Tait.

Brown, Stewart (1982) *Thomas Chalmers and the Godly Commonwealth in Scotland*. Oxford: Oxford University Press.

Carlyle, Thomas (1965 [1840]) *Past and Present*. New York: New York University Press.

Carpenter, Edward (1900) *Civilization. Its Cause and Cure*. London: Swan Sonneschein.

Charity Organisation Society (1924) *The Jubilee Book of the Glasgow Charity Organisation Society*. Glasgow: Charity Organisation Society.

Checkland, Sydney (1982) 'British Urban Health in a Single City', in Olive Checkland and Margaret Lamb (eds) *Health Care as Social History. The Glasgow Case*. Aberdeen: Aberdeen University Press.

Cohen, Nick (2000) 'Our Zero Privacy. Privacy on the Net: Special Report', *Observer* 18 June 2000.

Coleridge, Samuel Taylor (1972 [1830]) *On the Constitution of the Church and State According to the Idea of Each*. London: Dent.

Corporation of the City of Glasgow (1914) *Municipal Glasgow. Its Evolution and Enterprises*, Glasgow.

Dandekar, C. (1990) *Surveillance, Power and Modernity. Bureaucracy and Discipline from 1700 to the Present Day*. Cambridge: Polity Press.

Davis, M. (1992) 'Fortress Los Angeles: the Militarization of Urban Space', in M. Sorkin (ed.) *Variations on a Theme Park: The New American City and the End of Public Space*. New York: Hill & Wang.

De Swaan, Abram (1991) *In Care of the State*. Cambridge: Polity Press.

Donajgrodzki, A. P. (1977) *Social Control in Nineteenth Century Britain*. London: Croom Helm.

Engels, Friedrich (1987 [1845 (in German)]) *The Condition of the Working Class in England*. Harmondsworth: Penguin.

Escott, Thomas (1897) *Social Transformations of the Victorian Era*. London: Seeley.

Fitzpatrick, Michael (2001) *The Tyranny of Health: Doctors and the Regulation of Lifestyle*. London: Routledge.

Foucault, Michel (1991) *Discipline and Punish. The Birth of the Prison*. Harmondsworth: Penguin.

Fyfe, Nicholas R. and Jonathon Bannister (1996) 'City Watching: Closed Circuit Television Surveillance in Public Spaces', *Area* (Institute of British Geographers) 28(1): 37–46.

Fyfe, Nicholas R. and Jonathon Bannister (1998) 'The Eyes Upon the Street. Closed Circuit Television Surveillance in the City', in Nicholas R. Fyfe (ed.) *Images of the Street. Planning Identity and Public Control in Public Space*. London: Routledge.

Gaunt, William (1988 [1945]) *The Aesthetic Adventure*. London: Jonathan Cape.

GGDAT (Greater Glasgow Drug Action Team) (1999) *Tackling Drugs Together in Greater Glasgow: Strategy 1999–2003*. Glasgow: Greater Glasgow Drug Action Team.

Her Majesty's Chief Inspector of Constabulary for Scotland (2000) *Annual Report 1999/2000. A Year of Progress*. Edinburgh: HMSO.

Himmelfarb, Gertrude (1965) 'The Haunted House of Jeremy Bentham', in Gertrude Himmelfarb *Victorian Minds. A Study of Intellectuals in Crisis and Ideologies in Transition*. Chicago: Ivan Dee, 32–81.

Huysmans, Jorris-Karl (1891) *A Rebours*. Paris: Bibliotheque-Charpentier.

Ignatieff, Michael (1983) 'State, Civil Society and Total Institutions. A Critique of Recent Social Histories of Punishment', in Stanley Cohen and Andrew Scull (eds) *Social Control and the State*. Oxford: Blackwell.

Jackson, Holbrook (1988) *The 1890s*. London: The Cresset Library.

Jacobs, Jane (1961) *The Death and Life of Great American Cities*. Harmondsworth: Penguin.

King, Elspeth (1979) *Sober and Free. The Temperance Movement.* Glasgow: Tuckwell Press.

Lyon, David (1994) *The Electronic Eye: The Rise of Surveillance Society.* Cambridge: Polity Press.

McIlvanney, William (1981) 'Saturday Night', in Geddes Thomson (ed.) *Identities. An Anthology of West of Scotland Poetry, Prose and Drama.* London: Heinemann.

Muir, Edwin (1980) *An Autobiography.* London: Hogarth Press.

Nordau, Max (1968 [1892 (in German)]) *Degeneration.* Lincoln and London: University of Nebraska Press.

Norris, Clive and Gary Armstrong (1999) *The Maximum Surveillance Society: the Rise of CCTV.* Oxford: Berg.

Palmer, Brian (2000) *Cultures of Darkness. Night Travels in the Histories of Transgression.* New York: Monthly Review Press.

Raban, Jonathan (1976) *Soft City.* London: Collins Harvill.

Robertson, Edna (1998) *Glasgow's Doctor. James Burn Russell 1837–1904.* East Linton: Tuckwell Press.

Ryskamp, Charles and Frederick Pottle (eds) (1963) *Boswell. The Ominous Years 1774–76.* London: Heinemann.

Schlör, Joachim (1998 [1991]) *Nights in the Big City. Paris, Berlin, London 1840–1930.* London: Reaktion.

Scottish Executive (2000) *£1.8 Million to Provide Permanent Routes out of Prostitution* (Press Release SE2267/2000).

Scottish Office (1995) *Central Research Unit. Crime and Criminal Justice Research Findings No. 8.* Edinburgh: HMSO.

Scottish Office (1999a) *The Effect of Closed Circuit Television on Recorded Crime Rates and Public Concern about Crime in Glasgow* (Crime and Criminal Justice Research Findings No 30). Edinburgh: HMSO.

Scottish Office (1999b) *Research Report on the Hamilton Child Safety Initiative.* Edinburgh: HMSO.

Sennett, Richard (1996) *The Uses of Disorder: Personal Identity and City Life.* London: Faber & Faber.

'Shadow' (pseudonym of Alexander Brown) (1976 [1858]) *Midnight Scenes and Social Photographs. Being Sketches of Life in the Streets, Wynds and Dens of Glasgow.* Milngavie, Glasgow: Heatherbank Press.

Springham, Kay (1998) *Time to Go Home – Says Who? An Analysis of the Hamilton Curfew Experience.* Edinburgh: Scottish Human Rights Centre.

Stewart, Audrey (2000) *Where is She Tonight? Women, Street Prostitution and Homelessness in Glasgow.* Glasgow: BASE 75.

Symons, Arthur (1896) 'Ernest Dowson', *The Savoy* IV (August): 90–92.

Talbot Association (1999) *Annual Report*, Glasgow.

Thompson, Edward (1967) 'Time, Work, Discipline and Industrial Capitalism', *Past and Present* 38: 56–97.

Tilley, Charles (1995) 'Seeing off the Danger: Threat, Surveillance and Modes of Protection', *European Journal of Criminal Policy and Research* 3(3): 27–40.

Webster, William (1996) 'Closed Circuit Television and Governance: The Eve of a Surveillance Age', *Information Infrastructure and Policy* 5: 253–263.

Whitman, Walt (1993 [1855]) *Leaves of Grass and Selected Prose.* London: Dent.

Whyte, Hamish (ed.) (1983) *Noise and Smoky Breath.* Glasgow: Third Eye Centre and Glasgow District Libraries Publications Board.

Index